TERRORISM
THE MEDIA AND THE LAW

Edited by
Abraham H. Miller

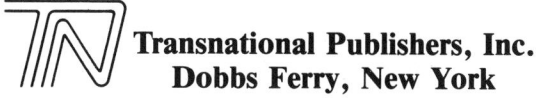 Transnational Publishers, Inc.
Dobbs Ferry, New York

This project was prepared under Contract Number-J-LEAA-005-79 from the National Institute of Justice, U.S. Department of Justice. Points of view or opinions stated in this document are those of the authors and do not necessarily represent the official position or policies of the U.S. Department of Justice.

Library of Congress Cataloging in Publication Data
Main entry under title:

Terrorism, the media, and the law.

Bibliography: p.
Includes index.
1. Terrorism—United States—Addresses, essays, lectures. 2. Terrorism in mass media—United States—Addresses, essays, lectures. 3. Law enforcement—United States—Addresses, essays, lectures. I. Miller, Abraham H., 1940-
HV6432.T47   1982   363.3'2'0973   82-11020
ISBN 0-941320-04-9

© Copyright 1982 by Transnational Publishers, Inc.

All Rights reserved. No part of this publication may be reproduced or transmitted in any form or by any means, electronic or mechanical, including photocopy, recording, xerography, or any information storage and retrieval system, without permission in writing from the publisher.

Manufactured in the United States of America

anizing the volume and bringing the project together reflected a superb command of the subject matter and a penetrating and professional understanding of the requirements of a good anthology. I am deeply grateful for the opportunity to work with a project monitor whose capabilities are very much those of a fellow colleague.

Charles Williams, of Koba Associates, Inc., Washington, D.C., deserves a very special note of thanks for his copyediting.

John Bellassai and Ilene Baylinson, both of Koba Associates, Inc., along with Charles Williams, helped to guide this project through some difficult times, and I wish to thank them for their assistance.

The support of the Charles Phelps Taft Foundation of the University of Cincinnati, which enabled me to conduct interviews at Scotland Yard during the summer of 1981, is gratefully acknowledged.

Molly Ross lent her skills to doing some of the proof reading and helped make the text more consistent and more accurate.

Abraham H. Miller
Cincinnati, Ohio

ACKNOWLEDGEMENTS

Earlier and draft versions of some of the papers in this volume were presented at the 1979 DePaul University (Chicago, Ill.) Conference, "On Terrorism: A Survey of the Problems Confronting Law Enforcement and the Mass Media in the Prevention and Control of Terror Violence." The Conference was funded by the Law Enforcement Assistance Administration pursuant to LEAA's International Authority, MBO 1.218. Professor M. Cherif Bassiouni, of DePaul University's College of Law, was the project director. His role in recruiting the participants and organizing the conference, which, in part, contributed to the production of this volume, is herewith gratefully acknowledged.

The papers presented in this volume have been, where appropriate, edited and updated since the 1979 DePaul Conference, and new material has been recruited to reflect recent events in this dramatic and ever-changing issue area. It was considered vital that we had a paper on the Iranian hostage situation, especially in view of the controversial interview aired by NBC News in December 1979. Robert Friedlander undertook this for us with his usual keen eye to the international and domestic legal and media aspects. Since the DePaul Conference, the Iranian Embassy in London had been taken over by Arab secessionists. I used materials acquired during my interviews with Scotland Yard during the summer of 1980 to bring that episode into the purview of our concerns.

As this volume is not intended to be a conference report but a series of related papers which stands by itself, several of the original conference papers, for a variety of editorial and organizational considerations, have not been included.

In accordance with the changed nature of the work, Professors Richard L. Moreland and Michael L. Berbaum prepared a new bibliography which honed in directly on the substantive concerns of the volume. I am grateful for their superb effort.

Throughout this project, Lois Felson Mock, of the National Institute of Justice, has been more than a Project Director. Her suggestions for reorg-

For their part the media have promulgated guidelines for the coverage of terrorist events. These are designed to prevent excesses by the media which in the gathering of news jeopardize human life or interfere with police procedures. The guidelines also caution the media about depicting terrorist events in a fashion that causes them to be emulated. Despite their existence, such guidelines are often violated when they are most needed—when the story is important and when the professional rewards for obtaining it are greatest. Although law enforcement has become somewhat more sensitive to the role of the press generally and to the functions the press can perform during in-progress terrorist situations, law enforcement has not learned either to communicate with or utilize the press as it should.

The balancing of both conflicting social values and social responsibilities against one another is always difficult. Under the stress and drama of an in-progress terrorist operation where life is at risk, such balancing can appear impossible. However, as the writings in this volume illustrate, the consequence of not finding that balancing point can be the loss of life itself. Only through strong dialog, based on mutual respect and understanding, can the media and law enforcement begin to even attempt to resolve these issues. It is to this end that the papers presented here were conceived and written.

Abraham H. Miller

times a not so unwitting accomplice. As terrorists need public attention, newspeople need news. Terrorists are all too ready to oblige with poignant drama, human interest stories, and spectacular visuals. And under such circumstances, the media are going to want to be as close as possible to the scene of those dramatic and fast-breaking stories. In a highly competitive, modern news business, with an emphasis on live action, modern terrorism not only presents opportunities for outstanding stories, but it confronts the media with some of their most difficult ethical, moral, and legal choices: choices between a free people's right to know and the right of terrorist victims to survive; between the media's right to disseminate information and a society's right to exist.

These are not abstract issues. They are day-to-day concerns which put in direct and sometimes heated conflict journalists in search of a story and law enforcement agencies trying to contain terrorism. These are the issues which our contributors address. Their responses run a gamut from calls for tough controls on the media to unrestricted support for freedom of the press. Surprisingly, the positions of our contributors are at times as uncharacteristic as they are varied. Some of the strongest criticisms of the media come from journalists, while some of the strongest words of support of the press come from the police. The issues are as complex as are the respective roles of the participants and the tensions between them. These have sometimes given rise to disputes which have gone all the way to the Supreme Court for resolution. The legal machinery, however, cannot resolve all the disputes, nor can it implement procedures for dealing with the multitude of complex issues which are generated in the course of terrorist episodes, especially while they are in progress. Even where legislation exists to restrict the media, democratic social and political norms can prevent the laws' implementation, as is the case in Britain. Obviously, other mechanisms for resolution must be found. And these will most likely come about through open and frank discussion between the media and law enforcement.

Those who scream for censorship and restrictive legislation to combat media excesses during ongoing terrorist events or the media's occasional favorable portrayal of terrorist groups, should consider that those procedures only accomplish for the terrorists what they cannot accomplish for themselves: extinguishing liberty to preserve order. Yet, those who call for complete and unrestricted freedom of the press should realize that other social values must be balanced with that freedom. The Supreme Court has not held that the right to publish inherently means there is an unrestricted corollary right to gather news.

Foreword

As an instrument of political violence, terrorism is not new. The propaganda of the deed as a means of creating political change through fear was carefully played out against the backdrop of the ancient marketplace of Jerusalem between the years 60 and 70 A.D. Long before Michkail Bakunin sought to establish a new political order in Russia through violent deeds which captured attention through fear, the Sicarii and the Zealots of ancient Israel had written their own propaganda in the blood of Roman soldiers and Roman sympathizers brought down with curved daggers in the broad daylight of the marketplace. As the victim fell to the ground, his assassin calmly slipped back into the crowd, his weapon covered by flowing robes, his manner indistinguishable from those around him. Fear of the terrorists spread, sympathizers of Rome became scarce; Roman repression provoked through these deeds increased and the populace revolted.

Terrorism was then and is now a mixture of propaganda and theatre. Terrorism is the weapon of the weak. It creates the allusion of strength to compensate for the reality of impotence. What terrorists cannot muster in political or military victory, they produce in spectacular, fear-gripping and attention-getting drama. The dream of contemporary terrorists is no different from that of the ancient Sicarri and Zealots: to produce fear in the masses and repression by authorities. This, the terrorists believe, will erode the legitimacy of the state, and like the ancient Israelites the populace will rise up in revolt. But where the religious fanatics of ancient Israel were successful, contemporary terrorists have not been. For instead of producing revolt through repression, they have simply produced repression, and generally publicly endorsed repression. In many states, freedom has also come to mean the right to go about one's business without the fear of being maimed or killed. Through publicity terrorists have been able to place their platform on the public agenda, but the response has not always been what the terrorists sought.

Always, terrorism is dependent on publicity. The quest for publicity has at times made the media an unwitting accomplice of terrorism; and at other

Chapter 6.	Terrorism in Britain: The Limits of Free Expression ... *Walter B. Jaehnig*	106

IV	RECOMMENDATIONS FOR COVERING TERRORISM	
Chapter 7.	Paper on Terrorism .... *The National News Council*	133
Chapter 8.	Guidelines for United States Government Spokespersons During Terrorist Incidents .... *U.S. Department of State*	148

APPENDIX A.   MEDIA GUIDELINE DOCUMENTS

News and Entertainment Media Responsibility for the Prevention of Extraordinary Violence 153
National Advisory Committee on Criminal Justice Standards and Goals

CBS News Production Standards 157

The Courier Journal and the Louisville (Ky.) Times Guidelines 158

The Chicago Sun-Times and Daily News Standards for Coverage of Terrorism 159

Guidelines of United Press International 160

APPENDIX B.

The Project on Media Coverage of Terrorism: A Summary of National Surveys and Other Investigations, 1977-79 161
Michael Sommer and Heidi Sommer

BIBLIOGRAPHY

Terrorism and the Mass Media: A Researcher's Bibliography 191
Richard L. Moreland and Michael L. Berbaum

INDEX 217

CONTENTS

Foreword		v
Acknowledgements		ix
List of Contributors		xi

	Terrorism, the Media, and Law Enforcement: An Introduction .... *Abraham H. Miller*	1
I	THE NATURE OF THE PROBLEM	
Chapter 1.	Terrorism, the Media, and the Law: A Discussion of the Issues .... *Abraham H. Miller*	13
Chapter 2.	Iran: The Hostage Seizure, the Media, and International Law .... *Robert A. Friedlander*	51
II	THE LAW ENFORCEMENT PERSPECTIVE	
Chapter 3.	The Journalist and the Hostage: How Their Rights Can Be Balanced .... *Robert L. Rabe*	69
Chapter 4.	The Police, the News Media, and the Coverage of Terrorism .... *Patrick V. Murphy*	76
III	A VIEW FROM THE FOURTH ESTATE	
Chapter 5.	The Media and Terrorism .... *James W. Hoge*	89

CONTRIBUTORS

Abraham H. Miller is a professor of political science at the University of Cincinnati.

Michael L. Berbaum is an assistant professor of psychology at Brandeis University.

Robert A. Friedlander is a professor of law at Ohio Northern University.

James W. Hoge is a publisher of the Chicago Sun-Times.

Walter B. Jaehnig is chairman and professor of journalism at the University of Wyoming.

Richard L. Morland is an assistant professor of psychology at the University of Pittsburg.

Patrick V. Murphy is president of the Police Foundation in Washington, D.C.

Robert L. Rabe is assistant chief (retired) of the Washington, D.C. Metropolitan Police.

Michael Sommer is publisher of New Worlds of Orange County (Calif.) and of the Irvine World News.

Heidi Sommer is a psychologist and counselor practising in Orange County, (Calif.)

TERRORISM, THE MEDIA, AND LAW ENFORCEMENT: AN INTRODUCTION AND OVERVIEW

Abraham H. Miller

As with the concept of revolution, there is no agreed-upon definition of terrorism. In his classic work on revolution, Crane Brinton solved the definitional problem by saying that his work referred to those events commonly called revolutions, such as the English, French, and Russian Revolutions.[1] Philosophers of science have recognized that men use ideas long before they learn to define them with anything resembling scientific precision.

Terrorism can be generally described as the systematic use of random violence against innocents in order to bring about political change through fear. Although the motivations, ideologies, and allegiances which separate terrorists are as diverse as any which can be found in the general political arena, there are several elements which, if not unique to terrorists, are strongly emphasized by them. These are their extensive reliance on both random and symbolic violence; their failure to distinguish between civilians and noncivilians as legitimate targets; their use of civilians as surrogate victims for the state; and their exploitation of the media to publicize their cause.

Even this general view of terrorism, which embraces concepts most academic researchers will recognize as important, must be further modified in light of the substance and orientation of this volume. Because our concern is with the interaction between law enforcement and the media and with their views on how terrorists should be depicted to the public, we have followed their usage of the term "terrorism." The police and the media use an operational definition, one which looks at methodology rather than cause. Their definition is similar to the one commonly used by the public and commonly described in dictionaries: violence, bomb throwing, or similar acts committed by groups or individuals in order to intimidate a population or government into granting demands.[2] The goals are inconsequential: the methodology is the distinguishing characteristic.

This view may not be received well by some students of terrorism, for it places common criminals and political terrorists in the same classification. Yet the police respond to crimes in terms of how those crimes are committed. Whether a bomb thrower, an assassin, or a hostage taker is or is not motivated by a political ideology is of little significance for the immediate tactical reaction of the police. Thus, scholars might still continue to debate whether the Hanafi Muslim seige in Washington, D.C., was a political or nonpolitical event, but for the police the tactical response was then, and would be in the future, independent of such concerns.

For the media as well, the methodology of an incident is the factor which determines whether or not the incident is appropriately called terrorism. It is the type of violence which makes an event newsworthy and creates pressure for access, for the scoop, and for the continual update of a fastbreaking story.

The problems which both the police and the press encounter during ongoing felonies are not dissimilar from those which arise during incidents involving political terrorists. Just as the police have used their experience with hostage taking in common felonies to develop tactical procedures to deal with political terrorists' taking hostages, so, too, have the police and the press learned about the problems of police/press relations during political terrorist incidents from their mutual experience with ordinary felony operations.

This is not to say that the differences between political and nonpolitical terrorists are irrelevant to the law enforcement and media responses. Rather, it is to say that for American law enforcement and American media, experience has shown that the similarities between nonpolitical and political terrorist episodes have overshadowed the differences. The most common examples of this observation are to be found in the hostage/barricade experience.[3] Hostage and barricade experiences involving nonpolitical terrorists have been generalizable to political terrorists.

This compilation of papers discusses issues of concern to both journalists and police who deal with various types of contemporary terrorism. Among the issues discussed in the papers are: The press' right to be at the scene where news is being made; the legal and ethical restrictions on the press' search for and dissemination of information; the accuracy with which the press portrays individual terrorists, terrorist groups, and terrorist incidents;

INTRODUCTION

the perceptions by the police and the press of each other's functions in terrorist cases; the advantages and disadvantages of the police' accommodating requests by the press for information; the implications for the larger society of police/press relations during ongoing terrorist situations; and the options the public will support when government must select policies to deal with terrorism. The two most important issues concerning terrorism which confront the police and the media are the issue of access by the media to in-progress terrorist events and the issue of the media's portrayal of terrorists. As these are of major concern to our contributors, let us examine them briefly.

The most common problem in police/press relations during a terrorist incident is the problem of access. This refers to attempts by the press to get first-hand information from the scene where an incident is taking place. The media believe strongly that if the first amendment means anything, it clearly means that the right to gather information is inherent in the right to publish: without the unimpaired right to gather information, the right to publish is meaningless. The media argue that strong, robust, and active coverage of events is not only guaranteed by our democracy; it is vital to its continued existence.

For their part, the police assert that the press' attempts to gather information all too frequently interfere with police operations. The police do not deny the validity of the press' need to gather independent, first-hand information, but the police caution that that right must be tempered by the right of all citizens to have their lives and safety protected.

The media's portrayal of terrorists—or sometimes how the media permit terrorists to portray themselves—is perhaps of somewhat less concern to local law enforcement than the issue of the media's intrusion. However, the problem of how the media portray terrorists appears to be of strong concern to society at large. Certainly, it has been of great concern to the media themselves and to policy makers dealing with issues related to terrorism. In a democracy, public perceptions of events will determine the policy course a government will be able to pursue. If the public's image of terrorists is one of "freedom fighters," "commandos," or "liberators," then that set of images will have profoundly different consequences for government policy than will a set of public perceptions which define terrorists as brutal murderers.

When the police speak among themselves or with the media about media coverage of terrorist episodes, the primary issue is whether the media's need for onsite coverage conflicts with law enforcement's needs for security. In sharp contrast, however, when journalists examine their roles in covering terrorism and terrorist operations, the issue of access quickly pales before the issue of how the media portray terrorists.

Although the issue of the press' intrusion into ongoing terrorist operations is of primary concern to the police, the issue of how terrorists are portrayed is also significant. The significance of this issue to the police can be seen from a rather insightful observation by the Task Force on Disorders and Terrorism:

> "Factual and fictional depictions of incidents of extraordinary violence in the mass media are an important part of the background against which individual choices whether or not to participate in crimes of this nature are made. They also are a significant influence on public fears and expectations."[4]

It is of interest to note that the Task Force on Disorders and Terrorism discussed the portrayal of events prior to its discussion of newsgathering. In this sense, the Task Force reflected a set of priorities very much in evidence in the community of journalists. In fact, it is this community which has been most concerned with and most critical of the media's portrayal of terrorism.

Journalists have traditionally asked how the media's ethical commitments to objectivity can be balanced against the day-to-day exigencies of a highly competitive business. The media's coverage of terrorism does not create new problems for journalists so much as it dramatizes, in an uncommon setting, common difficulties which journalists encounter in their search for "truth." This search takes place among self-serving sources who dispense highly subjective information. Journalists themselves are usually unable to establish the truth of an issue independent of the sources which provide information. Because publicity is such a large part of the terrorists' drama, both governments and the terrorists whom they combat have become highly proficient at conducting a symbolic war with each other through the media. In these circumstances, even the most consciencious and objective reporter might become the unwitting conduit for propaganda.

A media interview with a political terrorist is a situation ripe for exploitation. The degree to which the terrorist can successfully manipulate an interview will depend upon the terrorist's skill. Be they nationalists or anarchists, political terrorists attempt to portray themselves as outraged heroes who have been forced by society to commit acts of violence. Their crimes, they would have us believe, are inconsequential when compared to the evils of the larger society.

For terrorists, it is not really important if the self-portrayal is publicly approved or disapproved. The value of the propaganda lies in their getting the public to be so amazed at their description of reality that it will begin to question its own assumptions about morality and about the political system.

INTRODUCTION 5

The political implications of this type of redefinition of values will be obvious to students of revolution. Crane Brinton observed that a regime began its demise with the alienation of its intellectuals, who then proceeded to question the value system which sustained the regime.[5] Such issues of legitimacy are not abstractions, of interest only to scholars who seek to understand the conditions which give rise to revolution. These issues have profound implications for the operational procedures terrorists follow in their attempts to build a network of supporters, for political terrorists require a sympathetic cadre of fellow travelers alienated from the established order but not necessarily prepared to take direct violent action against it. In the short run, such individuals are important to the terrorists because they provide a base for logistical assistance: safe houses, money, and information. In the long run, they provide a base for new recruits, especially if the organization seeks to expand on the political front into a mass movement.

The importance of having a group of ideologically sympathetic fellow travelers was clearly evident in the ability of Patricia Campbell Hearst and her Symbionese Liberation Army comrades to elude a nationwide search. It is also seen today in West Germany in the re-emergence of the Red Army faction after the suicides of the original members of the Baader-Meinhof gang. The image terrorists project will influence public support for efforts by law enforcement to counteract terrorism. An unsupportive public is not simply detrimental to law enforcement morale: in a democratic society the public can influence the entire thrust of policy related to terrorism on both foreign and domestic fronts.

Because of America's place in the world community, American public opinion is all the more significant and might ultimately influence the way in which other Western nations deal with terrorism. Former Senator Jacob Javits (R.N.Y.), a strong critic of the Carter administration's policies dealing with international terrorism, stated: "I am becoming increasingly apprehensive that the Carter Administration has been relinquishing the lead expected of the United States in this struggle by the rest of the civilized world."[6]

In my paper which follows, I take a detailed look at some of the reasons behind Senator Javits' and others' criticisms of the counterterrorist policies of the past Administration and the media's lack of challenge to them. The reader is well advised that the issues still percolate with controversy, and they undoubtedly will for some time, for they involve concerns of whether the media have accurately portrayed an issue that the Government wished to play down.

The manner in which the media sometimes portray terrorists and the lengths to which journalists are willing to go to get access of information are dealt with by Robert Friedlander in the following paper. Friedlander discusses the larger implications of the controversial interview with Marine William Gallegos, then an American hostage in Tehran. According to Friedlander, the Gallegos interview raised serious questions about journalistic ethics because, as a condition of NBC's obtaining the interview, a militant spokeswoman named Mary was allotted time to launch a tirade against the United States.

Within the media community, there was disagreement over NBC's conduct. Some, such as NBC correspondent Ford Rowan, considered it to be the nadir of journalistic ethics. Others, such as the editors of the *Washington Post,* defended the broadcast of the Gallegos interview on the grounds that the propaganda was so blatantly transparent as to be useless to the Iranian militants.

Friedlander challenges us to consider the far-reaching implications of the Gallegos interview as they relate to public support for the media's fundamental role in democracy. The issue he raises runs counter to some of the thinking among law enforcement personnel—but not among journalists—about public tolerance of the media's excesses in covering terrorism. Most police have thought that public outrage against the media would most likely occur because of death or injury resulting from the media's intruding into police operations. Such is the way in which Chief Rabe portrays the issue in his paper.

Friedlander paints a different picture: according to Friedlander, the Gallegos interview presents a different type of problem for the media—one which occurs because of the manner in which the media either directly portray terrorists or permit the terrorists to portray themselves.

The issue Friedlander raises is not unlike the discussion Walter Jaehnig puts forth in his paper on the relationship between the police and the media in Great Britain. The Gallegos interview is similar to the British Broadcasting Company's (BBC) interview with members of the Irish National Liberation Army (INLA) who murdered Member of Parliament Airey Neave. In speaking of the BBC interview, Prime Minister Margaret Thatcher stated that the episode appalled her, and she went so far as to threaten legal action against the BBC. Her comments undoubtedly reflected the feelings of millions of her citizens.

The Metropolitan Police asked how it was possible to fight terrorism when the most respected media institution in the United Kingdom made heroes out of murderers. One only has to look at Italy and West Germany to see how the omnipresent problem of political terrorism had brought forth draconian

INTRODUCTION

restrictions on civil liberties, especially on those civil liberties which affect the press. In the United Kingdom, the legal bases for such actions were already on the books, but an historic tradition of common law mitigated strongly against their implementation. Even after the INLA interview, voluntary cooperation between the media and the Metropolitan police continued to be the basis for media/law enforcement relations.

Our contributors hold the same position on voluntary cooperation. Even in the face of certain excesses by the media, the tradition of a free press and its contribution to a democratic form of government are recognized as too important to be subject to government control. Our contributors conclude that voluntary cooperation and the use of guidelines drawn from traditional journalistic ethics should form the basis for media coverage of extraordinary violent events.

In his paper, Police Foundation President Patrick V. Murphy argues for a generally unrestricted press, not just for philosophical reasons, but for practical concerns related to police procedure. Murphy's statements are remarkably similar to those of James Hoge, publisher of the *Chicago Sun-Times.* Murphy and Hoge agree that the press play a highly functional role by covering ongoing terrorist operations. The press can crush rumors, prevent misinformation, and counter fear.

Murphy does agree with Chief Rabe that the press' intrusion into police operations has at times jeopardized the police. However, in contrast to Rabe's position, Murphy agrees with newsman Hoge that the excesses of the few should not be seen as representative of the actions of the many. Murphy also agrees with Leonard Downie, of the *Washington Post,* that overall, the press' handling of the Hanafi Muslim hostage-taking in Washington, D.C., showed more responsibility than irresponsibility.

In my paper, I raise the issue of whether or not there are factors inherent in the gathering and disseminating of news, and in the way that the journalism profession rewards those activities, which might indirectly promote certain kinds of abuses. When journalists formulate any set of voluntary standards to govern their conduct, they should take those issues into account.

The news media's codes for coverage of terrorism have generally been applauded by the media and by law enforcement. Walter Jaehnig's insightful paper discusses the application of voluntary standards in the United Kingdom. In an earlier paper he raised the question of the utility of such codes when the articulated journalistic ethics are already recognized as part of the bases of good journalism.[7] Friedlander raises a similar point when he notes that coverage of the American hostages held in Tehran was generally characterized by a flaunting of most of the codes, some of which are presented in this volume.

Does the existence of codes compromise journalists' claims to a first-amendment right to unrestricted news access? In the review of the case law, which follows in my paper, it is clear that in a number of major decisions, the Supreme Court has ruled against the press' claim to a constitutional right of privileged access in order to gather news. In *Houchins* v. *KQED*, Chief Justice Warren Burger reaffirmed earlier decisions to the effect that the right to speak and the right to publish do not carry with them the unrestrained right to gather information.

Nonetheless, I believe that the police would be well advised to follow Patrick Murphy's recommendations about the utilization of the functional role and capacity of the media. To totally proscribe the media's special access might be justifiable in terms of the law of the land, but it is simply not good police procedure.

This introduction was designed to provide neither solutions nor recommendations for the problems facing the police and the media as they execute their respective tasks in dealing with terrorism. Each contributor has articulated a number of ideas and points of view which can be incorporated in terms of a reader's own expertise, experience, and perspective on the types of situations discussed. The attitudes which separate our two major audiences, the police and the media, are empirically documented in the surveys undertaken by Drs. Michael and Heidi Sommer and are presented in this volume. The police often see media coverage as a threat to law enforcement operations while the press obviously do not. This fact, which Sommer and Sommer convey, illustrates the gap between the two.

Even though they are not in agreement, by exploring these problems, the police and the media might become more tolerant of one another's point of view. The formal and informal dialogs which this volume should inspire will help, I hope, to pave the way for voluntary agreements between the police and the media. This not only means media guidelines for dealing with terrorism in general and with ongoing terrorist situations in particular; it must also mean guidelines for the police to provide reasonable access to journalists. As James Hoge notes in his paper, there is little justification for a large, sophisticated metropolitan police force's being unable to provide orderly press releases during a dramatic terrorist episode. Failure to provide such information invites the press to interfere with police operations. If the media are going to commit themselves to restraint, then law enforcement must create an environment in which the violation of restraint is unnecessary.

INTRODUCTION 9

It is not appropriate to place blame in these sets of relationships. It is necessary to understand the problems of the past so that they can be avoided in the future. This volume was compiled for that purpose.

* * *

This volume is divided into four major sections, an appendix, and a bibliography. The first section delineates the nature of the problem confronting both law enforcement and the media as they attempt to execute their respective roles in dealing with terrorism. Two papers comprise this section. The first by Professor Abraham H. Miller, of the University of Cincinnati, looks at the two major themes which are the focal points of this volume: (1) the issue of media access to ongoing terrorist episodes, and (2) the issue of the media's portrayal of terrorists. The discussion is set against a background of actual cases and against a review of recent Supreme Court decisions which affect the media's first-amendment-based claims to access. The second paper, by Professor Robert Friedlander, of Ohio Northern University's College of Law, takes an in-depth look at the recent Iranian hostage crisis in order to explore the issue of how the media portray terrorists. Friedlander also looks at the role of the international legal system in the context of the Iranian hostage episode.

Section II looks at the two thematic issues, access and portrayal, from the perspective of law enforcement. Robert L. Rabe, deputy chief (retired) of the District of Columbia Police, opens this section with a very strong statement about press intrusion into police operations. Another policeman, Patrick V. Murphy, president of the Police Foundation, offers another view, one which describes a functional role for the media during terrorist operations.

James Hoge, publisher of the *Chicago Sun-Times,* opens Section III with a defense of the media. He cautions that it is a mistake to characterize the industry by the excesses of a few of its members. As our policemen are not in agreement, neither are our journalists. Walter Jaehnig, a former journalist, provides us with a comparative perspective on the media, by looking at the media's coverage of terrorism in Great Britain, and raises the question of whether attributes inherent in the way in which the media go about their business contribute to their problems with the police. Jaehnig also holds out an optimistic view toward the resolution of some of the issues separating the police and the media.

Section IV contains a number of guidelines for media coverage of terrorism. Included are guidelines from both Government and media sources: among them are the well-known guidelines of both CBS and the *Chicago Sun-Times.*

Appendix B contains a survey which empirically documents the views of law enforcement and the media on coverage of terrorism and extraordinary violence. This survey was conducted by Dr. Michael Sommer, a publisher with the Irvine Corporation, Irvine, California, and Dr. Heidi Sommer, a practicing psychologist in Orange County, California.

The extensive bibliography which completes this work was undertaken from a social psychological perspective by Professor Richard L. Moreland, of the University of Pittsburg, and Professor Michael L. Berbaum, of Brandeis University.

FOOTNOTES

1. Crane Brinton. *The anatomy of revolution*. New York: Vintage, 1965, p.3.
2. *Webster's new collegiate dictionary*. Springfield, Mass.: G. & C. Merriam and Co., 1980.
3. Abraham H. Miller. *Terrorism and hostage negotiations*. Boulder, Co.: Westview, 1980.
4. National Advisory Committee on Criminal Justice Standards and Goals. *Disorders and terrorism: Report of the Task Force on Disorders and Terrorism*. Washington, D.C.: Law Enforcement Assistance Administration, 1976.
5. Crane Brinton. Op. cit., p.45.
6. Jacob K. Javits. International terrorism: Apathy exacerbates the problem. *Terrorism: An International Journal*, 1(2), p. 112.
7. Walter Jaehnig. Journalism and terrorism: Captives of the libertarian tradition. *Indiana Law Journal*, 53(4), 717-747.

I THE NATURE OF THE PROBLEM

1. TERRORISM, THE MEDIA, AND THE LAW: A DISCUSSION OF THE ISSUES

Abraham H. Miller

Of the various types of events about which the media gather news, those episodes caused by terrorism, especially political terrorism, confront the media with some of their most difficult ethical, moral, and legal concerns. Such concerns are inherent in a variety of different kinds of newsmaking events. Terrorism does not bring forth a specter of new issues so much as it raises more distinct concerns which have potentially greater consequences for both the media and the larger political system.

The uniqueness of contemporary terrorism lies in its need, its almost incessant craving for publicity, whether favorable or unfavorable, at whatever cost. Terrorism and the media are entwined in an almost inexorable, symbiotic relationship. Terrorism is capable of writing any drama—no matter how horrific—to compel the media's attention. If initially ignored, terrorists do not hesitate to change the plot, the setting, and the characters so the performance will not be disregarded. Terrorism, like an ill-mannered enfant terrible, is the media's stepchild, a stepchild which the media, unfortunately, can neither completely ignore nor deny.

Terrorism is theater, and politics, generally, is dramaturgy. As Murray Edelman[1] and Richard Merleman[2] have insightfully been telling us, political life can imitate art. Terrorism, especially in its most extravagant and atrocious forms, is obviously undertaken for its spectacular, histrionic, and media-attracting effects. To recognize only those relationships is to see the more conspicuous linkages between terrorism and the media. Terrorists generate spectacles, and these are newsworthy items. This explains the symbiotic relationship between reporters' seeking news and terrorists' seeking an audience. There are, however, less vivid, less spectacular, and more common political components of terrorism. These too, and not just the brutal and dramatic episodes captured by spectacular visuals, are theater. And because this theater is not as spectacular nor as readily seen as drama, it is even more insidious.

Terrorists tend to portray themselves as outraged heroes and desperate individuals forced by brutal, repressive, and insensitive regimes to commit acts of violence for which the terrorists are not responsible. If the alleged brutality of the regimes is not enough to provide ample justification, then there is the alleged ubiquitous lack of sympathy of the international community, which is depicted as having abrogated its claim to moral outrage by not being concerned with the problem. The dramatic possibilities of media interviews with terrorists are ripe for exploitation; the situation is defined by the terrorists' view of reality. A terrorist hijacking, murder, or bombing, or an interview in an ongoing hostage/barricade situation, is clearly recognized as theater; and an interview with a terrorist who justifies the slaughter of innocents by appealing to a higher morality is less apparent but equally political theater. As James E. Cooms notes, such antics find little sympathy in mass audiences.[3] But it is not sympathy that the terrorist seeks; the terrorist seeks to define a new reality and to challenge existing values and modes of thought, and beyond that, he seeks what is inescapable in terrorism's brutal outrage—confrontation with publicly accepted morality. Confrontation will invariably cause some to ponder why terrorists commit atrocities and how terrorists are motivated to outrage morality with capricious violence. Once these questions are asked, it is a short step toward seeking an explanation. Explanation ipso facto is justification to a mass audience and helps set the stage for the redefinition of terrorism in a language constructed by the terrorists.

THE MEDIA'S PORTRAYAL OF TERRORISM: PROBLEMS IN GATHERING NEWS

Commenting on the tendency of the media to sometimes accept without questioning the most preposterous statements of terrorists, correspondent Louis Rukeyser has noted:

> "American news coverage of the Arab guerrillas in recent years has resembled nothing so much as American news coverage of the Black Panthers—and in neither case has my profession cov-

THE NATURE OF THE PROBLEM 15

ered itself with journalistic glory. With both groups there is a fascination with the reality and threat of violence. With both there was a tendency to overrate their influence and to take with grave seriousness the most nonsensical extremes of rhetoric."[4]

Rukeyser's observations are strikingly similar to those of John Lafflin, who, in writing about the publicity given Arab terrorists, noted:

> "Fedayeen have had extraordinarily good publicity in the West* * * being presented pretty much on their own terms as heroes and resistance fighters * * * a gallant few facing fearful odds. They were romanticized by the media in the U.S., Britain, and much of Europe to appear as idealistic daredevils and diehards."[5]

How does one explain reporting which portrays terrorists on their own terms? Perhaps some reporters are so naive as to not question inconsistencies between what they are told and what they know. Such explanations, however, are too facile to be taken seriously. Rather, the problem is undoubtedly inherent in the business of gathering and producing the news. Perhaps one of the most objective and insightful statements about this problem comes from Edward Jay Epstein:

> "The problem of journalism in America proceeds from a simple but inescapable bind: journalists are rarely, if ever, in a position to establish the truth about an issue for themselves, and they are therefore entirely dependent on self-interested 'sources' for the version of reality they report."[6]

The problem of source dependency is an important one to Epstein, and like his colleague Louis Rukeyser, he alludes to the situation involving the Black Panthers' allegations that in 1969, across the Nation, local police in conjunction with the Federal Bureau of Investigation conducted a systematic campaign of genocide against this black organization. The allegations themselves and the number (28) of alleged victims of the police campaign were taken by the media at face value, wholly unchallenged. One news source after another picked up the story without commentary, without even attribution, exactly as the Black Panthers had told it, and it soon became a part of the public's perception of the "truth." It was on the basis of this unchecked and false allegation that Ralph Abernathy, a respected black leader, accused the Nation of waging genocide.[7]

Close examination of the allegations revealed that of the numerous violent shootouts between the Panthers and the police only too remotely showed that they might have been executions under the cover of law. This number was far less than the 10 policemen known to have been killed by the Panthers.[8]

As Epstein continued to note, the discrepancies were known to the reporters closest to the Panthers; yet not one of those reporters came forward to dispute the Panthers' claim that an organized campaign of genocide was being waged against them. To do so would have jeopardized special access to information through Panther spokesmen.

A hostile or even assertive cross-examination of sources, especially those which become visible components of a story, will likely result in denial of access to those very sources, and it is by this access that a journalist lives.

A journalist is also limited by time, space, and the human resources that can be allotted to any story. As Walter Lippmann reflected in an assessment of his own profession, "[t]he final page is of a definite size and must be ready by a precise moment."[9]

My own experience with such constraints occurred in December 1968 when I was doing an observational study of the riots at San Francisco State College. One day a major confrontation between the police and the demonstrators occurred just before 4 o'clock in the afternoon. Most of the press crews were hastily leaving the scene. Naively I asked why. "If it doesn't happen by 3:30, it doesn't happen," one of the television people volunteered. "We have deadlines to consider."[10]

The pressures of the deadline and the scoop are inextricable components of the process of gathering the news. Jack Anderson, a well-known syndicated columnist, explained a blatantly false report about the arrest of Senator Thomas Eagleton, then the Vice-Presidential nominee of the Democratic party, by saying that if he had checked the story prior to publishing it, he probably would have been scooped by competitors.[11]

The constraints under which newspeople work are perhaps too easily criticized. Given the day-to-day economic exigencies of a highly competitive business, it is understandable how some excesses occur. Reporters take a lot of pride in the scoop and the dramatic interview with an inaccessible sourse, and irrespective of the secondary fallout from such successes, the fraternity of journalists rewards that kind of behavior. The Knight Newspaper Company, which disclosed the medical information on Senator Thomas Eagleton that ultimately led to his departure from the Democratic Vice-Presidential ticket, won a 1973 Pulitzer Prize for the story. Apparently the Pulitzer Committee was interested in neither the legality of Knight Newspapers' obtaining

THE NATURE OF THE PROBLEM 17

Eagleton's medical records nor the ethical problems of making someone's medical records public.

THE ISSUE OF MEDIA AS UNCRITICAL REFLECTOR OF GOVERNMENT OPINION

Self-interested sources, the rush for the scoop, the mass appeal of terroristic dramaturgy, the need to cultivate and maintain sources, and the more obvious limitations and exigencies of time, space, and resources are all ingredients of bias. Certainly these are not the only ingredients: the electronic media has added to the list by its concern with good visuals, simplicity, and an organizational orientation toward what is news and how it will be portrayed. But perhaps there is an even greater bias, one which the news does not originate but reflects; this is the bias of government. The news transmits rather than challenges government opinion.

Frequently the media serves as a strong challenger to government, and it almost violates our commonsense, if not our common experience, to think of the media as the conveyor and reflector rather than the critic of government's opinions and positions. Afterall, the imagery of Vietnam and Watergate is too fresh in our historic and collective memories. But let us reflect momentarily. Was it always quite that way? Certainly the case of Vietnam was not always one of challenge, especially in the early days. True, there were the "Bernard Falls" and the "David Halberstams," but early on there was also a time when it was too easy, too comfortable, and too safe to report the war from anywhere but Saigon, and at that time the "five o'clock follies" (the official briefings) were taken quite seriously. And let us also not remember Watergate simply from the investigative reporting of Bob Woodward and Carl Bernstein. We might also wish to give pause to the picture of George McGovern before the Washington press establishment, being ridiculed for his comment that the trail of Watergate led a lot farther and a lot higher than the unfortunate burglars surprised in the act at the Democratic Party's Watergate offices.

If access to self-serving terrorist sources is one problem for the media, access of self-serving government sources is an equal if not greater problem. These two forces seem to push in opposing directions. But this is not always the case, and when these forces move in the same direction one sees a strong reinforcing effect. Witness the changing attitude of the American press toward the Palestine Liberation Organization (PLO) since the 1973 war between Israel and Egypt and how that change coincided with the changing orientation of U.S. policy on the same issue. Until he was exposed to the heat of the 1980 election campaign, President Carter had been continuing a momentum toward what might be described as a less favorable stance toward Israel and a more positive attitude toward the PLO.[12] The meetings between U.N. Ambassador Andrew Young and the P.L.O's U.N. observer[13] are, in this vein, not to be seen as the naive action of an overly zealous individual who violated official policy in the quest for peace, but, rather, as the execution of a policy change which, although not publicly enunciated, began with the 1973 oil embargo and had become even more pronounced under the aegis of the Carter administration.

Beyond Middle East politics, there has been another impetus for the Government to downplay Middle East terrorism. It was a major concern of the Carter administration to keep the SALT II accords alive and to nurture them through the U.S. Senate. Prior to the Soviet invasion of Afghanistan, which killed any hope of Senate ratification of the treaty, SALT II was to be the keystone of Mr. Carter's foreign policy and perhaps the crown jewel of his administration. This meant that the linkages forged between the Soviet Secret Police (KGB) and the PLO had to be ignored and denied and that the PLO had to be portrayed in sympathetic terms.

As the Administration pushed this view, so did some of America's leading news sources—most prominently *Time* and the *Wall Street Journal*—and sometimes in language and with content not at all unlike that used by the Administration. (We will return to this issue in detail below.)

The occasional willingness of the press to become a mechanism for the dissemination of government material because of either source-based relationships which develop over time or their accepting uninvestigated government accounts as fact, is a problem in other Western societies as well. Simon Hoggart, writing of the British press accounts of the situation in Northern Ireland, notes:

> "When the British press prints an account of an incident as if it were an established fact and it is clear that the reporter himself was not on the spot, it is a 99 percent certainty that it is the army's version which is given."[14]

The media's dependency on sources and access has been incorporated in the British Government's very adroit response to the media in Northern Ireland. Journalists are treated as important guests by a large network of both army and Government press corps. Those who adhere to the official line and seek news from official sources are rewarded with continued access

THE NATURE OF THE PROBLEM 19

and even an occasional scoop. Those inclined to strike out on their own are cut off from official sources and may find themselves harassed out of Ulster.

Questions of bias and definition in the news industry's portrayal of terrorism are important in a democratic society because the public's appraisal of terrorism will have implications for foreign policy decisions. Public attitudes will not only influence how a government deals with terrorism as an internal or external threat: if an informed public sees terrorism as surrogate foreign policy for certain nations, e.g., Libya, Iraq, Syria, or the Soviet Union, the conduct of foreign policy toward those States will also be influenced. To the extent that the Carter administration wanted to deal in foreign policy negotiations unhampered by public distrust of the Soviets, especially in the area of the SALT II accords, it became necessary to ignore the issue of linkages between the KGB and foreign terrorists. Mr. Reagan's administration, in contrast, has been far and away less inclined to overlook the Soviet Union's involvement with and sponsorship of terrorist organizations. During the first days of the new Administration, Secretary of State General Alexander Haig struck out against Russian involvement with international terrorist groups.[15] To observers of the relationship between Government position and media portrayal, it should be interesting to detect if the media's description of the PLO, and Russian involvement with it and other terrorist groups, changes significantly over the next several months as a result of the State Department's new posture.

LOCAL LAW ENFORCEMENT AND THE MEDIA: DIFFERENCES IN PERSPECTIVE

Concerns of bias and definition in the media's portrayal of terrorism are significantly less important to local law enforcement than the issue of the media's intrusion into police operations. The journalist's desire to obtain news and the desire of the police to prevent loss of life come most directly into conflict in the local arena. Over this conflict, more than any other, most of the sometimes heated and sometimes fruitful dialog between the police and the media has taken place.

What the police often see as intrusion is to the media the right of the fourth estate to perform its traditional and historic role in a democratic society—to gather information and to be at the scene where news is made. This is an issue which a number of our contributors have addressed.

In the papers presented by newspaper publisher James Hoge and retired police chief Robert Rabe, we observe that not only philosophy separates the media and the police: apparently, interpretation of events does too. Both authors do show understanding, if not sympathy, for the professional concerns and responsibilities of the other; nonetheless, different professional orientations seem to have led to different perceptions and different interpretations. To some extent it is not simply that these men saw an event differently. Rather, from their respective professional vantage points, they chose to focus on different attributes of the same event. Robert Rabe notes that capturing the attention of the media is a prime ingredient in terrorists' tactical designs; the Hanafi Muslim incident (March 1977) in Washington, D.C. illustrated this, as did the manner in which the media handled some aspects of the episode. Rabe goes on to note that misreporting by some journalists, as well as premature factual disclosures of police tactics, seriously jeopardized the positions of both law enforcement and the hostages the police were trying to save. James Hoge, much to his credit, does note some of the same journalistic abuses but sees them not as inherent in the nature of reporting but rather as *unrepresentative* excesses. He argues that the *Washington Post*, for example, acted very responsibly. Realizing that the Hanafis hated the newspaper, Post editors made a decision to stop phoning the terrorists for interviews and became very careful about what they published, so as not to further incite the Hanafis.

Patrick Murphy, president of the Police Foundation, also shows that it is possible to transcend professional vantage point and role. Surprisingly, Murphy, like Hoge, sees the media's role in the Hanafi episode as largely professional, save for the excesses of a few. Moreover, Murphy agrees that the media's coverage provided a functional role of keeping people informed and away from the site; the otherwise spectators could watch the scene in the comfort and safety of their homes or read about it. He also argues that it is not just the media who should be concerned with guidelines; the police should do their part to create a set of access procedures which would promote responsible news coverage of a terrorist event. These are indeed strange words from a police officer, but they are worthy of our attention, serious reflection, and consideration.

How far the chasm separating the media and the police actually stretches can be seen by the precise quantitative descriptions rendered by Sommer and Sommer in the article describing their survey of news industry and law enforcement personnel. The Sommer and Sommer survey indicates that police chiefs in the Nation's 30 largest cities believe that television coverage of terrorist events has been insensitive and has served to encourage future acts of terrorism. When the data on police chiefs was paired with data on TV

THE NATURE OF THE PROBLEM 21

news directors and newspaper editors, sharp divergencies underscored differences in professional orientation and perception. One of the sharpest differences concerned the extent to which live television coverage of terrorist acts constituted a threat to hostage safety, with, as one might guess, the police seeing it as a substantial threat and the journalists seeing it in terms of a minimal threat. But the situation is not without remedy, for when asked about the desirability of promulgating the Columbia Broadcasting Company's (CBS) standards for covering terrorism (reprinted in this volume), there was, in contrast to so many areas, substantial agreement between police chiefs and TV news directors and journalists. The issue of guidelines is well discussed from a series of vantage points in the National News Council's "Paper on Terrorism," and examples of several guidelines, in addition to those of CBS, are also reprinted. Without striking too dissonant a chord in the midst of this optimistic refrain, most of what the guidelines call for is already part and parcel of the basic ethics of good journalism. In some important sense, the guidelines do not call our attention to new rules for covering terrorism so much as reiterate old rules for good journalism, irrespective of subject matter.

Most discussions between the police and the media tend to focus on the question of intrusion by the media into counterterrorist operation. Although there has been some concern about the media's portrayal of terrorists, when law enforcement and the press get together, this attention has usually been directed at the portrayal of a specific group or a specific incident. The public would be most likely to react against the media if the media's interference in a counterterrorist operation ended in the unnecessary loss of life.

This popular scenario is given a different slant in Robert Friedlander's chapter on the Iranian hostage situation. Friedlander recounts the December 10, 1979 NBC TV interview between Marine Corporal William Gallegos and his captors, which included a 5-minute anti-American tirade by a militant spokeswoman called Mary. Broadcast of the interview led veteran correspondent Ford Rowan to resign from the network in protest over what he termed "irresponsible journalism." Friedlander also reminds us that during the Iranian hostage crisis the much-touted guidelines for news coverage in terrorist situations were flaunted by all three networks. It is not unthinkable that such interviews, which appear to strain the ethical bounds of journalism and to permit the enemies of the Nation to use the American media for their own nefarious propaganda, might bring about a public reaction which calls for imposed rather than voluntary restraint. Friedlander's compelling piece gives us pause-for-thought, especially since the press do not enjoy an absolutist interpretation of the first amendment. The Supreme Court has recently moved to a less permissive position, and it is important to bear in mind that the press never did enjoy the same freedom as political speech. Access to information has generally been more narrowly prescribed by the high court.

The legal issues dealt with below do afford us one perspective on the future course of the dilemma between the sometimes contradictory goals of law enforcement and the news industry in these situations, but the experiences of other Western democratic societies offer us yet another perspective. Walter Jaehnig provides some important insights about the situation in Britain. When Irish Republican Army (IRA) attacks moved from the soil of Northern Ireland to that of England itself, the Government responded with the Prevention of Terrorism (Temporary Provisions) Act 1974. Although not constructed to deal with journalists, several of the Act's provisions had heavy-handed implications for the conduct of journalism in Great Britain. Their presence on the statute books led to two informal, voluntary statements of principle, which provided for cooperation between the media and the police.

LEGAL CONTROLS ON THE MEDIA AND THEIR PROBLEM FOR DEMOCRACY

These informal agreements, which in certain instances could be broken by the press, were seen as preferable to legal controls that could be applied under the Prevention of Terrorism Act. What happened in Great Britain through informal agreement, which preserved the independence of the press, happened more formally in West Germany and Italy under a series of draconian antiterrorist measures. Although the details differ, the tendencies and implications of the issue appear all too clear. In each society the tendency has been twofold: to meet force with force through greater use of police power and to yield liberty not only in the area of the press but in vital areas of civil rights protected by a constitution. The most haunting case is Northern Ireland, where antiterrorist measures dismiss the right of the accused to face his accuser in open court and abolish the tradition of habeas corpus.

Both the wisdom and the effectiveness of these acts have been questioned. One of the strongest objectives of terrorists is to create repressive social responses which will in turn serve as a foundation for revolution. Terrorists' use of random violence is calculated to destroy both the image of a government and the government's legitimacy. A government unable to insulate its populace from violence is ineffectual, and in contemporary societies a government's legitimacy is to no small measure a function of this effectiveness. Terrorists believe that if they bait the government into acts of repression the

THE NATURE OF THE PROBLEM

public will rebel against the government. This revolutionary plot originates with a rather limited understanding of Karl Marx's notion that revolutions come about through the increasing misery of society.[16] Whether this is accurate Marxism is debatable. Generally, Marx and Engels had little use for terrorism and saw it as a counterrevolutionary force. This is why they had such a harsh falling out with Michael Bakunin and his protege, Sergi Nechaev. "Catechism of a Revolutionary," revered by many contemporary theoreticians of terrorism, is an anarchist document created by Bakunin and eschewed by Marx and Engels.[17] Nonetheless, terrorists of a variety of persuasions claim to be the heirs of both these conflicting doctrines.

The actual operational unfolding of the doctrine, as distinct from its theoretical assertions, has not been what terrorists have sought or anticipated. In Uruguay, it did not cause a popular uprising against the Government, but the democratic Government, the target of the terrorists, fell to a military coup d'état. The military regime did away with both the terrorists and Latin America's oldest democracy. In Turkey, in September 1980, the same scenario repeated itself in another military coup. In West Germany and Italy, terrorism has caused the enactment of harsh antiterrorist legislation: the public has eagerly sacrificed liberty to preserve order.

Terrorism against the state occurs primarily in Western societies, and strong state counterterrorist action has had an awesome effect on freedom and civil rights. Terrorists are not all alike, and consequently the effectiveness of strong measures has not been the same. If the terrorist group is founded on a utopian vision of society and does not have a mass following, the society will either follow the government's lead toward stronger antiterrorist measures or take the initiative itself by pressing the government into stronger action. The utopian drama of revolution, which the terrorists believe they have created, fails to take place, and in the course of events the civil liberties of the entire society, including the media, are to some degree vanquished with the terrorists.

When the terrorists are nationalists, however, the utopian quest may in some sense be the same, but the popular reception is quite different.[18] The ensuing authoritarian response of the government only alienates intellectuals and hardens the resolve of the populace: witness Britain's dilemma in Northern Ireland, Israel's difficulties with West Bank Palestinians, and the gathering storm in South Africa. Repression may also be costly in terms of world public opinion and in the case of a colonial government, its own people. Nationalism garners a great deal of moral support in the international arena, and the international repercussions of such support are omnipresent. In these situations, a restrictive policy toward the media will be achieved at great cost: it will push local intellectuals onto the international stage and provide them with a forum, an audience, and a legitimacy they probably would never have had at home. The price a government will ultimately have to pay for curtailing civil rights and restricting the media will depend upon the kind of terrorists, their following among the public, and their realistic claims to legitimacy. Even when both precedent and the public support the curtailment of basic freedoms in an effort to deal with terrorism, the unanticipated consequences of such policies may demonstrate that they are not worth pursuing. As Paul Wilkinson has commented, "[t]o believe it is worth snuffing out all individual rights and sacrificing liberal values for the sake of order is to fall into the error of the terrorists themselves ★ ★ ★." To this we might add that in cases involving nationalist terrorists, the sacrifice of liberal values most likely will not bring about the cherished order for which liberty has been expended, and perhaps the society is unwittingly condemned under such circumstances to do some of the terrorists' work for them.

The issue of the media and terrorism is seen as a simple choice between freedom and order. From one perspective, to give the media unrestrained rights to print and air what they see fit is perceived as bordering on societal chaos. Accordingly, from this perspective, order can be maintained only through control of the media. Such thinking, often the outgrowth of direct experience with press abuse, is highly simplistic. The resolution of our dilemma, as our contributors acknowledge, lies not in choosing between simple alternatives but in finding a balance between cherished values. Any debate concerning the media is remiss if it ignores the functional consequences of the media, not only the obvious ones necessary for the preservation of a vigorous democracy but the less noticeable ones which can aid in defusing the threat of terrorism to the state. In the great crush of debate over the choice between freedom and order, these other aspects of the media are frequently ignored. The media have an immediate function to provide potential terrorists with a nonviolent alternative for disseminating a message.

THE MEDIA AS A NONVIOLENT ALTERNATIVE

If terrorism is a means of reaching the public forum, violence can be defused by providing accessibility to the media without the necessity of an entry fee of blood and agony. This was a conclusion that a number of us who met at the Ditchley Castle conference on terrorism came to several years back.[20] Beyond this function the media also provide an appropriate mechanism for a government to communicate with terrorists. One-time member of the notorious Baader-Meinhof gang, Horst Mahler, cited the efforts of the Government to communicate with terrorists, especially through the media, as one of the reasons for his and others' change of view toward the Government. The dialog initiated in the press by the West German Government served as a mechanism to bring about the capitulation of some terrorists, Mahler among them.[21]

Too often seen as unwitting accomplices in terrorists' quests for public attention, the media also act as forums for transmitting information and recasting images to extinguish terrorism. One of the most skillful users of the media for this purpose has been Irish Republic Prime Minister John Lynch. Repeatedly urging the media to speak out against the terrorism in Northern Ireland, Lynch took the matter into his own hands during a recent visit to the United States.[22] In appearances before the National Press Club in Washington, D.C. and before a sizable viewing audience on NBC TV's "Today" show, Lynch spoke out in unqualified terms about those Americans who support the IRA's Provisional Wing. Consider the image of the Prime Minister of the Irish Republic linking American fund raising with the bombings and killings in Northern Ireland and forcefully speaking out against Americans of Irish extraction who support the IRA. It is a moral and highly credible message, one that would cause all but the least sensitive or most committed Irish nationalists to reflect on the true implications of IRA support.

It is one thing, of course, to observe the intent of communication; it is quite another to know in any meaningful sense how such communications are received. Knowledgeable and informed observers will come to strikingly disparate conclusions about the impact of what is transmitted. Thus, Robert Friedlander's chapter raises the specter of public outrage because of NBC's transmitting the controversial interview from Iran with Marine Corporal William Gallegos. NBC newsman Ford Rowan called that interview "irresponsible journalism." However, support and justification for the interview came from one of the most responsible journalistic sources in America, the *Washington Post*.[23] While many observers saw the Gallegos interview as a cynical exploitation of the hostages' situation in order to obtain an audience, the *Washington Post* saw the accompanying propaganda as being so transparent as to amplify before Americans the outrage perpetrated by the Iranians on their captives. Drawing on that perception, the *Post* concluded that NBC was performing a legitimate public service in fulfilling its function as a conveyor of news.

There is also a valuable role for the media in squelching rumor and laying to rest erroneous and potentially harmful information, especially in ongoing hostage and barricade situations. The quality of that performance is, however, a controversial issue.

In his paper, Chief Robert Rabe sees the media as being as likely to contribute to the creation of rumor as to squelch it. Rabe's career as one of the Nation's best hostage negotiators gave him first-hand experience with the broadcast of unverified rumors and the dissemination of harmful, erroneous information. During the Hanafi seige, a live broadcast stated that the police were taking boxes of ammunition into the B'nai B'rith building in preparation for a no-holds-barred assault. What appeared to the reporter to be ammunition was food being taken in for the hostages. Leonard Downie, who managed the *Post's* coverage of the event, however, saw the media's handling of the crisis in terms more consonant with the positive contributions stemming from media coverage. Downie saw the media as having "contributed to an atmosphere in which the takeover could be more easily and more peacefully resolved."[24]

Chief Rabe would probably tell us that this view might be well and good if one were not on the other end of the phone trying to persuade an angry, heavily armed Hamass Abdul Khaalis that the boxes being brought into the B'nai B'rith building were food and not ammunition. He might also tell us that triggering an angry, vengeful, heavily armed man who has a history of mental illness and who holds the lives of dozens of people in his hands, is not aptly described as a journalistic "excess."

But if Rabe has his complaints about the press, *Chicago Sun-Times* publisher Hoge has his grievances about the police. In his own city, which has a large and sophisticated police department, Hoge found that attempts by the police to provide information during two important terrorist episodes were best described as chaotic.

Both men would agree that a hostage story is delicate and requires discrete and cautious coverage. At issue is their respective estimations of how discrete and cautious the press are capable of being. Giving the press a vote of confidence in both regards, Patrick Murphy indicates in his paper that for practical reasons the media should be generally unrestricted in their job of covering terrorist incidents. Primary among these practical considerations is the press' capacity to dispel rumors. To underscore this position, Murphy stands four-square behind Leonard Downie's view of the role of the press in the Hanafi incident.[26]

Often overlooked in the complexity and chaos of a hostage situation covered by hundreds of foreign and domestic reporters is that, as an institution,

THE NATURE OF THE PROBLEM 27

the media is not homogenous, but a group of people with different aspirations, different concerns, and different commitments to ethics. The media is not monolithic; it is coteries of people who descend on a dramatic event with an appetite for a morsel of news and with different notions of what lengths they would go to obtain that news. These people can be responsible or irresponsible. Different journalists will choose different roles, and over the course of a long seige it is not inconceivable that different characterizations would aptly describe the ethics of the same individual.

THE POLICE VIEW OF MEDIA

The police would like nothing better than for the news industry to deal responsibly with information so that its functional squelching of rumor can serve the interest of authorities, but by and large the police, at least from my conversations with them, are less concerned about the media's not fulfilling their civic responsibility than their restraining themselves from becoming part of the news instead of simply reporting it. The strongest friction between the police and the press occurs when the media become part of a drama and interfere with the attempts by police to bring a terrorist situation to a conclusion.

Some examples might be worth noting in this regard. Unfortunately, there are far and away too many from which to choose, but perhaps our viewing one in a foreign context will at least spare us some need for defensiveness.

On April 30, 1980, the Iranian Government, which had been holding American hostages at the U.S. Embassy in Tehran, had a bitter if not ironic taste of its own medicine when a group of Arab secessionists seized the Iranian Embassy in London. While the American public experienced some strong satisfaction in the Iranian's dilemma and enjoyed some relief from its own frustrations, when Iran comically denounced the seizure as a gross violation of international law, Scotland Yard found the situation anything but comic. The Yard was rapidly implementing plans and deploying men and resources to contain the situation and to deal with the deluge of reporters who flocked to the scene from London, the United Kingdom, and abroad.

Deputy Assistant Commissioner Peter C. Neivens, the Metropolitan Police's director of information, sought to secure the media's assistance to ease the tension and to squelch rumors surrounding the situation.[27] Neivens brought into play the media in its functional capacity almost as if drawing a leaf from the characterizations drawn by the *Washington Post's* Leonard Downie.[28] By stressing the aspirations of the authorities for a peaceful resolution of the situation, Neivens hoped to utilize the press to communicate to the terrorists that the British, who were neutral in the conflict, had no interest in becoming involved in violence and were deeply and optimistically committed to a peaceful resolution of the problem.

The terrorists had secured a good deal of publicity for their secessionist cause and had made their point before the world's press, many of whom had come to London expressly to cover the seizure. The fanatical revolutionary government of Iran's Ayatollah Khomeini could hardly be expected to yield to the terrorists' demands for self-determination simply because they were holding hostages. The authorities were calculating that the hostage situation would run its ritualistic course and that there would be an inevitable capitulation. It was all a matter of time. But thoughts of a peaceful resolution were quickly jolted by a strange and inexplicable turn of events—the terrorists killed a hostage. The authorities moved toward bringing in an assault team from the Special Air Services (SAS) of the Royal Air Force (RAF). These men, like our own SWAT teams, are specially trained in counterterrorist tactics, and as in any armed assault mandated by these situations, preparation, timing, and surprise are the watchwords for a successful operation.

But in this case the element of surprise was almost destroyed by members of the media. British ITV (Independent Television) had managed to get through the police barricades with a television camera and were able to transmit live the assault on the Embassy. One can only speculate what would have happened had the terrorists been watching Embassy televisions as the SAS men were televised as they attacked the building.

For their part, ITV claims there was a 2- to 3-minute delay in the transmission. The Yard responds that this occurred only because a decision had to be made to interrupt ongoing programs. The decision to transmit or not transmit was not even made at the highest levels but by whoever was at the station at the time.

According to the police, it appears that in the rush for a dramatic on-camera scoop, ITV was willing to jeopardize the lives of the captives and the dedicated men who had trained long and hard to risk their own lives to save hostages. Justifying these actions under the banner of the public's right to know seems rather empty under such circumstances.

Situations as dramatic and spectacular as the seizure of the Embassy draw coverage from the far corners of the world. As many as 200 correspondents were sent to report on the story. The flood of non-London reporters, who were unfamiliar with agreements between local press and the police and who had no interest in long-term accommodation with authorities, could have been

THE NATURE OF THE PROBLEM 29

expected to produce problems. Surprisingly it was not the flood of foreign reporters who washed away long-standing procedures: it was the local press who threatened procedure, accommodation, and nearly life itself.

Their actions could not be justified on the grounds that they were dealing with a police force that was neither equipped nor willing to give the media necessary access. As Walter Jaehnig notes in his paper on the police and the press in Great Britain, former police commissioner Sir Robert Mark and his successor Sir David McNee both realized the importance of maintaining good working relations with the media, and Deputy Assistant Commissioner Peter Nievens demonstrated a sophisticated understanding of the importance of good press relations.

AREAS OF DISAGREEMENT: SOME EXAMPLES

Despite areas of accord between the media and the Yard, sharp differences have repeatedly come forth. On July 5, 1979, the British Broadcasting Company (BBC) transmitted an interview with a disguised member of the Irish National Liberation Army (INLA), the group which claimed responsibility for killing Member of Parliament Airey Neave within Parliament's gates. The outrage extended beyond the halls of Scotland Yard to Number 10 Downing street. Prime Minister Margaret Thatcher said she was "appalled"[29] and later threatened legal proceedings against the BBC.

Overall, the London police maintain that the press have been cooperative, especially when covering an ongoing situation. As Peter C. Neivens informed me, during the Iranian Embassy siege, even with the sizable influx of foreign press, the press were given access to the periphery of the sealed inner perimeter and were conscientiously kept informed.[30] It is not lack of cooperation by authorities which motivates the press to violate the rules. Intrinsic and inherent differences in organizational goals bring the police and press into conflict.

Although no one was killed as a result of ITV's actions, this has not always been the case when the press have intruded where they should not. Referring to the October 1977 Lufthansa hijacking that ended in the daring raid by West German Police at Mogadishu, Somalia, Thomas M. Ashwood, chairman of flight security for the International Pilot's Association, noted that the head of the West German pilot's association held the media responsible for the summary execution of the Lufthansa captain. Apparently the captain had cleverly and skillfully passed information to authorities in the course of his normal radio transmissions overheard by the terrorists. The terrorists were unaware of the ruse until the media made the fact known.[31]

A similar case apparently took place earlier, in November 1974, when a British Airways plane travelling from Dubai to Libya was hijacked. Demands were made for the release of 13 terrorists incarcerated in Egypt. An aircraft supposedly carrying the 13 terrorists, arrived from Cairo. Suddenly a local reporter broadcasted that the operation was a ruse and that there were no freed terrorists on board the Cairo aircraft. In retaliation a German banker was selected from among the hostages and executed.[32]

Disclosures of information that have endangered hostages have unfortunately not only come from the media. This in no way absolves the media, but it does indicate how general the problem is. When terrorists seized U.S. diplomats George Curtis Moore and Cleo A. Noel in Khartoum in March 1973, and President Nixon responded with a public announcement reiterating the existing U.S. policy of non-negotiation, some State Department observers felt he had sealed the hostages' executions.[33]

Even where the hostages have not lost their lives, the premature and unwarranted disclosure of information that serves the terrorists has time and again threatened the lives of hostages or authorities. In the 1974 hostage episode in the cellblock of the D.C. Courthouse, the hostages and their captors were separated from the police by a two-way mirror which permitted the police to use snipers if the hostages' lives or safety came into jeopardy. Local media made that information public, and the hostages were rapidly dispatched to tape over the mirror.[34]

In the course of the same operation, a young, aggressive reporter conducted lengthy telephone interviews with the hostage takers and tried to get into the cell block. When I asked him if he had ever thought about this accidentally setting off the terrorists, he openly said:

> "I never thought about getting them riled up. My primary goal was to be let into ★ ★ ★ and to get a scoop. My gratification comes from doing something that is worthy of the front page ★ ★ ★ doing a story worth seeing. Probably, there in the back of my mind there was concern, but I didn't think about it."[35]

This reporter was concerned with not only getting the scoop but with getting it by gaining access to the cell block itself and getting into a face-to-face dialog with the terrorists—a very risky business. In fact, the difficulty and potential disaster of such undertakings are not readily apparent. A trained hostage negotiator spends months learning to negotiate, works with an experienced backup team, and is mentally prepared for the psychological drain of the process. An untrained reporter, especially one meeting face-to-face

THE NATURE OF THE PROBLEM

with the terrorists, is a liability not only to the hostages but in some real sense to his own mental well-being as well.

In the aftermath of a hostage situation in a large American city, I happened to interview a very sensitive and bright reporter whom, at the terrorists' request, the police had asked to negotiate. Although reluctant to undertake the task, he felt he really had no choice; were he to refuse and the situation go awry, in the public mind he would certainly be to blame. With this in mind, he accepted reluctantly and contributed to the captors' surrendering without any loss of life. Afterwards, for days he was psychologically drained; his emotional state had been severly rocked by the tension of the situation. He spent several sleepless nights and said that he would never again negotiate. Having acquired knowledge and experience of the psychological process of negotiation, upon reflection he marveled that the police would have acceded to the terrorists' request.

As long as media and terrorists share the common goals of reaching large, interested audiences, and terrorists continue to provide the media with dramatic and sensational material—often with the type of spectacular visual drama which the electronic media like—other social and human values will inevitably compete against the media's own definition of success. Not only will there be less than appropriate concern for the hostages during such crises; but this lack of sensitivity will continue even after the episode ends, when the human-interest stories may provide even more dramatic copy.

Journalist Charles Fenyvesi, who was a hostage in the Hanafi episode, found his colleagues had more sympathy for the terrorists than they had for the hostages—they had no compassion for the hostages' suffering. When the hostages were free but still disoriented and numb from the ordeal, the press descended on them "like a pack of hungry barracudas, pursuing hostages that had run away to elude them."[36]

The Hanafi episode produced a media spectacular—virtually continuous live television coverage and domination of most of the entire first section of the *Washington Post* for 2 days. The Hanafi hostage-taking so captured audience attention that TV news directors were reluctant to turn coverage away from the incident for fear of losing their audiences.[37]

The *Washington Post* so overexposed the Hanafi Muslims that it relegated a major address by President Carter to the inside pages and put the Hanafis on the front page.[38] Washington's WTOP TV spent between $70,000 and $75,000 for coverage of the Hanafis. Camera crews from as far away as Chicago and Burbank were flown in by the National Broadcasting Company (NBC) to make up their 18 camera crews which covered the story. For 3 days

NBC spent 53 percent of its total evening network newstime on the story; the other 2 networks followed suit, with the American Broadcast Company (ABC) spending 40 percent of its newstime, and Columbia Broadcasting System (CBS) spending 30 percent of its newstime on the episode for the 3 evenings of coverage. All 3 networks made it their lead story.[39]

This kind of investment to cover a little-known band of terrorists underscores the strong relationship between media and terrorists and their common goals in securing and keeping a large audience.

DEPICTION OF TERRORISTS BY THE MEDIA: SOME ISSUES

Concern over the media's attention to terrorism and intrusion into police operations is only one part of the issue. Equally if not more important are the debate over the way the media at times portray terrorists and the source-dependency of reporters in gathering information—a dependency which can result in biased accounts *for and against* terrorists. Source-dependency can operate in something as simple as the manner in which terrorists and their behaviors are described. Few words are neutral; each word chosen to describe terrorists and their operations has particular connotations and denotations. Afterall, calling a person a "terrorist" instead of a "guerrilla," "freedom fighter," or "commando" already establishes a point of view. The British press would never think of calling a terrorist "a commando," for such a designation would provide the terrorist with the aura that British commandos won at great sacrifice during World War II. Similarly, when a police officer is "executed," or simply "perishes" at the hands of terrorism, the media creates a cognitive image of something other than murder.[40]

Some of the strongest biases in the depiction of terrorism occurred when a strange constellation of events caused a Western government to portray a terrorist group as the terrorist group portrayed itself. The group is the Palestine Liberation Organization, and the government is the United States. The ironic public relations congruence came about, in this writer's opinion, because what was at stake far and away transcended terrorism, at least in the eyes of the Carter administration. Oil was only the obvious motivation; the less obvious motivation was the Strategic Arms Limitation Treaty (SALT) II.

The 1973 Middle East War, the corresponding Arab oil boycott, and the ensuing lines and sometimes violent conflicts over access to the gasoline pumps in America, set the stage for a major change in Middle East policy. Depicting the policy as more even-handed, the Carter administration contin-

THE NATURE OF THE PROBLEM 33

ued the momentum established under the Nixon administration toward a more positive posture vis-à-vis the PLO and, in the process, deferred to and recognized the powerful influence of Saudi Arabia as America's largest supplier of imported oil. When policy moved in this direction, other imperatives underscored by the SALT II agreements came into play. Here, the linkage with terrorism is less obvious, but perhaps the actions of both the Government and the media are all the more insidious because of this. At issue was Russian involvement with the PLO in fomenting Middle East terrorism. Prior to the Russian invasion of Afghanistan on December 27, 1979, the SALT II accords were still viable, and to link the Soviets with Middle Eastern terrorism was to create obstacles to its ratification by the Senate.

Robert Moss, of the *Economist* (London), has repeatedly spoken of a "conspiracy of silence" about Russian involvement in international terrorism, a conspiracy which has operated to preserve detente with the Soviet Union.[41] Somewhat in contrast, Charles Horner argues that the facts are known and accepted as a matter of course and that they "quickly succumb to a general lack of public interest."[42]

It is true as Dr. Horner asserts—the facts are known. However, it is also true that attempts to provide any meaningful attention to or commentary on those facts result in hastily drawn visions if not allegations of "anti-Soviet paranoia"; hence Moss' conspiracy of silence.

On Thursday July 26, 1979, the prestigious *Wall Street Journal* published an editorial-page article by Suzanne Weaver which covered a session of the Jonathan Institute (Jerusalem) Conference on Terrorism. The article reported Moss' charges concerning the use of terrorism by the Soviets, by Lybia, and by the PLO and that all three were heavily involved in the campaign to overthrow the Shah of Iran. Moss also asserted that the PLO had become a surrogate for the workings of Soviet policy interests in the Middle East. Given information generally available on the issue, Moss' comments should have been received as rather unexciting and common knowledge. Yet the reception he got was quite different from what one might have anticipated. According to Suzanne Weaver,

> "[a] considerable number in the press corps covering the conference were much annoyed by Mr. Moss' charges and told him so. Where was he getting his information? Was he really asking people to believe he had respectable evidence of a Soviet-lead conspiracy in this matter?"[43]

Pressured to hold a special press conference the following day, Moss obliged, and he chided journalists for not pushing Western governments to reveal the linkages between the Soviets and terrorism. Journalists, unfortunately, have gone to greater lengths to portray terrorists as victims of social injustice and soldiers of national liberation. In contrast to those motifs, the story of Soviet involvement is an obscure and pallid item.

Moss' approach, one which should be applauded, is to make us confront terrorism and see it for what it often is—surrogate warfare against the West. Both Moss' notion of a conspiracy of silence and Horner's idea of a general lack of interest are warranted because terrorism and Soviet involvement in it are not taken seriously. The differences between Moss and Horner may stimulate academic interest, but from my perspective both men are saying essentially the same thing—the media do not take terrorism and the Soviet involvement in it as seriously as they should. The reason is quite obvious: those committed to a broad world-view based on detente are reluctant to deal with the reality of the Soviet Union's contemporary political terrorism.

There is nothing new in the allegations that the Soviet Union trains terrorists. One State Department official confirmed such operations and in the same breath told me that there was nothing surprising or even reprehensible in those actions. "After all," he added, "they train their friendlies and we train ours. What is the difference?"[44] The difference, hopefully, is that although we train people in the use of violence, we are not involved in programs which concentrate on violence being randomly used against innocents.

The annoyance of the press with Robert Moss seems to raise the question of where the press have been. Moss' allegations about the PLO's involvement in the overthrow of the Shah appear borne out by the special relationship Arafat has with Ayatollah Khomeini. The PLO has been able to open offices throughout Iran, and, apparently, Iran has reciprocated Arafat's help by openly recruiting an army to be stationed in Lebanon under PLO direction. The bonds seem to be so tight that the American Government called upon Arafat to use his influence to assist in the American-Iranian discussions over the hostages. As Pierre Salinger revealed in the special edition of ABC's "20/20" broadcast on January 22, 1981, Arafat's relationship with Khomeini was so close that Arafat was able to secure the release of 13 hostages—5 women and 8 black men who were freed on November 20, 1979.[45] In Paris, three men arrested in the unsuccessful assassination attempt on former Iranian Premier Shapour Bakhtiar admitted that they had acted on behalf of the PLO and that Yasser Arafat had personally ordered the premier's elimination.[46]

Moss' allegations concerning Libya's use of terrorism were also well known.

THE NATURE OF THE PROBLEM 35

On March 27, 1980, Italian police discovered the decomposing body of Mohammed Salem Retaini in the trunk of a car parked in Rome. Retaini had left Libya in anger after Col. Muammar Qaddafi, Libya's strongman, had nationalized Retaini's business in 1977. Jacques deVernisy, writing in the socialist *Le Matin,* charged: "The assassinations in Europe arranged by Col. Muammar Qaddafi would fill a casebook."[47]

On October 31, 1980, David K. Shipler, in a special report to the *New York Times* from Hebron, on the Israeli-occupied West Bank, reported that the commander of the PLO terrorist group responsible for the murders of six religious Jews during a Sabbath attack admitted to having been trained in the Soviet Union. Adan Jaber, the terrorist, discussed steps taken by the Soviets to provide the Palestinians with better military skills and went on to discuss similar training provided by China, Vietnam, and North Korea.

The October 31, 1980 news item did follow Moss' comments, but that is hardly an excuse for the press to have attacked Moss, for such information—despite attempts by the State Department and many of the press to soft-peddle it—has been widely known. Eastern bloc defectors such as Czechoslovak General Sejna, a KGB Department V specialist, have long acknowledged the special training made available to the PLO in the Soviet Union and other Eastern bloc countries. The training has covered courses in terrorist methods and chemical and biological warfare; the military training institution at Simferopal has also offered courses especially tailored to Palestinians.

The press have reacted with annoyance and hostility, and State Department officials have even gone so far as to publicly criticize the ethics, competence, and credentials of journalists Claire Sterling and Jillian Becker, who wrote about the interlocking network of "terrorist international." When speaking of Moss' attempts to demonstrate the point to his fellow journalists, Suzanne Weaver observed:

> "If this attempt makes headway, the already-embattled idea of Western detente with the Soviets will be under even more intense challenge. And political leaders who try to push detente-based policies, from trade agreements to SALT, will have even harder going ahead."[48]

This may be the core of the issue.

The stakes of these policy options are very high, and if the choice is based on wrong assumptions, the consequences of error are costly. The choice of options, of course, does not proceed in an environment based purely on an objective, dispassionate cost-benefit basis. To no small extent these choices incorporate a view of the world based not only on what the present is but on what one aspires the future should look like. Noble sentiments might be influential here, but they probably produce dissonance when the facts are different from one's image of what the world is and should become.

It is not that some components of the press or some members of the State Department wish to promote terrorism: they see detente and the attendant SALT II treaty as far and away more vital to American and world interests than dealing with some of the objective realities of terrorism. Moreover, to some, America's dependence on imported oil primarily furnished by Saudi Arabia means that Arab terrorism should be viewed in a special light. This view is reflected in police collusion in the escape or the release of Arab terrorists, an open secret in some Western European countries,[49] and has caused some of the most influential of the American media to depict Arab terrorism in a fashion which the Carter administration's Department of State would not find offensive. Rael Jean Isaac's penetrating longitudinal analysis of *Time* magazine's coverage of the Middle East shows significant shifts in *Time's* position on Israel which correspond to the growth of the Arab oil weapon. At many points, *Time's* depiction of the PLO's position on major issues relevant to peace was clearly at variance with the PLO's own public statements.[50] Similar unabashed pro-Palestinian reporting that has either ignored or chosen to downplay the PLO's involvement with terrorism can be found in Ray Vicker's dispatches to the *Wall Street Journal*.[51] Vicker's catch phrase, "not just guerrillas," is unfortunately an echo of a very popular and disconcerting piece of the Carter administration's Department of State phraseology.

Clearly, there are no monoliths in this scenario. There is no organized media, for Robert Moss is very much a journalist and his charges at the Jonathan Institute Conference in Jerusalem were extended in a recent article in the *New York Times Magazine*.[52] If both *Time* magazine and Ray Vicker of the *Wall Street Journal* have taken positions which sound remarkably like PLO propaganda, we learn about the latter in surprisingly precise terms from the *New Republic*, another, although less popular, newsmagazine. If there are biases in depiction and if the imperatives of foreign policy and oil politics cater to the worst in journalism, then the remedy is to be found in a vigorous and dynamic competition of ideas. The best way to insure this is to preserve the free tradition of journalism. When we seek to make policy for what journalists write and how they write about it, we have gone a long way toward accomplishing for terrorists what they have been unable to accomplish for themselves. At the same time we must recognize that promoting the free marketplace of ideas is not synonymous with advocating an unimpaired access to information wherever the news is being made. Such access is not a corollary right inherent in the constitutional guarantee of a free press. When human life weighs in the balance against the news industry's search for information, an obstreperous media will not only find little support or solace in the law but will, if the European experience is instructive, run up against a public that will use the law to create publicly defined barriers to access. It is to that prospect which we will now turn.

THE MEDIA AND THE COURTS

Do the media have a privileged right under the first amendment to unrestricted access to news? Are restrictions placed on a journalist's access to information, paraphrasing the ideas of Thomas I. Emerson, going to cut off the search for truth, or the expression of it, and consequently create a despotic state?[53] Is unrestricted access so inimical to the process of democratic government that there can be no restrictions on gathering information? James Madison wrote:

> "A popular Government without popular information, or the means of acquiring it, is but a Prologue to a Farce or a Tragedy; or perhaps both. Knowledge will forever govern ignorance: And a people who mean to be their own Governors, must arm themselves with the power which Knowledge gives."[54]

The importance of James Madison's words can be noted by their appearance in the *dissenting* opinion by Justice William O. Douglas in *Environmental Protection Agency* v. *Mink*. In that opinion the Supreme Court ruled that a classified stamp on a Government file made everything in that file immune from disclosure. A United States district court, even in closed chambers, could not study classified documents for the purpose of releasing non-secret portions from them. It required a Congressional amendment to the Freedom of Information Act (Section 552, Title 5, U.S. Code) in 1974 to override the *EPA* v. *Mink* decision so that the district courts could go beyond the face of executive branch classification to determine whether documents are indeed properly classified. Where the right to gather news and its corollary, the public's right to know, have surfaced as issues before the Court, only *limited* recognition has been provided for the right to gather news.

The Court has also refused to give the press special status or immunities from warrants. In *Zurcher* v. *Stanford Daily* the Supreme Court rejected the idea that searches of newspaper offices for criminal evidence reasonably believed to be in the office will seriously threaten the ability of the press to gather, analyze, and disseminate news.[55] The Court upheld the search.

The case of *Zurcher* v. *Stanford Daily* is an important one and requires some detailed attention: a group of demonstrators had occupied the administrative offices of the Stanford University (Calif.) Hospital. Violence erupted when the police were removing the demonstrators; some police officers were injured, and some of their attackers escaped. Photographs which subsequently appeared in the *Stanford Daily,* the University's student newspaper, led authorities to believe that the newspaper possessed other film of the event which would enable the police to identify and apprehend their assailants. The district attorney obtained a search warrant from the municipal court for a search of the newspaper's offices. The warrant was issued by the court on grounds of just, probable, and reasonable cause for believing the evidence was in the hands of the newspaper's personnel. No allegations, in the warrant or in the district attorney's request for a warrant, were made concerning the culpability of any of the staff of the newspaper. The four officers who conducted the search, interestingly, did not open locked drawers and rooms. They had the opportunity to read notes and correspondence during the search but denied that they had exceeded the limits of the warrant. As it turned out, no evidence was found, and no material of any sort was removed from the newspaper's office.

The *Stanford Daily* brought suit against the local (Palo Alto, Calif.) police chief (Zurcher), the district attorney, and others, charging that the defendants, under "color" of State law, had violated the newspaper staff's rights under the 1st, 4th, and 14th amendments of the United States Constitution. The plaintiffs did not argue—and this is an important component of the issue—that the court was not entitled to a newspaper's evidence, but rather that the proper mechanism for obtaining such evidence was the subpena, whereby the newspaper would turn over such evidence to the court, and not the search warrant, which intimidated the press and enabled the authorities to seize evidence. The district court decided in favor of the *Stanford Daily,* and the decision was upheld by the court of appeals. The Supreme Court, however, overruled the lower courts and permitted the search. As the Court noted,

> "[t]hey [the framers of the Constitution of the United States] did not prohibit warrants where the press was involved, did not require

THE NATURE OF THE PROBLEM 39

special showings that subpoenas would be impractical and did not insist that the owner of the place to be searched, if connected with the press, must be shown to be implicated in the offense being investigated. Further, the prior cases do no more than insist that the courts apply the warrant requirements with particular exactitude when First Amendment interests would be endangered by the search. As we see it, no more than this is required where the warrant requested is for the seizure of criminal evidence reasonably believed to be on the premises occupied by a newspaper."[56]

The Court went on to argue that the procedure would not interfere with the timely publication process of newspapers, nor would it intrude into or deter normal editorial and publication decisions. The Court concluded that the Constitution did not give the press a special status which would make them immune from a duly executed search warrant. The Court majority, in balancing the freedom to gather news against the right of law enforcement agents to gather evidence pertinent to criminal prosecution, came down decisively in favor of the latter.

The issues at stake in this important case, and what they say about the value the Court places on the judicial process and the risks the Court is willing to take in deciding against the press, can be seen in Justice Stewart's dissent, which Justice Marshall joined. Justice Stewart saw both the presence of police in a pressroom and their search of it as interruptions of normal news operations that would impair or temporarily prevent the process of newsgathering, writing, editing, and publishing. He also focused on the *Stanford Daily's* willingness to yield information to subpena. He saw the use of the subpena as a means of protecting the freedom of the press and use of the search warrant as a direct threat to that freedom. To Justice Stewart it was self-evident that a search of newspaper offices by police would place a decisive burden on the freedom of the press and would be at variance with the first amendment and its function to provide an undiminished flow of potentially important information to the public.

The results of the Supreme Court's decision in *Zurcher* v. *Stanford Daily* were to be as poignant and dramatic as Justice Stewart feared. The decision had sent a shiver through the media community, and its chilling effects on the media's functioning were soon to be realized. In May 1980, police searched the printers of the Flint (Mich.) *Voice,* a monthly newspaper, and did precisely what Justice Stewart had feared would happen as a consequence of *Zurcher* v. *Stanford Daily.* Justice Stewart had expressed concern that the police would raid newspapers to seek the identity of confidential sources. In his dissenting opinion in the famous case of *Branzburg* v. *Hayes et al.*,[57] He stated that the Court had "invited state and federal authorities to undermine the historic independence of the press by attempting to annex the journalistic profession as an investigative arm of government."[58] He went on to note: "The right to gather news implies, in turn, a right to a confidential relationship between a reporter and his source."[59] In *Branzburg* v. *Hayes* the majority denied the right of a reporter to claim a constitutional privilege to protect a confidential source and upheld the propriety of courts to require the testimony of journalists before grand juries. In his dissent in *Zurcher* v. *Stanford Daily,* Justice Stewart cited his previous dissent in *Branzburg* v. *Hayes,* pointing out that opening the media's doors to police would remove any prospect of keeping a source confidential. The police, in effect, could now search the newsroom for information on confidential sources, and to the extent that confidentiality was a prime ingredient in newsgathering, this was impeded.

Two months after the Flint, Mich. search, seven plainclothesmen armed with a search warrant entered the facilities of KCBI TV in Boise, Idaho, and demanded film shot during a riot at the Idaho State Penitentiary. After rummaging through the office, the authorities left with two cassettes. Commenting on the aftermath of the experience, KCBI managing editor Bob Loy complained: "My desk looks like the Nazis went through it."[60]

Further ramifications of the results of the Court's difficult balancing of social values in *Zurcher* v. *Stanford Daily* and *Branzburg* v. *Hayes* were to be observed in a search conducted by the Georgia Bureau of Investigation (GBI) which followed on the heels of the forage of the KBCI TV offices. GBI went through the home-files of Albany (Ga.) *Herald* reporter Charles Postell. The GBI claimed they were looking for material relating to an escape of four convicted murderers from a Georgia prison. Postell, however, had earlier written stories critical of the GBI and had named a senior agent as a suspect in a drug investigation.[61]

In response to the *Zurcher* v. *Stanford Daily* decision and in anticipation of incidents like those described above—scenes which Mr. Justice Stewart conjured up in his dissenting opinion—nine States have passed laws limiting the search of newsrooms. And over Justice Department objections, the 96th Congress passed the Privacy Protection Act of 1980 (S.1790). This legislation makes it unlawful for Government officers and employees connected with a criminal investigation to seize work materials in the possession of persons engaged in some form of communication or publication. There are commonsense exceptions to the legislation which include: the person having

THE NATURE OF THE PROBLEM

possession allegedly committed the crime; immediate seizure would prevent loss of human life or bodily injury; the material is related to national defense; and a subpena would result in the destruction of the material, etc. In accordance with provisions of the legislation, on December 29, 1980, the Department of Justice released the Attorney General's guidelines for implementing the law.[62] These extended the legislative protection to confidential professional relationships, e.g., to lawyers, physicians, psychiatrists, or clergymen.

What is of interest here for our discussion is that the legislative branch of government had to override the action of the judiciary in weighing the interests of a free press against the needs of law enforcement agents to obtain evidence pursuant to criminal investigations. Moreover, the Privacy Protection Act of 1980 refers to seizure *by warrant* of confidential materials held by a disinterested third party. Although this deals with the concerns for press freedom addressed in *Zurcher* v. *Stanford Daily*, it does not in any way shield the press from *subpena*, the issue in *Branzburg* v. *Hayes*. This controversy over reporter's privilege dates as far back as 1848 when John Nugent, a reporter for the *New York Herald*, was served with a subpena by the U.S. Senate after having made public a confidential draft of the proposed treaty to end the Mexican-American war. In 1896, Maryland became the first of 26 States to enact laws giving reporters testimonial privilege protecting confidential news sources.

This statutory approach was not without its problems. Who, afterall, is a reporter? Psychiatrists, physicians, and attorneys, also covered by the statute, are licensed; hence, they are distinguishable. Reporters are not licensed, and it is difficult to determine who qualifies for the legal privilege and who does not. The statutes have granted limited protection, which varies from state to state. In Ohio, for example, the law shields only the identity of the source, not the information involved, thus failing to protect information that is deliberately given off-the-record. State shield, of course, has no bearing on procedures involving the Federal courts, and the recent Federal guidelines issued by the Department of Justice have no bearing on State law. The Privacy Protection Act of 1980 pertains to both the communication and publication involved in interstate *and* foreign commerce—which comes under Federal jurisdiction and may not be of assistance if the material in question can be shown to be purely for local consumption (although given wire services and affiliate relationships this limitation may be difficult for a State law enforcement agency to demonstrate). Consequently it would appear that despite the Privacy Protection Act of 1980, the privileged claims of the press have been eroded since the Court's decision in *Branzburg* v. *Hayes*. Moreover, decisions by the Supreme Court based on first-amendment interpretations transcend the limitations of legislative enactments.

With regard to obtaining information from the press by subpena as opposed to search warrant, since 1970 there has been a modest Federal shield law in the form of guidelines promulgated by former Attorney General John Mitchell. These guidelines are now part of the Code of Federal Regulations. Although in the Court's opinion in *Branzburg*, Justice White alluded to the guidelines as controlling potential abuse of the subpena power, the protection they afford is limited. Basically, they use negotiation to balance the interests of the trial or grand jury with the interests of the media and attempt to create the most unobtrusive situation possible within the context of a particular investigation. If the negotiations prove fruitless, direct authorization by the Attorney General is required before a subpena can be issued against any member of the news industry. However, the guidelines tend to be about as honored in the breach as adhered to in practice. According to Mark Neubauer, of 76 subpenas requested against news industry personnel from March 1973 to May 1975, 22 were never approved by the Attorney General.[63]

In addition to denying special testimonial privilege, the court has also denied special access rights to the media. In *Pell* v. *Procunier,* three journalists sought interviews with several specific inmates of California prisons.[64] The request was denied because of a regulation (415.071) of the California Department of Corrections which prohibited media interviews with specific individuals. Both the inmates and the journalists sought injunctions under the Civil Rights Act (42 U.S.C. 81983). The district court held in favor of the inmates but ruled against the journalists. The Supreme Court ruled against both arguing that the first amendment does not guarantee the press a constitutional right of special access to information not available to the general public, and that reporters do not have a constitutional right of access to the scenes of crime or disaster from which the general public is excluded.

The Court administered the same ruling in a companion case, *Saxbe* v. *Washington Post*, in which the Court rejected a challenge to an almost identical regulation of the Federal prison system.[65] Justice Stewart, speaking for the majority, found the key issue (whether there is a constitutional guarantee of superior access for the press than the general public) indistinguishable from the issue in *Pell*. Justice Douglas dissented, arguing that the average citizen is highly unlikely to seek information about a prison system by requesting an interview with a particular inmate with whom there is no prior relationship. It is the practice in our society, Justice Douglas argued, to rely upon a free press for this kind of information. Douglas's dissent in *Pell* applied also to *Saxbe*.

THE NATURE OF THE PROBLEM 43

The Supreme Court did not again confront the issue of media access and newsgathering until June 1978 in the case of *Houchins* v. *KQED, Inc.*[66] Again the case involved access to a prison, and again it took place in California. Pacific Foundation station KQED challenged the Alameda County Sheriff's ban on their inspecting and photographing a section of the county jail. The press, however, did have the same access to the jail as the general public, no better and no worse. In response to the challenge of KQED, the district court enjoined the Sheriff from denying KQED, and other responsible news media "reasonable access" to the jail, including the prohibited area, and from preventing interviews with inmates and the use of both photographic and sound equipment. By a unanimous decision, the Ninth Circuit Court of Appeals affirmed the district court's decision. There were, however, some disagreements among the judges concerning the holdings in *Pell* and in *Saxbe*.[67] In overruling the court of appeals, Chief Justice Warren Burger framed the primary question in terms of the issues which the Court addressed in *Pell* and in *Saxbe*.[67] Did KQED as a member of the media have a first-amendment right which entitled it to access superior to that of the general public? Clearly, in terms of both *Pell* and *Saxbe* the answer was "No." Chief Justice Burger also noted that the right to speak and the right to publish do not carry with them the unrestrained right to gather information.

What can we conclude regarding the media's assertion of a first-amendment right during terrorist sieges, particularly the right to be at the scene of the news and the right to interview terrorists and hostages? Clearly the Burger Court is telling the media that their right to access is not superior to that of the general public. In *Pell* specifically, the Court noted that when the public is excluded from the scene of a crime or disaster, the press may be excluded.

The Court's rulings also imply that access to the perimeter between the tactical squad and the public (often set up by the police in siege situations for the purpose of press access) is not a first-amendment right but a privilege granted at the discretion of the law enforcement agency. Access to the site where news is being made cannot be claimed by the press if the general public is also excluded. Press access, largely a privilege under the most sanguine circumstances, can be revoked, and where the situation is fraught with imminent danger of people being injured or killed, the media's claim to special access rings especially hollow. Given the present composition of the Supreme Court and reasonable expectations about future appointments, it is difficult to imagine the Court moving to a more liberal position.

TERRORISM, THE MEDIA, AND THE RESPONSE OF THE LEGISLATIVE BRANCH

The legislative branch has been the most responsive to the media's demand for greater access. The amendment to the Freedom of Information Act permitting a district court to disseminate nonclassified information contained within a classified file came from the U.S. Congress in direct response to the Court's ruling in *Environmental Protection Agency* v. *Mink*. State legislatures and the Congress have also been responsive to the media's request for shield laws in order to prevent the forced disclosure of confidential sources by subpena and, after the decision in *Zurcher* v. *California*, by warrant.

Legislatures, however, are elected institutions and their members keep an ear to the ground listening to the political footsteps of the public. In the face of the particularly vicious and brutal menaces of terrorism, legislatures can seldom be expected to uphold a libertarian view of the law, especially if law enforcement calls for greater restrictions not only on the press but on other forms of civil liberties as well.

When terrorists strike frequently and leave horrible carnage in their wake, the public will see due process and democratic components of the rule of law as luxurious and dysfunctional abstractions irrelevant to its immediate need for personal security. Citizens will clamor for emergency measures, and the legislature will be most responsive. This is precisely what has been happening within constitutional democracies in Western Europe. Over the past 3 years, West Germany has passed restrictive legislation to deal with terrorism. Even earlier, on May 16, 1968, the West German Government, with approval from the U.S., Britain, and France, as required by the Occupation Statute, endorsed emergency legislation to deal with mass, leftist, student demonstrations which were considered a threat to the Government. The emergency legislation passed the Bundestag by a vote of 384 to 100, with 1 abstention.

The increase in terrorist activities during the early 1970s led to the passage of additional restrictive legislation. The new laws dealt with special provisions of the Criminal Code and aimed to give authorities a more efficient means of combating the growing problem of terrorist activities. This legislation makes "association" for purposes of terrorism an offense punishable by up to 5 years imprisonment even if an act of terrorism is not committed. Simply, the attempt to create an association is also an offense. Another section of the 1970s legislation (88A) makes just *verbal support* of an unlawful act directed against the West German Constitution a violation of law. Verbal "glorification of violence" and public "approval of criminal acts" are also punishable.[68]

Besieged by terrorists, Italy was zealous in adopting strong antiterrorist legislation and found support for its efforts from a strange quarter. The Communist Party's newspaper, *Unita*, endorsed the promulgation of the December 5, 1979 emergency measures. The Red Brigade terrorists reacted swiftly to the legislation by murdering four magistrates. Undoubtedly, their action only served to underscore public endorsement of the harsh measures.

In 1973, terrorism in the United Kingdom crossed the Irish Sea. Once complacent Great Britain soon found that the dangers of Northern Ireland were not just something to be viewed at a safe distance on the evening news. Casualties of terrorist violence began to be tallied on British soil. In the aftermath of an explosion in Birmingham in November 1974 which killed 21 and wounded 180, Parliament summarily passed the Prevention of Terrorism Act without debate. Stunned and dismayed by the carnage at Birmingham, Britain was, despite its democratic traditions, not about to choose abstract legal formalities over life and limb. As Lord Shackleton, who reported on the impact of the legislation at the request of the Home Office, was to put it, "Basic civil liberties include the rights to stay alive and go about one's business without fear."[69]

CONCLUSIONS

The experiences of Western European democracies with terrorism clearly demonstrate that in the face of visible, dramatic, and psychologically threatening violence, the legislature can hardly be counted on to continually shield the press against assaults by society and the judiciary. The best defense of cherished first-amendment freedoms, which sustain the vitality and development of any democracy, lies with the press themselves. I would not argue that the press submit to censorship, even self-censorship, but to a reasonable code of professional conduct of the type illustrated in the guidelines presented in later chapters. These guidelines suggest that reporters are observers of events, not participants in them, and should make every effort to avoid lapsing into the role of participants. The guidelines also make reporters cognizant of the otherwise symbiotic relationship which occurs in the interaction between terrorists and journalists. In an extraordinarily competitive business, an effect of that omnipresent but too-often-ignored fact of life is that the media become propaganda platforms for the shibboleths of terrorist babble. And sometimes, as we have noted, and as some of our contributors elaborate below, the media have become the eyes, ears, and general intelligence service of the terrorists. At other times, the media have weighed the importance of the scoop and the concern for ratings over the risk to human life. Most likely they have done this less in malice or mendacity than in the pure unreflective zeal of getting a job done and done well, and they have used a set of standards and goals unrecognizably dissonant with the imperatives of a hostage/barricade siege.

Despite guidelines and related attempts to grant senior news executives the opportunity to apply sound, experienced, and ethical judgments to the control of story coverage, human failings play an unrehearsed part. In an insightful piece, Walter B. Jaehnig relates that the Associated Press released the story of the *false* immunity offer to Indianapolis gunman Anthony Kiritsis when two lives were still at stake and when a zealous reporter's over-dramatic description of the activities of the local bomb squad had already pushed Kiritsis toward making good his threats of violence.[70] The decision to go ahead with the story was made not in Indianapolis but hundreds of miles away in New York. A decision came about because no one locally "wanted to take responsibility for involving two lives."[71] What should have worked as a safety mechanism preventing irresponsibility by transferring the story to a more distant, more senior, and more responsible authority had the reverse effect. A distant authority was willing to take risks with other people's lives that a local reporter could not and would not take. This poignantly demonstrates that mechanisms for dealing with these issues will not provide the safeguards we seek if they do not inculcate the common ethos of valuing human life over ratings and circulation.

Walter Jaehnig asks a rather telling question of his journalism colleagues: Most of the guidelines for the coverage of terrorism are nothing more than a restatement of the common basics of good journalism; why are these basics pushed aside, ignored, or forgotten when they are most needed?[72]

As we reflect on the problems which the media have at times created, it is of the utmost importance to maintain a sense of balance, to realize how vital a free media is to our democracy and to acknowledge the personal risks that journalists take to bring us news from the world's danger spots. The soldier who falls in battle receives medals and recognition, but there are precious few accolades for a reporter who falls in the streets of Nicaragua or El Salvador, the mountains of Afghanistan, or any of the world's temporary and long-term shooting galleries. The media is not a monolith, although given the parsimony that comes so easily with generalization, we tend to think of the media in those terms. It is also important to be reminded that if some reporters in the heat of story-seeking have violated the canons of responsible journalism, it has been other journalists who have called these excesses to

THE NATURE OF THE PROBLEM 47

our attention. Long before it was popular for the news industry to show introspection about its coverage of terrorism and before the inhibitions of first-amendment rights were psychologically loosened to allow criticism of the media from other quarters, Stephen Rosenfeld, of the *Washington Post,* wrote:

> "We of the Western press have yet to come to terms with the international terror. If we thought about it more and understood its essence, we would probably stop writing about it, or we would write about it with a great deal of restraint."[73]

The following papers view media and terrorism from a variety of perspectives. They do not come to resounding agreement, nor do they even see the issues the same way. As Drs. Sommer and Sommer indicate, police chiefs see live television coverage as a great threat to hostage safety, while TV news directors and newspaper editors do not. That alone illustrates the intellectual and attitudinal distance that must be traveled just to generate meaningful dialog on the topic. Though they are not represented as definitive solutions, it is hoped that the following papers will generate thought, dialog, and ethical introspection among law enforcement agents and journalists. Establishing methods of compromise and conciliation will permit each group to perform their respective jobs and to contribute to both the democratic vitality and the security of the political system. Afterall, in a society such as ours, the choice is not between freedom and order but rather *for* freedom and order.

FOOTNOTES

1. Murray Edelman. *Politics as symbolic action: Mass arousal and quiescence.* Chicago: Markham, 1971; *The symbolic uses of politics.* Urbana: University of Illinois Press, 1967.
2. Richard M. Merleman. The dramaturgy of politics. *Sociological Quarterly,* 1969, X.
3. James E. Cooms. *Dimensions of political drama.* Santa Monica: Goodyear, 1984, P. 184.
4. Louis Rukeyser. American Information Radio Network, March 4, 1972.
5. John Lafflin. *Fedayeen.* Glencoe: The Free Press, 1973, p. 113.
6. Edward Jay Epstein. *Between fact and fiction: The problem of journalism.* New York: Vintage Press, 1975, p. 3.
7. Ibid.
8. Eugene H. Methvin. *The rise of radicalism: The social psychology of messianic extremism.* New Rochelle, N.Y.: Arlington House, 1973, p.511.
9. Walter Lippmann quoted in Epstein, op. cit., p.5.
10. See: James McEvoy & Abraham Miller, On strike . . . shut it down: The crisis at San Francisco State College. In J. McEvoy and A. Miller (Eds.), *Black power and student rebellion.* Belmont, Ca.: Wadsworth, 1969.
11. Epstein. Op. cit., p.15.

12. See, for example: Collision course over the PLO. *Newsweek*, September 3, 1979, 18–25; Behind the shift in U.S. policy on Mideast. *U.S. News and World Report*, May 29, 1978, 20–21; Norman Podhoretz. The U.S. v. Israel. *New York Times*, June 28, 1978; Amos Perlmutter. The Saudis and peace. *New York Times*, June 29, 1978; Stephen L. Spiegel. Where is Carter going in the Middle East? *American professors for peace in the Middle East: Background paper.* October 17, 1977; Karen Elliot House & Felix Kessler. Mideast chill. *Wall Street Journal*, July 15, 1980, 1&14.
13. On July 26, 1979, Andrew Young met with Zehdi Labib Terzi, the PLO's observer at the U.N., in the New York apartment of Kuwait's U.N. Ambassador, Abdullah Yacoub Bishara. This unauthorized, clandestine meeting, which Young later denied to the State Department, resulted in his resignation and the so called "Andrew Young Affair."
14. Cited in: Philip Elliot. Reporting Northern Ireland: A study of news in Britain, Ulster and the Irish Republic. In *Ethnicity and the media.* Unesco, 1976, p.v–5.
15. *Cincinnati Enquirer*, January 29, 1981, p.1.
16. The application of this and other theories is dealt with in: Abraham H. Miller et al. The J-curve theory and the black urban riots. *American Political Science Review*, September 1977, *LXXI*, 964–982.
17. For a discussion of the Bakunin v. Marx conflict, see: Paul Avrich. *The Russian anarchists.* New York: W.W. Norton, 1978, 20–26.
18. For an engaging discussion of the influence of nationalism see: Robert A. Friedlander. Self-determination: A legal-political inquiry. In Y. Alexander & R.A. Friedlander (Eds.), *Self-determination.* Boulder, Co.: Western Press, 1980, 307–331.
19. Paul Wilkinson. *Terrorism and the liberal state.* London: MacMillan Press, Ltd., 1977, p.122.
20. November 1978, Oxfordshire, England.
21. *Times* (London), January 12, 1980, p.12, C-1.
22. *New York Times*, September 23, 1979, p.16, C-5, UPI.
23. *Washington Post*, December 13, 1979, p.18, C-1.
24. Leonard Downie cited in: James Hoge. The media and terrorism. Included in this volume, p.96.
25. Ibid.
26. Patrick Murphy. The police, the news media, and coverage of terrorism. Included in this volume, pp.76–86.
27. From a personal interview with Deputy Assistant Commissioner Peter C. Neivens, August 11–12, 1980, at New Scotland Yard, London, England.
28. Quoted in: James Hoge. Op. cit. p.96.
29. *Daily Telegraph* (London), July 13, 1979, p.7.
30. See note 27, above.
31. From a personal conversation with Thomas M. Ashwood, November 17, 1977, at the City University of New York, New York, N.Y.
32. J. Chester Stern. News media relations during a major incident. *Police Journal*, October 1976, (4), 257–260.
33. From personal conversations.
34. From personal interviews with members of the D.C. Metropolitan Police Barricade Squad and members of the team which directed this operation.
35. From a personal interview. See also: Abraham Miller. *Terrorism and hostage negotiations*, Boulder, Co.: Westview Press, 1980, Chapter 5.
36. Charles Fenyvesi's remarks to the conference on terrorism sponsored by the City University of New York, November 17, 1977, New York, N.Y.
37. Charles B. Seib. The Hanafi episode: A media event. *Washington Post*, March 18, 1977, p.1. For a full discussion of the episode, see: Abraham H. Miller. *Terrorism and hostage negotiations.* Op. cit., 14–32.
38. William R. Catton, Jr. Militants and the media: Partners in terrorism. *Indiana Law Journal*, 1978, *53*(4), p.713.
39. Herbert A. Terry. Television and terrorism: Professionalism not quite the answer. *Indiana Law Journal*, 1978, *53*(4), p.754.
40. See: Juan Tomas De Salas. *Responsibility of the press and other information media with*

THE NATURE OF THE PROBLEM 49

regard to terrorism. Paper presented to the Council of Europe, Strasbourg, France, November 1980, 12–14.
41. Robert Moss. The terrorist state. *International terrorism: The Soviet connection.* Jerusalem, Israel: The Jonathan Institute, 1979, p.23.
42. Charles Horner. *"The usual suspects": The state and the status of terrorism.* Paper presented to the Totalitarianism and Terrorism conference, Washington, D.C., April 24, 1980, p.4.
43. *Wall Street Journal,* July 26, 1979, editorial page.
44. From personal conversation.
45. According to correspondent Salinger, the contact was made through the offices of Austrian Prime Minister Bruno Kreisky.
46. According to the Sunday *London Times,* July 21, 1980, the PLO receives a royalty from Iran for the disposal of troublesome opponents to the Iranian revolution. And according to Ali Akhbar Tabatabai, assassinated 3 months after his revelations about the PLO connection, "There are 15,000 PLO mercenaries in Iran." WRC Radio, Washington, D.C., April 9, 1980.
47. *Le Matin* (Paris), July 31-August 4, 1980. For a look at Gaddafi's expansionist foreign policy, see: *Economist* (London), January 31-February 6, 1981, 11–12.
48. *Wall Street Journal,* July 26, 1979.
49. See: Victor S. Pisano. *Contemporary Italian terrorism analysis and countermeasures.* Washington, D.C.: Law Library, Library of Congress, 22–23.
50. Rael Jean Isaac. *Time* against Israel. *New Republic,* October 18, 1980, 18–23.
51. See, for example: Ray Vicker. Not just guerillas. *Wall Street Journal,* October 22, 1979, p.1. It is instructive to go back through the Journal and read Vicker's earlier dispatches, all part of a similar theme.
52. Robert Moss. Terror: A Soviet export. *New York Times Magazine,* November 2, 1980, 41–58. For additional writing on the Soviet connection, see: Neil Livingston. Terrorism: The international connection. *Army,* December 1980, 14–21; Samuel T. Francis. *The Soviet strategy of terror.* Washington, D.C.: The Heritage Foundation, 1981; Claire Sterling. *The terror network.* New York: Holt, Rhinehart, & Winston, 1981.
53. Thomas I. Emerson. *The system of freedom of expression.* New York: Random House, 1970, p.6.
54. James Madison. Letter to W.T. Barry, August 4, 1822. Quoted in *Environmental Protection Agency* v. *Mink,* 410 U.S. 73, 110–111, 1973, dissenting opinion of Justice Douglas.
55. *Zurcher v. Stanford Daily,* 436 U.S. 547, (1978).
56. Ibid., p.565.
57. *Branzburg v. Hayes et al.,* 408 U.S. 605, (1972).
58. Ibid., p.2671.
59. Ibid., p.2673.
60. *Newsweek,* August 11, 1980, p.52.
61. Ibid., p.52.
62. *Guidelines on methods of obtaining documentary materials held by third parties.* 28CFR, Part 59, U.S. Department of Justice, December 29, 1980.
63. Mark Neubauer. The newsman's privilege Branzburg: The case for a Federal shield law. *U.C.L.A. Law Review,* 1976, *24,* 185–186.
64. *Pell v. Procunier,* 417 U.S. 817, (1974).
65. *Saxbe v. Washington Post,* 417 U.S. 843, (1974).
66. *Houchins v. KQED, Inc.* 438 U.S. 1 (1978).
67. KQED, Inc. v. Houchins, 546 F 2d 284, 9th Circuit, (1976).
68. Miklos Radvani. *Anti-terrorist legislation in the Federal Republic of Germany.* Washington, D.C.: Law Library, Library of Congress, 1979, 70–71.
69. From personal conversation with Lord Shackleton, Ditchley Castle, Oxfordshire, England, November 25, 1978.
70. Walter B. Jaehnig. Journalism and terrorism: Captives of the libertarian tradition. *Indiana Law Journal,* 1978, *53*(4), 717–747.
71. Ibid., p.738.
72. Ibid.

73. Stephen Rosenfeld quoted in: Abraham H. Miller. *Terrorism and hostage negotiations*. Op. cit., p.85.

2. IRAN: THE HOSTAGE SEIZURE, THE MEDIA, AND INTERNATIONAL LAW

Robert A. Friedlander

On November 4, 1979, more than 60 American nationals were seized by young Iranian militants and held hostage at the U.S. Embassy in Teheran.[1] The precipitate seizure of the Embassy personnel not only symbolized a major breakdown of international law;[2] but also starkly revealed America's powerlessness to deal with an act of state-encouraged terrorism within a foreign jurisdiction.[3] Not surprisingly, serious questions were soon raised about the nature and efficacy of the international legal system.[4] Ultimate resolution of the hostage crisis, irrespective of the Interim and Final Judgments of the International Court of Justice,[5] has further tarnished the American public's distorted image of international law and its processes.

The United Nations has similarly been found wanting in the Anglo-American court of public opinion for failing to persuade the Iranian Government to release the captives and for failing to enforce either judgment of the International Court.[6] However, since the world organization is demonstrably unable to control individual and group terrorism throughout the globe, it should not be surprising that the U.N. likewise cannot affect the malfeasance or nonfeasance of nation-states. One month after the Embassy seizure, the *New Republic* editorialized:

> "Without these [diplomatic] rules the UN itself could not exist. If the UN can't act decisively for these canons of intercourse among nations that are essential to its own survival, what is it worth?"[7]

Over 1 year later that question has still not been answered.

Neither the U.S. Government nor the American media were prepared for the takeover, despite an earlier attack against the U.S. Embassy on February 14, 1979. In that incident, 70 persons, including the U.S. Ambassador, were taken temporary prisoners, and 2 staff persons suffered injuries.[8] But the incident was soon forgotten, and not even a menacing demonstration on November 1, 1979, in front of the Teheran Embassy, prepared the Carter administration and the U.S. media for what was to follow.[9] The sudden and overwhelming shock of the unanticipated events of November 4, which brought the earlier threat to its ultimate conclusion, may well have been responsible for the President's week-long silence, finally broken by his press conference on November 12.[10]

A paralysis of communication on the highest level (the President did not even involve himself in the crisis for the first 48 hours[11]) caused the Chief Executive to remain in the background until his appearance in the White House Press Room on November 12.[12] The President's behavior might also explain the subdued initial reaction to the Embassy takeover on the part of most newspapers, such as the *Chicago Tribune* and the *New York Daily News*.[13] That mood, however, did not last for long, and the change was forecast by the outraged reaction of the *Atlanta Constitution:*

> "We cannot allow an uncivilized government in Iran to dictate American foreign policy ★ ★ ★ we should take the sternest retaliatory measures possible against any government that encourages violence and blackmail as a means of imposing its own peculiar brand of justice on some of its deposed leaders."[14]

By the end of the first week of the hostage crisis, the American public's patience had worn thin, and the President was confronted with a growing national resentment.[15] His first personal appearance during the crisis, on November 12, utilized television as a presidential forum, and at 2 o'clock in the afternoon (a time of minimum audience impact), the Chief Executive announced immediate suspension of oil imports from Iran and simultaneously exhorted the American public to save more oil. He also admitted that no progress had been made in the diplomatic efforts to secure the hostages' release.[16] Not until the end of the second week, on November 15, did President Carter rhetorically lash out against the Iranian Government.

Appearing before a cheering crowd of 3,000 delegates to the AFL-CIO Convention in Washington, D.C., the President combined domestic politics with the deepening Iranian political crisis and accused Iran of committing "an act of international terrorism totally outside the bounds of international law."[17] His subsequent comment described not only the prevailing popular

THE NATURE OF THE PROBLEM 53

sentiment; it was to become the epitaph of the Carter administration: "Every American feels anger and outrage over what is happening."[18] Seizing on the opportunity to attack his political opponents in both parties, the President, in effect, set the tone of the entire Democratic pre-Convention campaign.[19] By using the media to publicize his role as national leader and outraged first citizen, Mr. Carter was able to turn disastrous foreign events to domestic political advantage. But the hostage crisis continued to worsen.

In retrospect, the growing militancy of Ayatollah Khomeini seems to have been based, at least in part, upon the inability of the United States to back up its harsh words with strong deeds. As noted by one defense analyst, "[i]t is hard to believe that perception of a United States unwilling to use force and unable to do so effectively failed to influence the actions of Khomeini * * * during the past eighteen months."[20] By the third week of November, Iranian invective had escalated to the point where the Ayatollah, in a growing series of threats, warned that Iran might put the hostages on trial as enemy spies.[21] This not only added insult to injury; it defied both international custom and Moslem tradition.[22] Khomeini's view, however, was that the United States and Iran were effectively at war, and thus the seizure was justified.[23]

Former Secretary of State Dean Rusk has remarked that "[t]he safety of the American people is perhaps the primary goal of [our] foreign policy."[25] But in the case of Iran, under the unexpected and rapidly deteriorating circumstances, what were the U.S. options? When could the Carter administration respond, and how could a legal response be effectuated? Customary international law permits an injured states party to seek four different methods of relief, providing that they are utilized proportionally to the degree of harm inflicted: (1) retorsion (legal measures short of force more often than not economic in nature), (2) reprisals, (3) humanitarian intervention, and (4) self-defense. Several remedies are controversial, but all are permissible depending upon the extent of the injury and the nature of the response.[26]

An Entebbe- or Mogadishu-type rescue was undeniably within the parameters of the international law, but it was not feasible due to the precautions taken against such a possibility by the Iranian militants. In fact, the Iranians made it quite clear to the American media, which in turn unequivocally relayed the message to the American people and their Government, that if the United States attempted military action of any sort, the hostages would be killed outright.[27] Moreover, the United States was actually unprepared to mount any successful military rescue mission,[28] though Washington's inability to exercise that option was neither openly admitted nor widely discussed. Unmindful of this paralyzing weakness, the tide of public anger continued to rise.[29]

In addition to threat-inspired fear, the stimulation of doubt and the spread of disarray and panic are among the unarticulated purposes of terrorism. During the second week of the hostage crisis, the popular perception was that the U.S. Government itself had become hostage to events beyond its control. For whatever reason, it soon was clearly apparent that the Carter administration was unable to take independent action and could only offer a disproportionate response to the challenge of the moment. It has been argued "that the great movements of history are nothing more than the accumulation of small decisions taken by individuals only imperfectly understanding what they are doing."[30] This is as good an explanation as any of the pattern of decisions taken throughout November 1979 by Iranian and American leadership.

On November 10, in the first of a series of uncoordinated moves, President Carter ordered his Attorney General to initiate deportation proceedings against Iranian students who were residing illegally in the United States.[31] Three days later Attorney General Benjamin R. Civiletti issued immigration regulations which provided for the deportation of Iranian students who were not enrolled as full-time students or who had committed crimes of violence. The burden of proof was placed upon the Iranians, estimated at 50,000.[32] Although the Presidential order withstood constitutional attack,[33] and there is reason to believe that the Government could have expelled all of the Iranian students if a national emergency so required,[34] the impact of the decree was largely vitiated by the lengthy requirements of due process and by the fact that over half those ordered to be deported went into hiding.[35]

On November 11, partly in response to public pressure and partly to demonstrate to the Iranians a hardening U.S. resolve, the President declared an immediate suspension of the importation of Iranian oil.[36] In his television address to the nation, he called the oil cutoff "a real challenge to our country" and sternly promised his audience: "We refuse to permit the use of terrorism and the seizure and holding of hostages to impose political demands."[37] No attempt seemed to be made, however, to seek Allied support.[38] On the same day as the oil ban, a "quick reflex exercise" was held at Fort Hood, Tex., by units belonging to the new Rapid Deployment Force. This operation took place over the protests of the State Department, which feared that any military maneuvers might be viewed by Iran as a provocation.[39]

The oil cutoff was vigorously supported by the *New York Times* in an editorial entitled "The Right Way to Get Tough," which at the time seemed

THE NATURE OF THE PROBLEM 55

to reflect the opinion of most newspapers and commentators. "The President has skirted the twin dangers of inaction and over-reaction," the editorial declared. "He deserves admiration and support."[40] But the real test was yet to come.

It is now clear that the one significant action taken by the Carter administration during the first 10 days of the hostage seizure, and arguably during the entire time of detention with the exception of the U.S.-Iran hostage agreements, was his freezing Iranian Government assets held in American banks. The pre-dawn Executive order of November 14, 1979, decided upon by the President and his Treasury Secretary, was merely a hasty response to the announced Iranian intention to withdraw its funds from U.S. banks and their overseas branches.[41] Thirteen months later, the Office of Foreign Assets Control (OFAC) of the Treasury Department estimated the 1979 value of Iran's blocked assets to be approximately $8 billion.[42] But, astonishingly, not until late October 1980 (2 weeks before the presidential election) did the Chief Executive mention using the assets as a means of bargaining for the hostages' release.[43] The response of Iran's American legal representative, and then the Majlis itself, first on October 26, and again on November 8, 1980,[44] indicated for the first time that the other side was responding to American financial pressure. One month earlier, on September 26, the legal validity of the assets' seizure had been decided in favor of the Carter administration by a U.S. District Court for the Southern District of New York,[45] which concluded: "I find the President's determination to be most persuasive ★ ★ ★ ."[46] Thanks to a fortuitous combination of public policy and national self-interest, mixed with the unanticipated circumstance of the prolonged Iranian-Iraqi War, the November 14, 1979 freezing of the assets proved to be the decisive factor in the ultimate liberation of the hostages on January 20, 1980.[47]

Well into the third week of captivity, threats and counter threats between the American President and the Iranian Ayatollah continued to escalate—on the same day that Jimmy Carter labeled the Iranian Government terrorists and blackmailers, Ayatollah Khomeini called the American leadership criminals and thieves. Shortly thereafter, Khomeini again threatened a hostage massacre.[48] Yet despite an increasingly violent rhetoric on both sides the Iranian cleric was to dumbfound everyone by ordering the release of five women and eight black hostages.[49]

As a widely recognized security analyst observed 12 months after the initial seizure, "[n]o hostage-taker is persuaded to let his victim go in response to a simple humanitarian appeal."[50] It may very well be that the combination of legally permissible retorsive acts, plus the rising anger of the American public and the increased pressures upon its Government (in addition to public outrage throughout Western Europe which was, after all, a prime customer for Iranian oil[51]), led the Iranian leaders to make a gesture of conciliation.* Lost in the maelstrom of accusations and counteraccusations, denunciations and recriminations, was the fact that whatever the intention of the gesture, the release of the 13 hostages—5 women and 8 black men—was undeniable evidence that the Iranian Government exercised power in the situation and was an accomplice, both during and after the fact, in an internationally prohibited terrorist act.[52]

If the Iranians had actually intended a message, it certainly was misunderstood on the American side. A nervous and exasperated Jimmy Carter, who could not have been unmindful of his low standing in the pre-primary Presidential polls,[53] chose at that moment both to escalate the war of words with his Iranian nemesis and to re-emphasize the threat of military action. The militants and the Ayatollah countered with their own colorful invective and again threatened the lives of the remaining hostages.[54] Although it was not apparent at the time, deadlock had given way to stalemate, and henceforth, to the Ayatollah and his fanatic subordinates, the United States would be a toothless, albeit posturing tiger. To send a carrier task force to the Persian Gulf, without utilizing its military capabilities, was to the Iranians but another empty gesture.[55]

The Iranians had in fact guessed correctly. Unwillingness by the Carter administration to apply even a modicum of force proved its undoing.[56] It is hard to explain, even with hindsight, the failure of the U.S. Government to break diplomatic relations with Iran until April 7, 1980, 2 weeks prior to the abortive rescue mission of April 24. Reliance upon the United Nations was, at best, pursuit of a diplomatic will-o'-the-wisp, as evidenced by the Security Council's initial reaction to the U.S. appeal. (The Council unanimously voiced its "profound concern" over Iranian actions and urged a release "without delay," but at the same time refused to call for any concrete measures.[57]) Failure to take a decisive stand when it was most needed foretold further U.N. helplessness, whether due to a Soviet veto or to the embarrassing personal mission of Secretary General Kurt Waldheim.[58] If the U.N. was to be utilized as an instrument of conflict resolution, it might have been better

---

*According to Pierre Salinger, of ABC News, during a special report broadcast after the hostages' release, this release was the result of the intervention of Yasser Arafat, the PLO leader. Others claim this was less an act of goodwill than an indication of earlier collusion between the PLO and the Iranian militants. - Ed.

THE NATURE OF THE PROBLEM 57

to have had the Secretary General ask for an advisory opinion from the International Court of Justice regarding the hostage seizure, rather than having the United States appear before the Court as the moving party.[59] At least the pressure of world opinion would have reinforced the Court's finding, a condition lacking with the first Interim Judgment.

The truth of the matter is that even if there had been a desire on both sides to find some way out of the impasse, the two heads of Government had painted themselves into blind corners. In the view of a member of the State Department's Iranian Task Force, resolution of the hostage conundrum had become virtually impossible due to the need to simultaneously satisfy two domestic constituencies—Carter's and Khomeini's.[60] Though it is now apparent that the Administration's policy was one of "flailing in countless desperate directions for the next 14 1/2 months,"[61] there was a far different perception on the part of both the media and the American public during the first 8 weeks of the hostage crisis. The *New York Times* probably spoke for the majority of the Nation, when it cautioned on November 21, 1979:

> "But President Carter has woefully few instruments of foreign suasion and domestic reassurance * * * [M]oderation, calm and a sense of proportion are America's greatest assets. Cool heads, we think, do not begrudge the President the immediate opportunity to buy time, even if they also watch closely to see that he does not in the bargain buy long-term trouble."[62]

This message was borne out by a mid-December Gallup/*Newsweek* poll, which revealed that President Carter's overall approval rating had jumped dramatically from 30 to 61 percent within the first month of the hostage imbroglio, and that 77 percent of the respondents approved of his reactions to Iranian pressures.[63]

Small wonder, then, that the President chose to inject presidential politics into the U.S.-Iranian confrontation. According to former Assistant Secretary of State (and current editor of *Foreign Policy* magazine) C. William Maynes, "[t]he impact of the primary campaign on our policy was critical—unspoken but critical."[64] An even more pointed assessment was given by a southern Senator 3 weeks into the hostage crisis:

> "If Carter secures the release of the hostages and demonstrates that this country will no longer allow itself to be humiliated, he can win the election. If he fails, he's finished."[65]

That politically oriented prediction would stand the test of time.

After leaving the practice of diplomacy and taking on the role of observer of the diplomatic function, Maynes shrewdly observed that the real beneficiaries of the Iranian impasse were the media, particularly the television networks. With a breakdown of communication between the two Governments, both heads-of-state utilized the press and the camera as the prime means of communicating first to their own citizenry and only then to the other side. It was the journalists rather than the politicians or diplomats that had access to the Iranian mobs and to the changing cast of characters who represented the Iranian leadership. Television enabled Khomeini and the hostage takers to speak directly to the American people, and they cleverly sought to exploit American public opinion.[66] George Ball, a past Under Secretary of State and current foreign policy commentator, provided the harshest view of the media's influence and effect upon the hostage seizure. It was, he claims, a relatively trivial incident inflated way beyond any legitimate proportions by media coverage. Denying its historical importance, Ball has relegated the entire affair to the status of "a television soap opera."[67]

Throughout the previous decade, media and terrorism were engaged in an incestuous relationship. Bluntly stated, terrorism is a creature of the media. In the words of psychiatrist Frederick J. Hacker, a distinguished authority on terrorism,

> "[m]ass media thrive on the sensational, surprising, and exceptional event that occupies total audience attention for a period of time. Terrorists intentionally manufacture, direct, and perfect the sensations they need to captivate their fascinated audiences, who temporarily forget their private concerns and worries."[68]

Thus, terrorism is an act of theater, designed to have a strong psychological impact upon a vast audience. The image becomes as important as the reality, for the terrorist victim is rarely the ultimate target. Particularly for political and ideological terrorists, to borrow a phrase from noted hostage expert Abraham H. Miller, "terrorism seeks access to the public agenda ★ ★ ★ ."[69]

It can no longer be said, as may have been true a half dozen years ago, that the media are unaware of their operative role in the terror syndrome. This is now clearly evident from such diverse sources as the March 1977 report to the National News Council,[70]★ by numerous conferences and symposia,[71] and from observations of journalists themselves.[72] Nor have those venerated commentators of the American scene for most of this century been

---

★ See the National News Council's "Paper on Terrorism," reprinted as Chapter 8 of this volume. - Ed.

THE NATURE OF THE PROBLEM

unaware of the apparent causal relationship between news reporting and actual events. In his famous study of American democracy, which appeared during the early years of the Truman era, British political scientist Harold J. Laski complained of the American news industry's methods of presentation and of techniques which focused the reader's attention "on the personal and trivial." The result, Laski maintained, was to distort the reader's sense of proportion and to consciously pervert the ordinary citizen's ability to separate fact from opinion.[73] Writing at the beginning of the 1920s, news analyst Walter Lippmann acknowledged "the economic necessity of interesting the reader quickly, and the economic risk involved in not interesting him at all ★ ★ ★ ."[74] A contemporary, somewhat controversial critic of the news media put it more directly: "Noteworthiness in the eyes of the *Times* is like money: It takes some to get some."[75]

In the context of the Iranian hostage crisis, the question then becomes, with respect to television and the press, whether event-oriented sensationalism is inextricably linked with mundane commercialism. Iran proved once again, beyond any doubt, that terrorism is quintessentially the propaganda of the deed.[76] That "progaganda" also sells newspapers and increases Nielsen ratings. In April 1977, CBS News issued a series of internal guidelines for the coverage of terrorist incidents.[77] Yet throughout the Iranian captivity these guidelines were ignored to a far greater extent than they were observed. All three television networks, taking advantage of the Iranian drama, developed a blind eye to professional, ethical considerations in a fervent competitive quest for audiences. For example, despite network policies prohibiting non-spontaneous interviews, ABC, NBC, and CBS jumped at the chance to broadcast their correspondent's controlled conversations with the Ayatollah on Sunday evening, November 18, 1979. Robert Chandler, director of public affairs for CBS, offered no alibis for his network's justification in ignoring their own rules. "What it came down to," he frankly admitted, "was do we get an interview with the Ayatollah or don't we?"[78]

As veteran ABC political reporter Sander Vanocur observed on Northwestern University's Seminar Day, April 12, 1980, television news can be likened to an omniverous carnivore which requires fresh meat every day.[79] Likewise, the networks' appetite for Iran-related events became insatiable for the entire period the hostages were captive, plus the week following their release. During the Iranian Revolution of 1978, each of the three major networks produced on the average less than one story a week.[80] During 1979, especially in the wake of the Embassy takeover, ABC showed 261 reports, CBS 252, and NBC 208.[81] Similarly, the *Washington Post* carried 35 articles on Iran in 1977, 134 articles in 1978, and 476 articles after the hostages were seized. In 1980 that paper carried a total of 916 articles, or an average of nearly 3 a day.[82] A cursory examination of the *New York Times* index for 1979-1980 seems to indicate an even larger figure.

But this is not the entire picture. Beginning on November 15, 1979, and continuing for several months after the Embassy takeover, ABC Television ran a late evening news show entitled "America Held Hostage,"[83] which eventually proved so profitable that it was turned into a regular nightly program called "Nightline." Each day of the hostages' imprisonment was carefully counted, as it was also by Walter Cronkite at his sign-off on the CBS evening news. One newspaper columnist, himself not noted for dispassionate prose, has referred to the ABC production as "the propagation of rumor, gossip, and haranguing opinion."[84] The nadir of network coverage, however, was plumbed by NBC Television on December 10, when it played an interview between Marine Corporal William Gallegos and his captors that included a 5-minute harangue by a militant spokeswoman called Mary. Three days later, NBC reporter Ford Rowan resigned in protest, accusing the network of "irresponsible journalism."[85]

There is no doubt that at this period of time the Embassy militants proved themselves masters of manipulation vis-à-vis American television:

> "The students in the embassy would frequently schedule "events" to meet satellite and nightly news broadcast deadlines in the United States. From time to time Iranian officials indicated this was how they planned to turn the American people against the policy of their own government."[86]

Well might *Newsweek* magazine, during the last week of December 1979, raise the question of just who is actually the hostage of whom? "When are the media being manipulated? When are they influencing the events they seek to cover?"[87] Or to quote columnist Bill Green of the *Washington Post*, reflecting on the entire relationship between the media and the hostage story after its emotional denouement:

> "Was the press, in any degree a party to Iranian tactics, interpreting moves and pronouncements as possible concessions to American will? Should it have been more cautious? Did it lose its cool? ★ ★ ★ Did the press, by writing and broadcasting feverish bits of news, inflame the situation? And if so, did it have alternatives."[88]

THE NATURE OF THE PROBLEM 61

These are hard questions, and as yet no one has been able to provide wholly satisfactory answers.

One cannot but conclude that the 52 American hostages' 14 1/2-months of Iranian captivity represented an American national trauma. Yet though the victims of the Embassy invasion suffered real physical abuse and psychological deprivation, "there never was a physical threat to the United States itself, nor was the scale of the threat to Americans as great as has been the case in some other circumstances."[89] In only one respect is the Iranian legacy clear: The resolute and unambiguously determined declaration by Secretary of State Alexander Haig, that concern with international terrorism and its tragic consequences now takes priority in American foreign policy over that of human rights, has changed the foreign policy direction—if not the governmental image—of the United States.[90]

The role of the U.S. media with respect to the global terrorist challenge is much less clear, though just as relevant to the present course of national affairs. If television and the press are unwilling or unable to adopt meaningful professional standards and to adhere to reasonable voluntary guidelines relative to the coverage of terrorist violence and the motives of its perpetrators, then it is conceivable that at some future date assertions of national interest may ultimately take priority over the public's historic right to be informed.[91] It is far better to debate the issue now, than to trust to luck and to crisis management. This may be the most important lesson of the hostage seizure.

FOOTNOTES

1. *New York Times*, November 5, 1979, p.1, c.5–6; *Newsweek*, November 19, 1979, 61–73; *U.S. News & World Report*, November 19, 1979, 23–25; *Time*, November 19, 1979, 14–17; *Macleans*, November 19, 1979, 23–26. The first reports were that approximately 100 hostages were seized, 90 of whom were American. See: *New York Times*, November 5, 1979, p. 1, c.5–6.
2. Cf., for example: Vienna Convention on Diplomatic Relations, 23 U.S.T. 3227, T.I.A.S. No. 7052, 500 U.N.T.S. 95, April 18, 1961, entered into force December 13, 1972; International Covenant on Civil and Political Rights, G.A. Res. 2200 (XXI), 21 U.N. GAOR, Supp. No. 16, U.N. Doc. A/6316, December 1966, entered into force, March 23, 1976; Convention on the Prevention and Punishment of Crimes Against Internationally Protected Persons, Including Diplomatic Agents, G.A. Res. 3166 (XXVIII), 28 U.N. GAOR, U.N. Doc. A/9407, and Annex, December 1973, entered into force, February 20, 1977. See, also: American Bar Association Board of Governors. Resolution of the rule of law in Iran. *American Bar Association Journal*, January 1980, *66*, p.8; and the extensive analysis of L.C. Green in: The Teheran Embassy incident—legal aspects. *Archiv Des Völkerrechts*, 1980, *19*(1), 1-22.
3. See: *Newsweek*, November 1979, 61–75; ibid., November 26, 1979, 34–39; ibid., December 3, 1979, 44–55; *U.S. News & World Report*, November 26, 1979, 29–33. Attacks on the

security of diplomats and other internationally protected persons have, for the past decade, been considered acts of international terrorism. It soon became evident that the Iranian Government aided and abetted the hostage seizure and therefor was an accomplice in the illegal activities of the terrorist militants. See: *Washington Post*, November 16, 1979, p. 1, c.5; ibid., November 24, 1980, p. 1.,c.1; and infra, note 52.

4. The *New York Times* editorialized, 2 days after the Embassy seizure, that kidnaping U.S. personnel was "a declaration of war on diplomacy itself ★ ★ ★ ." See: *New York Times*, November 6, 1979, p.A18, c.1. For a contra view, see: Roger Fisher. Helping the Iranians to change their minds. Ibid., November 10, 1979, p.23, c.1.; Alfred P. Rubin. How international law bolsters the U.S. hand. *Christian Science Monitor*, January 21, 1980, p.23, c.1.

5. Interim judgment, case concerning United States diplomatic and consular staff in Iran (*United States of America* v. *Iran*). In Marilou Righini (Ed.), *International Legal Materials*, January 1980, *19*(1), 139–147, (hereinafter cited as *I.L.M.*); Final judgment, case concerning United States diplomatic and consular staff in Iran (*United States of America* v. *Iran*). In ibid., May 1980, *19*(3), 553–584, (hereinafter cited as *I.C.J. Final Judgment*).

6. Cf. *I.C.J. Final Judgment*, 559–564; *U.N. CHRONICLE*, January 1980, *17*(1), 5–13; ibid., March 1980, *17*(2), 18–27.

7. Quarantining the ayatollah. *New Republic*, December 8, 1979, p.8; Georg Schwarzenberger. Detente and international law. *Yearbook of World Affairs*, 1981, *35*, p.277. Schwarzenberger is highly sceptical of the good faith adherence to treaty obligations by Third World countries. But, then, this distinguished legalist is likewise unimpressed with the efficacy of the United Nations.

8. *I.C.J. Final Judgment*, p.557. Incredibly, the Embassy had been left basically unguarded on the morning of November 4. See: *Chicago Tribune*, November 13, 1979, p.1, c.2. But according to an informed State Department source, a minimal Embassy security system was in operation at all times. Conversation with author, January 23, 1981, hereinafter cites as State Department Source.

9. *I.C.J. Final Judgment*, p.557. Yet President Carter is reported by a high-level assistant to have demanded of his National Security Adviser, who had urged allowing the Shah to enter the U.S. for medical treatment, "[w]hen the Iranians take our representatives hostage in Teheran, what will you advise me to do?" See: Anthony Sampson. Le Chah, le banquiers et les otages. *Le Nouvel Observateur*, 1980, *17*, p.59.

10. This point is made by John Osborne in: The hostage game. *New Republic*, November 8, 1980, p.6. Administration uncertainly over the proper course to follow was immediately evident. See: *New York Times*, November 6, 1979, p.1.,c.1.

11. *Chicago Tribune*, November 7, 1979, p.1, c.6. The State Department had first decided to treat the Embassy seizure as though it were an aircraft terrorist hijacking. "The important thing was to cool it," according to an Administration official. See: *New York Times*, November 11, 1979, p.14, c.3.

12. Osborne. *The hostage game*, p.6.

13. Iran ungoverned. *Chicago Tribune*, November 7, 1979, Sec.1, p.8, c.1, which stressed "careful and quiet negotiation with whatever forces are involved ★ ★ ★ ." See, especially: U.S. papers comment on Iran. Ibid., November 11, 1979, Sec.1, p.25, c.3.

14. Idem. Many mid-level State Department personnel favored a forcible response to the hostage seizure and detention. State Department Source, January 23, 1981. A number of hostages had expected a stronger reaction by the U.S. and clearly indicated their displeasure to former President Jimmy Carter during their meeting in Wiesbaden, Germany. See: *Washington Post*, January 23, 1981, p.1, c.6.

15. Furor over Iranian students. *Chicago Tribune*, November 11, 1979, Sec.1, p.1, c.2; Sec.1, p.19, c.2.

16. *New York Times*, November 13, 1979, p.1, c.6; *Chicago Tribune*, November 13, p.1, c.6.

17. *Chicago Tribune*, November 16, 1979, p.1, c.2.

18. Idem.

19. See infra, note 64.

20. Jeffrey Record. Is our military incompetent? *Newsweek*, December 22, 1980, p.9.

THE NATURE OF THE PROBLEM 63

21. See particularly: *Chicago Tribune*, November 19, 1979, p.1, c.2; *New York Times*, November 21, 1979, p.1, c.3; *Washington Post*, November 23, 1979, p.1, c.6.
22. See especially: M. Cherif Bassiouni. Protection of diplomats under Islamic Law. *American Journal of International Law*, July 1980, 74(3), 609–633; Herman F. Eilts, Security considerations in the Persian Gulf. *International Security*, Fall 1980, 5(2), p.106. Eilts adds that leaders of the Persian Gulf countries acknowledged that the hostage seizure "violated both Islamic law and custom." See, also: Roy Parviz Mottahedeh. Iran's foreign devils. *Foreign Policy*, Spring 1980, 38, 19–20.
23. *U.S. News & World Report*, December 1979, 11–13.
24. Mottahedeh. Iran's foreign devils, 32–34. He adds that Khomeini and the Mullahs may very well have been consciously repudiating Western international law for their own purposes. Ibid, p.34.
25. Speech to ABA Law Professor Workshop on "The Economic Aspects of National Security and Foreign Policy." St. Louis University School of Law, St. Louis, Miss., December 12, 1980.
26. See the discussion in: Robert Friedlander. The "Mayaguez" in Reprospect: Humanitarian intervention or showing the flag? *St. Louis University Law Journal*, 1979, 22(4), 601–613; Robert Friedlander. Retaliation as an anti-terrorist weapon: The Israeli Lebanon incursion and international law. *Israel Yearbook on Human Rights*, 1978, 8, 63–77.
27. Cf. *New York Times*, November 6, 1979, p.A12, c.1; *Chicago Tribune*, November 7, 1979, p.1, c.5. The latter carried a headline statement.
28. See: U.S. military "helpless" to aid hostages. *Chicago Tribune*, November 11, 1979, Sec.1, p.19, c.1; David Tinnin & David Halevy. Strike teams: Can the U.S. handle the terrorist threat? *Playboy*, February 1979, 90–94 & 191–197. On December 2, the Soviet Army newspaper, *Krasnaya Zevezda*, warned of possible U.S. armed intervention in the Persian Gulf. See: *New York Times*, December 3, 1979, p.A5, c.1.
29. *Chicago Tribune*. November 11, 1979, Sec.1, p.1, c.2; idem., Sec.1, p.19, c.2.
30. Shaul Bakhash. Before the fall. *New Republic*, November 22, 1979, p.33.
31. *New York Times*, November 11, 1979, p.1., c.4.
32. 8 C.F.R. §214.5. See also: *Washington Post*, November 14, 1979, p.A1, c.4; *Chicago Tribune*, November 15, 1979, Sec.1, p.1, c.1, and Sec.1, p.6, c.1. The Institute for International Education set the 1980 figure at 51,870. See: *Chronicle of Higher Education*, October 21, 1980, p.18, c.1.
33. *Narenji v. Civiletti* 617 F.2d 745 (D.C. Cir. 1979).
34. *Korematsu v. United States*, 323 U.S. 214 (1944). See: Arthur Miller. Presidential power. St. Paul-Minneapolis: West Publishing Co., 1977, p.178. Miller claims that the Court read into the Constitution "a theory of raison d'état." Korematsu still controls in wartime emergencies.
35. See: *Washington Post*, November 20, 1980, p.A1, c.1, which states that "[m]ore than half of the 7,700 Iranian students identified by immigration agents in the last year have failed to appear for deportation hearings or to leave the United States when ordered to do so ★ ★ ★ ."
36. *New York Times*, November 13, 1979, p.A1, c.3&5; *Chicago Tribune*, November 13, 1979, p.1, c.6.
37. *New York Times*, November 13, 1979, p.A10, c.5.
38. Idem., p.A10, c.3. Allied support for economic sanctions was not sought until mid-December. *New York Times*, December 12, 1979, p.1, c.4.
39. Ibid., November 13, 1979, p.A11, c.1. Apparently, the maneuvers had been scheduled months before the hostage seizure.
40. Idem., p.A22, c.1. Even conservative columnist Patrick Buchanan was in agreement: "Public saber-rattling makes little sense ★ ★ ★ To do so would only incite the crazies." See: Patrick Buchanan. What we should do about Iran. *Chicago Tribune*, November 13, 1979, Sec.1, p.9, c.5.
41. *New York Times*, November 15, 1979, p.A1, c.5&6; *Washington Post*, November 15, 1979, p.A1, c.4; *Chicago Tribune*, November 15, 1979, Sec.1, p.1, c.5 & 6. See, also: Iranian assets control regulation, 44 F.R. 65956-65988.

42. *Blade* (Toledo), December 6, 1980, p.13, c.1; Russ Hoyle. Endgame. *New Republic*, November 15, 1980, p.10. Hoyle puts the total amount of blocked Iranian assets as high as "$10 to $13 billion". As of December 1980, there were over 3,000 claimants, of whom 250 had already sought court action. See: *Blade* (Toledo), December 6, 1980, p.13, c.1.
43. Hoyle. Endgame, p.10.
44. Edward Gordon. Trends: The blocking of Iranian assets. *International Lawyer* Fall 1980, *14*(4), 659–688. This is an excellent and carefully detailed survey of the entire assets question. Cf. a more recent short statement: Edward Gordon. Freeze, thaw may squeeze law: What's happening to those Iranian assets? *International Practitioner's Notebook*, November 19, 1980, 1–7.
45. *New England Merchants Bank* v. *Iran Power Generation and Transmission Company et al.*. *I.L.M.*, September 1980, *19*(5), 1298–1329.
46. Ibid., p.1324.
47. See the U.S.-Iranian Accords signed in Algiers on January 19, 1981. *Courier* (Findlay, Oh.), January 20, 1981, c.1–6. One may argue that Article One of the Algerian Declaration was in part an American admission of past illegality, although as of this writing, most commentators have refrained from making that inference.
48. Cf. *Chicago Tribune*, November 16, 1979, p.1, c.2&6; ibid., November 18, 1979, Sec.1, p.1, c.2; *New York Times*, November 16, 1979, p.A1, c.6; *Chicago Tribune*, November 19, 1979, Sec.1, p.1, c.3; *New York Times*, November 21, 1979, p.A1, c.3; *Washington Post*, November 23, 1979, p.A1, c.6; the European Parliament by means of a November 16 resolution denounced Iranian "blackmail" and "violence." *Chicago Tribune*, November 17, 1979, Sec.1, p.1, c.3.
49. See: *Chicago Tribune*, November 18, 1979, Sec.1, p.1, c.2; *New York Times*, November 18, 1979, p.1, c.6; *Chicago Tribune*, November 19, 1979, Sec. 1, p.1, c.6; *New York Times*, November 19, 1979, p.A1, c.6; *Washington Post*, November 19, 1979, p.A1, c.5 & 6; *Chicago Tribune*, November 20, 1979, Sec.1, p.1, c.2; *Washington Post*, November 20, 1979, p.A1, c.1-6; and ibid., November 22, 1979, p.A1, c.6.
50. H.H.A. Cooper. Let my people go. *Atlantean Era*, November 1, 1980.
51. See: *New York Times*, November 16, 1979, p.A17, c.3. Asian and Middle Eastern Governments were prone to tergiversation.
52. It now appears that some Iranian clerics were co-conspirators as well. See: *Plain Dealer* (Cleveland), January 28, 1980, p.14A, c.1. Cf. supra, note 3.
53. See, particularly, the New York Times/CBS News Poll of November 5 in: *New York Times*, November 6, 1979, p.A1, c.5 & p.B8, c.1; and the Harris Poll of early November in: *Plain Dealer* (Cleveland), November 9, 1979, p.29-A, c.1.
54. See: *Washington Post*, November 21, 1979, p.A1, c.1; *New York Times*, November 21, 1979, p.A1, c.6; *Washington Post*, November 22, 1979, p.A1, c.1; *New York Times*, November 22, 1979, p.A1, c.6; *Washington Post*, November 23, 1979, p.A1, c.6; *New York Times*, November 23, 1979, p.A1, c.6; and *Washington Post*, November 24, 1979, p.A1, c.1.
55. *New York Times*, November 21, 1979, p.A1, c.5&6.
56. Cf. the comments of former Assistant Secretary of State Charles William Maynes in: After freedom, the lessons. *Miami Herald*, January 25, 1981, p.4M, c.4; Grim lessons of the long crisis. *Newsweek*, November 10, 1980, p.58; Robert W. Tucker. American power & the Persian Gulf. *Commentary*, November 1980, p.29; Osborne. The hostage game, p.6&7; and the admission by President Carter in his final State of the Union Message that the U.S. abstained from "other remedies to us in international law." See: *Courier* (Findlay, Ohio), January 17, 1981, p.A2, c.2.
57. *New York Times*, November 7, 1979, p.1, c.1. See also the remarks of Bernard D. Nossiter in: Nobody blinked. Ibid., December 2, 1979, Section 4, p.E1, c.1. On December 17, 1979, the U.N. General Assembly—after almost 4 years—adopted an International Convention against the Taking of Hostages. It appears to have been still-born. *U.N. Chronicle*, January 1980, *17*(1), p.85.
58. Russian veto of a sanctions program occurred on January 13, 1980. See: *U.N. Doc. S/PV.219/Add.1*, January 13, 1980, 54–55. The failure of the Waldheim mission is described

THE NATURE OF THE PROBLEM 65

in: *New York Times*, January 4, 1980, p.A1, c.3; ibid. January 5, 1980, p.A4, c.4; *Time*, January 14, 1980, p.24.

59. *New York Times*, November 30, 1979, p.A1, c.4. Technically, the U.S. was in violation of Article 13 of the 1973 U.N. Convention on the Protection of Diplomats, since it calls for a 6-month period of negotiation and arbitration before submission of any dispute to the I.C.J. See: Robert A. Friedlander. *Terrorism: Documents of international and local control*, Vol. 1. Dobbs Ferry, N.Y.: Oceana Publications, 1979, p.505.

60. State Department Source, January 23, 1981. Iranian expert James Bill, of the University of Texas, defined the problem succinctly: "Informed and sensitive leadership was lacking on both sides." Quoted in: *Blade* (Toledo), January 25, 1981, Sec.B, p.1, c.2.

61. Bill Prochenau. U.S. traveled a maze to get hostages freed. *Blade* (Toledo), January 25, 1981, Sec.B, p.1, c.2. See, also: Grim lessons of the long crisis. *Newsweek*, November 10, 1980, 57–60; and Elie Kedourie. The illusions of powerlessness. *New Republic*, November 29, 1980, 17–18, among others. See, also: Robert W. Tucker. The purposes of American power. *Foreign Affairs*, Winter 1980/81, *59*(2), 241–274. Tucker gives a wide-ranging critique on the Persian Gulf, but does not directly mentioning the hostages.

62. Editorial: The rights of Iran. *New York Times*, November 21, 1979, p.A18, c.1. See, also the editorial in: Ibid., December 5, 1979, p.A30, c.1. This approach seems to have reflected the European view throughout the crisis. See: Lord Chalfont. Triad of influence? *Europe*, November-December 1980, 9–10. For a contra editorial comment of the same period, see: Marvin Stone. Iran and after. *U.S. News & World Report*, Report, November 26, 1979, p.108.

63. *Newsweek*, December 17, 1979, 29 & 45. Only 27 percent indicated they would approve of military action.

64. Quoted in: Ibid., November 10, 1980, p.58.

65. *U.S. News & World Report*, November 26, 1979, p.32.

66. Charles William Maynes & Richard H. Ullman. Ten years of foreign policy. *Foreign Policy*, Fall 1980, (40), 16–17. Cf., also: *Newsweek*, December 24, 1979, p.27. U.S. State Department officials actually complained 1 month after the seizure that American television reporters were practicing "TV diplomacy" and had more access to the Iranian Government than did the State Department. See: *New York Times*, December 11, 1979, p.A18, c.5.

67. Quoted by: Jim Klurfeld. Legacy of Iran impasse. *Pittsburgh Press*, January 24, 1981, p.B-3, c.4. U.N. Secretary-General Kurt Waldheim, on the other hand, believed that the U.S.-Iranian confrontation represented the gravest threat to world peace since the 1962 Cuban missile crisis. See: Quarantining the Ayatollah, p.8. Paul Nitze and Robert Tucker appear to hold similar views, although their focus centers on the entire Persian Gulf. See: Tucker. American Power and the Persian Gulf, p.37.

68. Frederick J. Hacker. *Crusaders, criminals, crazies: Terror and terrorism in our time*. New York: W.W. Norton, 1977, p.292. See, also: J. Bowyer Bell. *A time of terror: How democratic societies respond to revolutionary violence*. New York: Basic Books, 1978, 110–116.

69. Abraham Miller. *Terrorism and hostage negotiations*. Boulder, Colo.: Westview Press, 1980, p.83.

70. Statement of the National News Council, New York, March 22, 1977.

71. See, for example: Symposium, "Terrorism and the media: Legal response." *Indiana Law Journal*, Summer 1978, *53*(4), 619–777. This is one of the most informative of its genre, hereinafter cited as *Indiana Law Journal*.

72. See, especially: David Anable. Media, the reluctant participant in terrorism. In Marie Snyder (Ed.), *Media and terrorism: The psychological impact*. North Newton, Kansas: Mennonite Press, 1978, 15–22.

73. Harold J. Laski. *The American democracy: A commentary and an interpretation*. New York: The Viking Press, 1948, p.648.

74. Walter Lippman. *Public opinion*. New York: The Free Press, 1965, p.221.

75. Todd Gitlin. The whole world is watching. Quoted in: Richard J. Margolis. "Framed" by the evening news: Media images of the new left. *Chronicle of Higher Education*, November 10, 1980, p.15, c.2.

76. The originator of that phrase was 19th century Russian anarchist Michael Bakunin.

77. CBS Press Release, April 14, 1977, reprinted in: *Indiana Law Journal*, 776–777.
78. *New York Times*, November 19, 1979, p.A12, c.1.
79. *Northwestern Alumni News*, April-May 1980, p.1, c.1.
80. *Washington Post*, January 23, 1981, p.A10, c.4.
81. Ibid., January 24, 1981, p.A2. c.1. These are corrected figures relating to the previously cited article of the day before.
82. Ibid., January 23, 1981, p.A10. c.4.
83. Cf. *New York Times*, November 16, 1979, p.C28, c.2; Edward W. Said. Inside Islam. *Harper's*, January 19, 1981, p.25; Nicholas von Hoffman. ABC held hostage. *New Republic*, May 10, 1980, 15–16.
84. Nicholas von Hoffman. Op. cit., p.15.
85. See: *New York Times*, December 11, 1979, p.A1, c.4, & p.A16, c.1; ibid. December 14, 1979, p.A16, c.6; *Newsweek*, December 24, 1979, p.27; *U.S. News & World Report*, December 24, 1979, p.7; and Nicholas von Hoffman. Op. cit., p.16. The latter misdates "Mary Militant's" appearance by 2 weeks.
86. Said. Inside Islam, p.25.
87. *Newsweek*, December 24, 1979, p.27.
88. *Washington Post*, January 23, 1981, p.A16, c.5.
89. Don Oberdorfer. Hostage seizure: Enormous consequences. *Washington Post*, January 23, 1981, p.A1, c.2.
90. *Blade* (Toledo), January 29, 1981, p.1, c.4. This was meant to counter such statements as that of columnist William Safire, that the hostage settlement "set a precedent that encourages terrorists, and endangers innocents, everywhere." *New York Times*, January 19, 1981, p.A25. c.1. See, also, the comments of George Ball in: *Pittsburgh Press*, January 24, 1981, p.B-3, c.1.
91. Presidential Press Secretary Jody Powell, in the aftermath of the Hanafi Muslim incident, raised by indirect implication a future possibility of government controls. *New York Times*, March 15, 1977, p.A16, c.4. For a law enforcement perspective on this pressing issue, see: Miller. *Terrorism and hostage negotiations*, 86–92.

II THE LAW ENFORCEMENT PERSPECTIVE

3. THE JOURNALIST AND THE HOSTAGE: HOW THEIR RIGHTS CAN BE BALANCED

Robert L. Rabe

Terrorism is an ugly phenomenon and has no place in a free society, yet in light of the increasing incidence of terrorist acts, it is apparently no longer a last resort. Terrorism is calculated to shock and draw attention to any real or imagined grievance; its nature is to capture the attention of the public. The basic goals of terrorism—not only to jeopardize lives and destroy property, but to break the spirit of the opposition—depend on extensive coverage by the media, and the viewing public is precisely the segment of people that the terrorist wishes to impress.

Let's look at terrorism for what it really is: Criminal acts in violation of specific Federal, State, or local statutes, to which are added the victims' reactions of intense fear. While the news industry is considered somewhat legitimate when reporting criminal activity, it is called to task when terrorists use the media to obtain their objectives. Reporters can become newsmakers. This type of involvement not only contributes to greater subjectivity; it can bring about a change in the course of the news event as well.

What of the contagion caused by such detailed coverage of a terrorist incident? When terrorist activities are glorified with extensive news coverage, an event is projected as an attraction for others to emulate. When this happens, terrorism has truly made television a pawn in the great game of propaganda. Let's look at an example. In the 1975 Baader-Meinhof kidnaping of mayoral candidate Peter Lorenz, control of the media was at the beck and call of the terrorists for almost 72 hours. Regularly scheduled programs were shifted and even canceled in order to meet the terrorists' timetable; news coverage included statements prepared by the terrorists.* The script for this drama was being written by the terrorists, not the reporters. This episode is a prime example of just how effective such criminals can be in using the media for their purposes.

The ability to capture the attention of the media has changed not only terrorists' tactics but their potential to reach the public and their perception of their role. Terrorists' attacks are often carefully choreographed to attract the attention of both the print and electronic media on an international scale. The Hanafi incident in Washington, D.C. (1977) is an outstanding example of this. The Metropolitan Police Department not only had to deal with live coverage on local and national television; they also had to deal with reporters who called from places like Ottawa, London, and Sydney directly into the hostage site to interview the terrorists.

Such theatrics are possible because the electronic camera has set a wide stage and has created a large captive audience. The electronic media can travel all over the world, to wherever the news is breaking, and the viewing public would be dismayed if terrorist episodes were ignored. It is not the coverage of these events that gives rise to concern, but the manner in which the coverage is presented. Because the terrorists provide the drama and make the news, media publicity tends to favor the terrorists. This tendency, together with the competitive nature of the news industry, gives rise to a real danger for police, for frequently the media do not merely report the news—they become participants in their own stories. Journalists cease to be merely the recorders of the news; they become part of the audience the terrorists try to reach. There are two sides to every story, and the media would be remiss in their duty if they were unable to report a nonofficial side of a story; yet even they must question their intervention and participation in the news.

The media are by no means confined to reporting newsworthy events; they play an influential role in the formation of public opinion. The public's interest in the news lies in the subjectivity of its presentation—the distinctive angles the media adopts and the way relatively standard news can be made to provide an element of entertainment. When we find one sector of the press that is more diligent, more up-to-date, or more expansive in its news coverage, we think that we are so much better informed. After all, this is why we read one newspaper over another and why we allow ourselves to be entertained by one radio or television station in preference to a competitor.

---

* For a detailed description of the Lorenz kidnaping and its implications, see: Neil Hickey. Terrorism and television, Parts I and II. *TV Guide*, July 31 - August 31, 1976. - Ed.

THE LAW ENFORCEMENT PERSPECTIVE

This is the ratings-and-revenue game; competition for audiences is very intense. It would be irresponsible of and impractical for the news industry to ignore this reality; if one sector of the press ignored something newsworthy, it is certain that another would be only too eager to pay it the proper amount of attention.

It would be unrealistic to say that terrorist acts might not be covered. Their nature is to gain the media's attention and ultimately the attention of the public. Imposing a partial or total news blackout is both unrealistic and counterproductive for it would mask some of the problems this country faces. Therefore, we must deal with the fact that the news must be reported and the public informed.

This is the dilemma faced by both news industry and law enforcement officials: Can the right to report news be claimed when there is an equal if not a more compelling public interest—saving the lives of hostages? The public's right to be informed is somewhat compromised by the need to deny terrorists the means to communicate their propaganda and instill in the public the element of fear so necessary for their operations and survival. The media, commonly referred to as the fourth estate, have been described as a powerful force, sometimes more influential than government itself. There are those in the media who, under the guise of the first amendment and the public's right to know, claim not just the sacred right, but veritable duty to publish anything remotely newsworthy. The media's first-amendment rights—to gather and to disseminate news—must be examined against other rights and interests also protected. The first amendment states:

> "Congress shall make no law respecting an establishment of religion; or prohibiting the free exercise thereof; or abridging the freedom of the speech, or of the press; or the right of the people peaceably to assemble, and to petition the Government for a redress of grievances."

Obviously, there are first-amendment rights involved. But in an early case, *Schenck* v. *U.S.*, the Supreme Court compellingly acknowledged that "the most stringent protection of free speech would not protect a man in falsely shouting fire in a theatre and causing panic."[1] More than two decades later, the Court reaffirmed that

> "when particular conduct is regulated in the interest of public order and the regulation results in an indirect, conditional, partial abridgement of speech, the duty of the courts is to determine

which of these two conflicting interests demands the greater protection under the particular circumstances presented."[2]

In another important decision in 1950, *American Communications Association v. Douds*, the Court further reaffirmed that first-amendment freedoms, while fundamental, are not absolute.[3]

Today, the problem confronting local law enforcement and the news industry during some ongoing terrorist events is to balance the rights of the press—the right of access to newsworthy events, the right to freely gather news, the right to freely publish, and the right to disseminate information that becomes news—against potential injury to hostages and loss of life. First-amendment rights are not absolute, and specifically, "[t]he right to speak and publish does not carry with it the unrestrained right to gather information."[4] Just as the Government has both the right and the duty to prohibit forms of speech, such as libel and slander, the Government must also expend every effort to protect the safety and lives of hostages, even if the latter dictates limiting the rights of the press. The right to live is, of course, most basic and paramount, and it is recognized that free speech can be limited when the right to live is in jeopardy.

A useful analogy or parallel can be assembled from several cases dealing with the issue of press bans on interviews with Federal and State prisoners. In *Garrett* v. *Estelle*,[5] *Pell* v. *Procunier*,[6] and *Saxbe* v. *Washington Post*,[7] the courts emphasized that the media do not have an absolute, constitutionally protected right of access to information which is distinct from the right of access held by members of the general public. They frankly admitted that the Government does not have an affirmative duty to make available to journalists sources of information not available to the general public. I know of no authority which asserts that the public has a right to interview or talk with either hostages or hostage takers during an incident—and journalists have no greater right.

As recently as June 26, 1978, in *Houchins* v. *KQED, Inc.*, the Court stated: "We must not confuse what is 'good,' 'desirable,' or 'expedient' with what is constitutionally commanded by the First Amendment. To do so is to trivialize constitutional adjudication." The Court further commented that "neither the First Amendment nor Fourteenth Amendment mandates a right of access to government information or sources of information within government's control."[8]

Clearly, any practical solution depends almost entirely on the voluntary cooperation of the media. This will require a reasonable measure of agree-

THE LAW ENFORCEMENT PERSPECTIVE 73

ment between journalists and the networks, but first, news industry representatives must be aware of the problem and recognize that the media are a part of it. For example, although terrorists create an incident, to be effective their propaganda needs the help and encouragement of the media. This is one of the greatest concerns of the law enforcement community—the propagandizing of terrorism rather than the straightforward, objective reporting of an incident. Again, the problem lies in the presentation of the news, the drama which must accompany it. Television's particular appeal is its immediacy, the sense the public has of being present while history is made, and the thrill of participating from a safe distance. The camera certainly allows this, and it is what the public wants. But the real question is whether or not what the public wants is good for it.

The dilemma facing journalists is that they must report the horror of a terrorist incident without the partial revelations and speculations likely to increase the public's fear. In this regard, there needs to be communication between police and journalists to avoid having stories break before the police are ready to release them. I believe the media will find that the police are surprisingly cooperative in this regard, for a legitimately acquired scoop will only in the rarest instance prejudice the security and effectiveness of ongoing operations against terrorists. However, for their own part, journalists should be content with the inherent drama in a story and not exaggerate.

Journalists can provide the police a substantial service. Factual reporting can squelch many half-truths and unsubstantiated rumors that might be rampant in a community. In addition, if terrorists want to publicize their cause through the media, police negotiators can use this service as a bargaining point for the release of hostages.

Neither the public, nor journalists on the public's behalf, need to have direct access to hostage takers. Although this may be considered to restrict access,

> "[t]here are few restrictions on action which could not be clothed by ingenious argument in the garb of decreased data flow. For example, the prohibition of unauthorized entry into the White House diminishes the citizen's opportunity to gather information he might find relevant to his opinion on the way the country is being run, but that does not make entry into the White House a First Amendment right."[9]

Negotiating the release of hostages cannot be accomplished under the glaring lights of a mini-camera. This kind of coverage promotes a circus-like atmosphere at odds with the delicacy of the process. Professional integrity and discipline should discourage journalists from attempting to report such events.

Police negotiators should not have to compete with journalists for the time and attention of the terrorists. It is a very dangerous situation, indeed, when telephone lines are constantly tied up by reporters trying to scoop the latest breaking story; it prevents negotiators from establishing contact with the hostage takers and prevents negotiators from doing their job. Reporters must come to realize that they are not trained in the delicate and sensitive art of hostage negotiation. When you have inexperienced reporters talking to highly volatile terrorists, one wrong word, one slip of the tongue, or one question improperly phrased by a reporter could cause a hostage to lose his life. This is why police departments spend so much time and money to train personnel in the psychological techniques of hostage negotiations. Direct communication between journalists and terrorists is best limited to those times when the terrorist himself initiates the request to speak to the media. As indicated previously, this can be an important bargaining point for the safe release of hostages, and it allows police to conduct negotiations free of outside distractions.

Another area in which members of the press must exercise care when reporting is police operations. Indiscriminate live coverage of police operations on radio and television gives terrorists the latest information on police activities, a distinct tactical advantage not available to the police. In any case, an operation may be different from what the press see and report. During the Hanafi incident, for example, a local journalist reported live over the radio and television that boxes of ammunition were being taken into the 'B'nai-B'rith building in preparation for an all-out police assault, when, in fact, what was being taken in were boxes of food for the hostages. Just imagine the repercussions if the hostage takers had been monitoring their radios or televisions at the precise moment. Imagine too, the tactical advantage hostage takers have in knowing where and how many police sharpshooters are on the rooftops when the police are attempting to ascertain how many terrorists are involved. It is obvious that there will be critical information that the police just cannot release, especially concerning tactical operations.

Another reason the press should limit coverage of a terrorist incident is to protect a terrorist's constitutional right to a fair trial. Both adverse pretrial publicity and contamination of a crime scene by the press can become grounds for a mistrial or even case dismissal. There is also the possibility that the media could prolong an incident by bolstering terrorists' egos. The Anthony Kiritsis incident in Indianapolis (1977) seemed to be such a case.

THE LAW ENFORCEMENT PERSPECTIVE

Also, law enforcement agencies need to reevaluate their positions on news coverage; there is a critical need for police departments' public information offices to release timely and factual information about law enforcement activities. With police information officers always accessible, journalists will find it a relatively easy task to determine if broadcasting information obtained from other sources could damage current negotiations. The responsibility would then lie with the police to advise the media why they feel it would be harmful, but the decision to use or hold the information will ultimately rest with the media.

News coverage represents a real potential for harm in a hostage situation, but it also can be of tremendous value to the police and the community. Freedom of the press must be logically (and constitutionally) balanced with the interests of public safety and the lives of hostages. Having the media take responsibility for this balance would insure the protection of all involved in terrorist incidents, while at the same time allowing the first-amendment right of freedom of the press. On the whole, the law enforcement community has always received splendid cooperation from the majority of the news media represented at terrorist and hostage incidents. It has been the actions of a small segment of the media that have caused us the greatest concern for the safety and welfare of the hostages.

I believe the problem can be solved, and I would like to propose that officials from both the law enforcement and media communities sit down together and make a sincere effort to develop recommendations which allow the police and journalists to work more closely without jeopardizing the lives of innocent hostages, police officers, or reporters.

FOOTNOTES

1 *Schenk* v. *U.S.*, 249 U.S. 47 (1919).
2. *Cox* v. *New Hampshire*, 312 U.S. 569 (1941).
3. *American Communications Association* v. *Douds*, 339 U.S. 382 (1950).
4. *Zemel* v. *Rusk*, 381 U.S. 1, 16–17 (1965).
5. *Garrett* v. *Estelle*, 556 F. 2nd 1274 (5th Cir.d 1977).
6. *Pell* v. *Procunier*, 417 U.S. 817, 834 (1974).
7. *Saxbe* v. *Washington Post*, 417 U.S. 843 (1974).
8. *Houchins* v. *KQED, Inc*, 438 U.S. 1 (1978).
9. *Zemel* v. *Rusk*, 381 U.S. 1, 16–17 (1965).

4. THE POLICE, THE NEWS MEDIA, AND THE COVERAGE OF TERRORISM

Patrick V. Murphy

This paper discusses the practical problems the police encounter when dealing with the news media during terrorist events. Although the subject is a vivid one, of the many concerns of American police leadership today, it probably takes low priority. Teenage vandalism, convenience-store robberies, newly formed and sometimes insurgent police unions, the fiscal crunch affecting all municipal services—these are more real and pressing problems.

American policing is fragmented into 17,000 autonomous, insular agencies. This means that there are 17,000 police chiefs working in the 50 states. Some may occasionally daydream about what they would do if a dramatic terrorist event occurred within their jurisdictions, but few will ever have to deal with an ongoing incident. Indeed, the subject of this paper is as remote from what American police usually encounter as meteorites. But meteorites do fall and terrorists incidents do occur, and because the status of American policing affects how the police will handle both meteorites and terrorism (as well as everyday occurrences), either is a good excuse to note key aspects of American policing.

I mentioned that American policing is fragmented into 17,000 agencies. This fragmentation is a principal factor inhibiting the growth and development of a superior American police service. Perhaps 16,500 of these agencies are so small and usually suffer such poor training, education, and professional expertise, that routine criminal occurrences are often too much for them. For 5-, or 10-, or 20-member police departments the question is not what to do when a terrorist incident occurs in their backyards; the question is what to do about a routine felony.

Another problem with American police is the insularity of its personnel. I know of only a few exceptions to the rule that after 20 or 30 years of service police officers retire from the same department they joined as young people. Because there is virtually no lateral movement among police agencies, an officer is stuck in the same department for an entire career, subject to the folkways of that particular department. The police officer has virtually no chance to enjoy the sort of professional growth that comes in other fields, where changing jobs is a way of going up the ladder to better pay and promotions, a way of broadening experience and increasing expertise. This insularity breeds narrowness, resentfulness, and a cynicism which manifests itself in an us-against-them attitude.

A third problem of American policing is a stolid resistance to change and innovation, particularly when change and innovation may mean that authority held by top brass and middle management is transfered to officers in the street so that the officers can get closer to the communities they serve, in a sustained, productive manner. During the past 30 years, partly because of the necessity of using the automobile for patrol, the police have become remote from neighborhoods and citizens. In practical terms, this has meant that the police are not close enough to sources of information, to what is going on in communities. The information and confidence that the police need from citizens in order to control crime are not as ample as they once were.

When I was a young police officer patrolling the Red Hook section of Brooklyn, it was natural for me and my colleagues to know the community and to be aware of the good guys and the bad guys. Since then, policing has become more impersonal, again thanks, in part, to the impersonality of automobile patrol.

There are other problems which face policing: the need to increase, by more than has been accomplished, the number of women and minorities in policing; the need to test and introduce measures of productivity into police work; the need to turn policing into a profession (something it is not now) through education, research, and debate. But I will limit my discussion to the three problems I have mentioned because they relate directly to the practical problems that law enforcement encounters when dealing with the news media during terrorist events.

Fragmentation means that the police in many areas lack the coordination and the staff, the training and skills to deal with a wide range of criminal activities. Insularity means that in most departments, the police are not as sophisticated and enlightened as they should be in dealing with the extremes of human nature. Their remoteness from citizens and communities means that they often lack sufficient intelligence about what is happening in their jurisdictions and can neither anticipate criminal events as well as they might, nor effectively deal with those events once they occur.

For this discussion, terrorism is defined as "a strategy of unlawful violence calculated to inspire terror in the general public, or a significant segment thereof, in order to achieve a power-outcome or to propagandize a particular crime or grievance." By using criminal violence to bring attention to political or ideological claims, terrorists become their own press agents. An explanation for the relatively infrequent occurrence of politically or ideologically inspired terrorist sieges in the United States may lie in the fact that, with a little skill and planning, any fool promoting virtually any cause can grab the media's attention and trumpet a belief without resorting to violence. By exercising first-amendment rights to cover anything and everything, the U.S. media may be helping law enforcement keep down the nation's level of terrorism. If so, I relish the irony.

As terrorists seek to be their own press agents, capturing the media's attention is their primary goal—not cash, or property, or the death or injury of an estranged lover or friend, as is common in most crimes. Terrorists plant bombs or lay siege, for maximum public visibility; they endanger lives, even kill, to extort as much printed space and broadcast time as possible. The immediate purpose of their extortion may be a plane abroad or a ransom, but this purpose is almost always secondary to the goal of propagandizing a belief or course of political action.

Their actions change the rules of the game between the police and the news media, two frequent adversaries who ordinarily operate in an established manner. The police patrol the streets, enforce the law, investigate crimes, and capture criminals. The news media stand aside, observing this process and reporting its outcome. That's the way it's supposed to be, except that sometimes the reporters get the facts wrong or misplace the emphasis of a police matter, and the police boil in resentment. Sometimes the police lie to journalists or bungle a case, and the press catch on and write a tough story. To this mix of often strained relations add the police chief's realization that, at least in many localities, the press—particularly the local newspaper—can make or break him.

In events of criminal terrorism, particularly ongoing events, the accustomed pattern of relations between the police and the news media is markedly transformed. The news media not only cover the crime the police are handling; their power to disseminate information is the reason for the crime.

THE LAW ENFORCEMENT PERSPECTIVE

Crime stories usually deal with a bank being robbed, a house burgled, a lover slain—all criminal acts. In terrorist events, wittingly or not, the news media cover occurrences which are intended to elicit that very coverage—the more the better, as far as terrorists are concerned.

Of course, a great deal of what the news media report is designed to capture coverage—prepackaged news conferences, politician's travels, ribboncuttings, and staged confrontations. But with terrorism, the device used to gain attention is the threat of criminal violence in any number of manifestations. Relations between the police and the news media change substantially, and as a consequence, the usual understandings between the police and media are less clear, and the usual tensions more subject to strain.

When a felony unfolds, the police reflex is to stop its course or, if that is not possible, to limit its damage. When the felony involves terrorism, which almost always involves a threat to life, the police' instinct is, at the least, to save lives and to deny the terrorists a full realization of their goal to gather as much publicity as possible. The media's instinct is to give a terrorist event as much coverage as they think it deserves. With the rules of the police-media game transformed, the police are apt to bridle at the media's intrusiveness, and the media are apt to resist attempts by the police to limit their coverage.

This observation recalls the subject of this paper—the practical problems of law enforcement and the media during ongoing terrorist events. The discussion would be different if it could be said that the police in the United States were uniformly trained and educated, and able—ready at the break of a terrorist incident to swing into action in a coordinated, professional manner. Lines of communication would be clear; hostage negotiators and other specially trained officers would be near at hand to help defuse the passions of terrorists and calm down the situation; seasoned media liaison officers, skilled at handling both local and national media, would quickly set up a media center for the rapid dissemination of up-to-date information. The press and the public would have a police operation working as smoothly as possible to save lives and to bring the event to an end.

But this cannot be said about American policing, now or for many years. The fragmentation of American policing forestalls the development of the coordination, the specialized training, and the skills necessary to deal with terrorism in most local police jurisdictions.

For most police agencies, if terrorists strike within their jurisdictions, the best that can be hoped for is rapid State or Federal intervention. Even many U.S. police agencies of workable size—those with a minimum of 200 officers—are not prepared to deal with terrorism. As noted earlier, police chiefs are concerned primarily with problems of a far more immediate nature, and although some larger departments are able to send managers to seminars and training sessions designed to guide the police in dealing with terrorism, the shelf life of that training is often quite short. This year's chief of operations, a graduate of a seminar on terrorism, is next year's chief of traffic or personnel. This calls for an occupational confession: as in most other human endeavors, knowledge is power in law enforcement, and police don't usually will their successors the expertise and training manuals they picked up at special seminars or training institutes.

In sum, most police agencies are usually inadequately prepared to deal with terrorist events, particularly the ongoing kind which involve delicate negotiations and demand a trained, calming hand.

Summing up the October 1978 testimony of Glen King, then executive director of the International Association of Chiefs of Police, the staff of the House Judiciary Subcommittee on Civil and Constitutional Rights said King testified that

> "state and local police officials are better trained than they were five years ago. However, he indicated that significant training remains to be done if these officials are to respond effectively to a domestic incident of terrorism in the future."[1]

King's testimony, in my view, understates the matter.

So far, the Nation has been fortunate that most recent ongoing terrorist incidents have occurred in large cities whose police agencies have been of a size and sophistication that could begin to deal with the situations. The incident which seems to be cited most in discussions of domestic terrorism—certainly the one which received the most thorough recent news coverage—was the 1977 Hanafi Muslim siege in Washington, D.C.

Overall, the Metropolitan Police of the District of Columbia handled the incident very ably, though the department's ability could have been predicted. Washington police, unique in having to serve the diverse constituencies of the Nation's capital, have been tempered for 15 years through dealing with riots and massive antiwar demonstrations. The department is geared to expect the rare occurrence.

Suppose an incident similar to the Hanafi siege occurred in a New England village, a small midwestern city, an Arizona county, or even an industrial city with a population of a few hundred thousand? I question whether the police in these localities would be as close to being prepared as the police in

THE LAW ENFORCEMENT PERSPECTIVE

Washington, New York, Chicago, or Los Angeles. If I am correct, that almost all police jurisdictions are unready to deal with terrorism, how are these same agencies prepared to deal with the media coverage of a terrorist incident? My answer is that they are not prepared, for several reasons.

The first reason—to hark back to my observation about the fragmentation of policing—is that policing in this Nation is not consolidated into a few hundred agencies and so cannot afford the economy of scale that would mean not only skilled, quickly deployable units which would open negotiations with terrorists and seek to save lives, but also police officers trained to deal with the media in all types of incidents.

Perhaps in a department of 50 or 100 officers, one officer may be assigned to deal with the local media. But does he or she have the savvy and experience to operate effectively when the national wire services and network radio and television crews descend on a big terrorist story? The lights, the cameras, the media's competitiveness, the pressure of deadlines, and other demands of a harried press corps can overwhelm untrained police officers attempting to deal with the media and can feed too easily into the unfolding situation at hand.

The second reason refers to my observations about the insularity of police personnel. Police officers, penned into one department for all of their careers, tend to become narrow in outlook and suspicious, particularly of the news media. In fact, it's fair to say, if not almost an understatement, that many law enforcement officers neither trust nor like reporters. And it's sad to say that this is a great impediment to effective policing. Police don't know how to tell their good stories, nor do they inform the public of their successes and productive efforts to serve the communities as well as they might.

In the typically tense and delicate surroundings of a terrorist incident, the dislike and resentment which the police have for the media easily surface and complicate attempts to deal with terrorists, whose goal, after all, is the media's attention. Some reporters have disdain for the police and in order to obtain more extensive news coverage, invent schemes to outwit them; I am certain that this also contributes to the problems between law enforcement and the news media during these incidents. The point is that, ideally, the police should be sufficiently sophisticated to deal with the media in an even-handed, fair manner. The insularity of policing works against achieving this goal.

The third reason the police are unprepared to deal with the media's coverage of terrorism is that we in policing waste time by trying to blinker or curtail it. Like the rest of the police—and many citizens—I am outraged when a media personality chats on the phone with gunmen during a hostage situation and when a disc jockey asks a terrorist if he has set a deadline on his demands. These are stupid, dangerous actions on the part of irresponsible members of the media. But the police should not attempt to restrict the media's job of covering terrorism. Apart from the first-amendment rights which the media enjoy, there are practical reasons for this position.

First, it has been my experience that in the event of extraordinary violence or the threat of such violence, extensive, balanced coverage is better than restricted news coverage. Once the news media are allowed to determine what is going on in a situation and report it accurately, rumors and excessive fears tend to be dispelled. For example, restrictions on the media's coverage of the Hanafi Muslims could have had damaging results. The Hanafi Muslims had captured three key positions in the Nation's capital, including City Hall. This drastic takeover in the heart of Washington could have easily been fertile ground for wild speculation and rumors. But the media were allowed to do their job, and despite the excesses of a few, the stories were presented generally in a fair and balanced manner. In fact, the media benefited the police because their reporting kept citizens from becoming overly concerned, and because news reports assured citizens that the police had the situation well in hand.

At a very helpful seminar sponsored by the *Chicago Sun-Times* in the spring of 1977, Leonard Downie, who coordinated the *Washington Post's* coverage of the Hanafi siege, said of coverage of the event:

> "It was our impression that once the first day was over and all of the media, broadcast and print, had given the public a rather full picture of what was going on, that city seemed to ease a great deal. The jams of traffic and gawkers were not that great around the three sites, and I feel that's because people could watch what was going on on television. Tourists continued to come to town and continued to go to the White House. People went to work ★ ★ ★ saturation coverage allowed the city to relax, in a way, to know that information was coming to them ★ ★ ★ ."[2]

I agree with Downie's conclusion.

A second reason why the police should not attempt to restrict the news media's coverage of terrorist events is that police are not trained to run news operations any more than journalists are trained to run police departments. If the media were to be formally restrained from covering certain aspects of terrorist incidents, the police would be immediately in the business of censorship, something for which they are not, and should not, be prepared.

THE LAW ENFORCEMENT PERSPECTIVE

I extend these remarks to the point of saying that police should keep to a minimum their requests for news media to regulate themselves. Many news organizations are aware of the operational problems involved in terrorist incidents and have already issued their own self-imposed rules for covering such events. These organizations should be congratulated for their thoughtful study and their attempts to achieve noninflammatory, balanced coverage of terrorist incidents.

None of these observations mean that, when asked by the media, the police should not explain the issues involved in dealing with terrorism.

The news media can create problems for the police during terrorist incidents in many ways, including:

- By attempting to negotiate with terrorists, thus depriving the police of their official responsibility for dealing with terrorists;
- By talking directly with terrorists, thereby reinforcing the terrorists' sense of power and diluting the influence of police negotiators;
- By casting doubt upon the veracity or reliability of what the police say and do;
- By disclosing tactical information which might endanger hostages and others under the threat of terrorist violence; and
- By raising the anxiety of terrorists by disclosing police plans and tactics, for example, that a police sharpshooter squadron may be on scene.

There is another area which I can only mention because neither I nor others in policing have had much experience with it: the news media have a responsibility to balance coverage of terrorist incidents in a way that does not encourage imitation. This is a delicate issue. I realize that one news organization's interpretation of what is fair and balanced coverage is another news organization's sensationalism. But the fact remains—and it is one for debate among members of the press—that incidents such as plane hijackings, bombings, and terrorist sieges, can carry an element of contagion.

There are several things the police can do to promote responsible coverage of terrorist incidents. Police agencies, as a matter of course, should develop clear guidelines governing the news media's access to the scene of terrorist incidents and clear rules governing police lines and press identification passes. The media should be made aware of these guidelines and conditions before terrorist incidents and similar events occur. This step seeks to avoid the arguments and recriminations that can develop between individual reporters and police officers during the rush and confusion of violent incidents.

Police departments, if they have the organizational capability, should have contingency plans for dealing with events likely to draw national news media attention, particularly extensive television coverage, with its attendant lights, cameras, and technicians.

The police should encourage meetings in which news media personnel and police officials discuss a wide range of issues involved in the media's coverage of terrorist incidents. The Report of the Task Force on Disorders and Terrorism of the National Advisory Committee on Criminal Justice Standards and Goals makes a good point in suggesting frequent forums for the exchange of local police and media viewpoints.

From these forums, the media should be aware of the substantial problems terrorist incidents and similar occurrences create for the police. Of course, a good police department already has on the books some basic planning and training for emergency events. This planning and training is designed to ensure that police are in control of the scene of an incident as soon as possible and that they are able to work toward its nonviolent conclusion. Complicating the police administrator's job of dealing with terrorist incidents are not only the demands of the media, but also the sometime presence of elected city officials, city managers, and others in government who are natural targets for the media's attention. The media want to know what the mayor or city council member has to say about the terrorist event, just as they wish to interview as many police officials and officers as possible.

Perhaps the single most important thing the police officer in charge can do to help establish control at the scene of a terrorist incident is to make certain that police media liaison officers, practiced in dealing with reporters, have on hand at all times accurate information about the incident. Reporters should be made aware that the most complete information about the incident is available from these officers. In return, the media liaison officers should be made aware of what is being published and broadcast so that inaccurate or misleading coverage can be called to the journalists' attention.

Finally, common sense should prevail on the part of both the media and the police. As noted, this Nation has had relatively few terrorist incidents, particularly of the kind that go on for several hours or several days. Neither the police nor the press are as practiced in dealing with these incidents as they might be. But there is another sort of occurrence relevant to this discussion with which both the news media and the police have had a great deal of experience: I refer to kidnapings.

Generally, the news media have cooperated with the police and Federal officers by withholding information involving a kidnaping if that information posed a threat to the life of a victim. Of course, terrorist incidents are different in that they occur in an immediately public way and are designed to grab the media's attention. But if the media use common sense in kidnaping incidents and agree to withhold information to save the life of a victim, they may also be expected to withhold delicate information concerning a terrorist incident if the police have the credibility to show that its release could be fatal to hostages.

I note a recent debate in the media about the actions of a New York television station monitoring FBI radio conversations in connection with the kidnaping of a New Jersey woman. The television station deployed a camera crew to trail the victim's husband during his attempts to deposit the ransom. Some members of the media defended the TV station's attempted coverage, but most of those interviewed in a recent issue of *Editor and Publisher* deplored the coverage.[3]

Benjamin C. Bradlee, executive editor of the *Washington Post*, said the television station's actions sounded like "an intolerable interference. We wouldn't do that. We have called off kidnaping stories when asked to do so by the FBI." Earl Moses, city editor of the *Chicago Sun-Times*, said that "our general policy is not to endanger the lives of any kidnaping victims. We've called off photographers in cases like that."[4]

Terrorist incidents can be very different from kidnaping incidents. The point is that if the news media are responsible and the police have credibility by not misusing requests to delay reporting specific items of information, then common sense may prevail in the coverage of terrorist incidents. The burden of using common sense lies equally with both parties. It is up to the news media to establish their own standards of conduct in terrorist incidents. It is up to the police to be wary of issuing requests for self-regulation to the news media and to not damage their own credibility by making unnecessary requests.

At the beginning of this paper, I mentioned that the police generally have become remote from the communities they serve. This point seems far afield from a discussion of dealing with terrorist incidents, but it is not.

To be productive, the police must have the trust of the community when extraordinary events such as terrorist incidents occur. When the Hanafi siege struck in Washington, D.C., I wondered whether the incident might have been forestalled if the police had had some clue to the Hanafi's dissatisfaction. This observation is not meant as a criticism of the very fine Washington, D.C., police department. Rather, it is meant as a reflection on the importance of the police' having the trust of communities and their receiving intelligence from the communities about pockets of discontent and the possibility of radical action by disgruntled citizens.

This is a tricky point. The police should not be snooping about the ideological and political beliefs of citizens, nor should they be poking into their private lives. But at the same time, a police department which is close to the community develops an intelligence base which can alert the department to the possibility of criminal actions.

If, as some predict, there is increase of domestic-bred terrorism in the United States during the next years, the police can play an important role in forestalling terrorist events by knowing their communities and enjoying their confidence. Meanwhile, they must be prepared to deal effectively with terrorism, to save lives, and to protect property. And they must use their common sense in dealing with the news media during terrorist incidents. I believe the news media can be expected to respond in kind when they understand the problems the police face. The exercise of common sense is the best prescription for all police dealings with the media.

FOOTNOTES

1. U.S. House of Representatives, Committee on the Judiciary, Subcommittee on Civil and Constitutional Rights, Staff Report. *Federal capabilities in crisis: Management and terrorism.* 95th Congress, 2d Session, December, 1978. Washington, D.C.: U.S. Government Printing Office, 1979, p.15.
2. Leonard Downie, Jr. The breaking story: How the Washington Post covered the siege. *The media and terrorism: A seminar sponsored by the Chicago Sun-Times and the Chicago Daily News.* Chicago: Field Enterprises, 1977, 21–21.
3. See, for example, the comments of Ben Bradlee and Earl Moses, quoted in: Andrew Radolf. Editors disagree with TV station's kidnap coverage. *Editor & Publisher*, July 28, 1977, p.9.
4. Andrew Radolf. Op. cit.

III A VIEW FROM THE FOURTH ESTATE

5. THE MEDIA AND TERRORISM

James W. Hoge

For an editor or a news director, concerns about the coverage of terrorism differ greatly, depending on whether an incident occurs at home or abroad. The terrorist execution of an English lord in Ireland, for example, will compete with school board meetings and oil slicks in the Gulf of Mexico for space on a managing editor's evening news budget. A wide array of intangibles—the rest of the day's news, the prominence the organization gives foreign news, the significance of the event, and how spectacular it was—will determine how the terrorist story will be displayed.

Terrorism in an editor's backyard is admittedly a different kind of story. But it is not *drastically* different; civil rights marches, Nazi rallies, student riots, gang wars, even auto gas lines might all be considered special cases requiring more sensitivity and a more thoughtful reporting touch. But a terrorist incident is certainly one of those crucial stories where an editor and his reporters have to be particularly sensitive to a fundamental caveat of the news business: Don't become a part of the story. Rather than deciding how to display copy from a correspondent or wire service, the editor is creating copy from an evolving situation. Most often there are hostages' lives at stake, and the actions of reporters could conceivably jeopardize those lives. In these situations not only news judgment is important; the procedure used to collect the news is too.

Terrorist stories, depending on proximity, raise special but related questions. The first is a strategic question: Whether to cover the incident and, if so, how much emphasis to put on the story. The second is a tactical question: How to go about obtaining as much information as possible without adding to the dangers of hostages and officials.

Acts of terrorism should be covered consistently and completely as legitimate news events. As in similar conflict situations—for example, wars, demonstrations, elections—the rules of balance and perspective should apply. Common sense and sound news judgment should be the prevailing guidelines for the direct coverage of a terrorist situation and protection of human life should be the highest goal. Some advance preparation is necessary, and communication with the authorities is essential.

The context for these recommendations is that political terrorism in the United States is not a major problem. It may or may not become one, but throughout our history there have been only sporadic, random outbursts of terrorist violence. More generally, terrorism is politically unsuccessful, and, despite its horror, not among the major dangers facing mankind.

Press coverage is often cited as a contributing factor to the spread of terrorism, but there is no empirical evidence in the U.S.—or for that matter the world—that the actions of the press have caused the spread of terrorism or the loss of a single human life in a terrorism situation. A better case can be made for reporters on the scene, acting as a check on both terrorists and law enforcement officials and actually saving lives.

It is also important to remember the diverse composition and role of what is called the media. "Media" includes everything from the metropolitan and rural dailies to the television and radio networks; it includes local television outlets, the news magazines, special and general interest magazines, and political journals. It also includes suburban weeklies, radio journalists, and broadcast personalities such as disc jockeys and talk-show hosts who, although they don't carry press cards, can become an obtrusive part of a terrorist situation. The media are present at terrorist incidents to report the news, not to participate in the functions of police or government. The media are not there to hinder the process, but only on rare occasions should they be expected to help.

The diversity of media outlets will report the news with varying degrees of competence. A recent terrorist takeover of a Chicago office was covered by student journalists, freelancers, yearling reporters from suburban papers, experienced police reporters, and veteran foreign correspondents home on leave—as well as a healthy contingent of out-of-town reporters and European and Japanese correspondents. It was a group that spoke with many voices.

Of this conglomeration, most will file accurate reports and a few will not; most will conduct themselves properly and a few will not. Yet taken together, the story will come out, and with reasonable planning and cooperation the press will not be the cause of major disruptions. One might ask whether this amalgam of organizations and individuals should be covering terrorism incidents at all and, if so, how extensively.

Media critics contend that the intent of the terrorist is to gain media exposure; that the terrorist is concerned with the quantity not the quality of that coverage; that the incidents are portrayed as much more significant than they really are; and that coverage causes contagion, encouraging others to try the same techniques. Although there seems to be little or no empirical evidence to support them, these criticisms are probably valid, at least in the short run. If fictional violence on television sometimes spurs violence in real life, why shouldn't the portrayal of real violence do the same? More convincing arguments could be made that, in the long run, media coverage has the opposite effect, at least with regard to terrorism. It eventually focuses public scrutiny on the demands and actions of the terrorists and, as in Italy after the Aldo Moro kidnaping, promotes public outrage.

As for contagion, terrorist groups may be prompted to act because they see another band of terrorists receiving media exposure, but in the long run, media exposure must cause terrorists more harm than good. Given the amount of attention the media pays to terrorist incidents, one might expect armies of terrorists to be roaming the globe, daily committing acts of violence in the media-saturated United States alone. But that is clearly not the case: in the age of live television and instant communication, terrorism has continued to follow its traditional, sporadic pattern.

Take, for instance, the case of the Symbionese Liberation Army (SLA) and its kidnaping of newspaper heiress Patty Hearst in 1974. At the time of the kidnaping, critics claimed that the media magnified the case beyond its real significance, providing sensational mass entertainment and serving the publicity needs of the SLA as well. Yet what can one say of the SLA as a political force today? It received as much air time as any two candidates in the Presidential primaries, but today the SLA is extinct. Through the coverage, which varied in competence and seriousness, emerged a picture of a bank of social misfits with an unappealing message.

Yet the question of whether the coverage of terrorism is advantageous or disadvantageous is really secondary to the most important question a journalist must ask himself: Why cover terrorism? The reason is that terrorism is news. Terrorism is different, dramatic, and potentially violent. It frequently develops over a period of time, occurs in exotic locations, offers a clear confrontation, involves bizarre characters, and is politically noteworthy. Finally, it is of concern to the public.

When reporting a foreign or national (as opposed to local) terrorist incident, most journalists do not agonize over questions of contagion and whether they too are being held hostage by the terrorists; they use the same news judgment that would apply to a plane crash, a war, or a natural disaster. None are everyday stories, and all may require different displays in the newspaper or on the evening news. Then again, sometimes they will not be given different treatment, depending on the nature of other news and the preference of the individual editor.

As suggested earlier, a lot of factors go into the display of any news story, and a story on far-away terrorism is just another story. One editor's definition of proper play is another's example of excess. The hijacking that ended at Entebbe Airport on July 4, 1976, took place over a "slow news" summer weekend and took up more space than if it had occurred during an election week. The news business is an imperfect institution; it does not follow a systematic pattern of covering news because news does not occur systematically.

Then there is the question of how much air time or how many column inches actually *are* devoted to terrorism. While there are no empirical data available, studies have shown that violent or extraordinary incidents, particularly on television, leave a greater impact on the viewer. A close parallel might be found in the television coverage of the tumultuous 1968 Democratic Convention in Chicago. NBC and CBS calculated that only 3 percent of their total convention coverage dealt with the street violence; ABC, whose coverage was limited to excerpts, devoted 1.1 percent to the demonstration. "The stream was forgotten, the trickle remembered," wrote former CBS executive William Small in an analysis of the convention coverage. Can the press be responsible for how people perceive an event?

Perception was an important question in the debate over the media's coverage of the Vietnam War. Arguments have been made that the U.S. war effort in Vietnam was defeated by television's portrayal of the war's violence. Even if correct, does this justify regulating coverage of an undeclared war? Television did not upend the war effort, but perhaps people's perception of what they saw did. Critics claim that the media's excesses and lack of proportion amounted to an abuse of the first amendment, that they cried "Fire!" in a crowded theater. But the spirit of the first amendment demands that the press shout "Fire!" if the crowded theater is burning. Once the warning is given, people can do as they choose.

Finally, even if someone were to prove that the news media's coverage of violence spawns more violence, that it leads people to believe that violence is unusually pervasive, or that it makes people see the horror of a war in which, consequently, they refuse to fight, the newsman's reply would have to be that his responsibility is to tell the public what is going on.

A VIEW FROM THE FOURTH ESTATE

Another reason the media must be aggressive in their coverage of subjects such as terrorism is that a policy of benign neglect or selective coverage may allow government to take such restraint for granted and to eventually institutionalize it. The suppression of news is an important element in an authoritarian regime.

In West Germany, the rash of terrorism in the mid 1970s produced what has been called "an extreme reaction to extremism." Pressure for media restraint had been building throughout the exploits of the Baader-Meinhof gang but the cataclysmic event was probably the kidnaping of Hans Martin Schleyer on September 5, 1977. Censorship laws were enforced with such absurd results as the cancellation in Bonn of a 19th century comic operetta because it depicted a farcical kidnaping. Germans soon found that much of the subtle repression was directed against leftwing liberal opinion rather than against extremist action. Leftists likened it to a "McCarthy period," and writers such as Heinrich Böll found themselves chilled by what one called, "a general uncertainty as to what may or may not be articulated, written, learned or even taught." For their part, the press were remarkably docile, first agreeing not to cover the Schleyer kidnaping in detail and eventually minimizing all coverage of terrorist acts. This prevailing attitude of self-censorship has come to be known by the Germans as "scissors in the head" and has prompted Böll to say:

> "I wonder if it's necessary to do away with democracy. People are so intimidated, the media have become so careful, that the laws don't actually have to be changed ★ ★ ★ even liberal newspapers have become so conformist and careful that it isn't necessary to do anything."

A further progression of this kind of situation can be seen in Uruguay where spiraling extremism by the Government and the Tupamaros guerrillas ended in the destruction of the strongest democracy in Latin America and its being replaced by a rightwing military dictatorship. For the guerrillas and the Government, their war was mutually suicidal. The next step was that terror by dissidents was completely replaced with terror by the state. Shielded from any criticism by the press, Stalin and Hitler were able to conduct the most ruthless campaigns of state terrorism. In Argentina, terrorism-by-the-right is indistinguishable from that by-the-left because the press cannot write about it. The situation is one of chaos, with the public, and often the Government, unaware of what's going on.

Carlos Marighella wrote in "Minimanual of the Urban Guerrilla" that the terrorist begins to make substantial gains when he induces government officials to shut off the media. Government, he says,

> "winds up in a defensive position by not allowing anything against it to filter through. At this point it becomes desperate, is involved in greater contradictions and loss of prestige, and loses time and energy in an exhausting effort at control which is subject to being broken at any minute."[1]

Such a scenario for the United States is as hypothetical as a mass outbreak of terrorist violence. But if we are to deal with hypotheses, then it's necessary to look at all the implications. One of the greatest detriments to even discrete restrictions on the press is that the media lose credibility in the eyes of the public. If media's coverage of terrorism was even voluntarily restricted, the public could legitimately ask: "If you're not giving us the whole story on this, what else are you holding back?" A reputation for attempting to report the news completely and accurately is an important asset at all times, particularly during public crises such as terrorist incidents. At these times, citizens need reliable sources of information lest they be left with only rumors.

If an aggressively reported story causes someone harm, the newspaper's credibility may be intact but its respect damaged. But as press critic Ben Bagdikian asks,

> "Should the reporter and editor be responsible for the ill effects of printing truthful news? If so, then each editor and reporter has to decide ahead of time what he wants the reader to think and do, and only report those events that lead the reader to that end."[2]

This would eventually undermine the media's credibility as badly as government censorship would. The most appropriate course is to report the news and to encourage reporters and editors to give the clearest possible picture of what's happening. Bagdikian cautioned that when a reporter begins to filter his stories through a concern for whether the reader will "react correctly," he has ceased being a reporter. And people cease believing him.

But much of the foregoing discussion has presumed that there is something dangerous about the coverage of terrorism—or at least something dangerous in what is nebulously perceived as "too much coverage." To the contrary, the coverage of terrorism can be beneficial, and the proper response of government is to encourage *more* rather than less coverage.

This argument finds considerable support from many outside the news business. H.H.A. Cooper, staff director of the National Advisory Committee

Task Force on Disorders and Terrorism, has written of the "greater mischief" of "partial revelations, half-truths, and frightening speculation" that occur when there is not comprehensive media coverage of an extraordinary situation such as a terrorist siege. He reiterates that it causes a loss of confidence in the media and calls the authority of the government itself into question.

In Israel, where terrorism is much more than hypothetical, there is strong recognition of the necessity of press coverage. Although the country does have laws against live television coverage, it doesn't discourage other reporting of terrorist violence. As an Israeli army spokesman said in a *Harper's* magazine article, "[w]hether we release the news or not, there is no vacuum of information, and this would only allow the other side to come out with their own distorted version." He added that journalistic silence would also jeopardize the Government's credibility with the Israeli population.

Richard Clutterbuck, the British scholar who has often been very critical of the media, nonetheless offers a strong argument for robust coverage. In "Guerrillas and Terrorists," he wrote:

> "The overwhelming majority of the public detest political violence and terrorism and wish to help the police to defeat them. So, given the chance, the media will reflect that feeling."[3]

Clutterbuck also cited examples of law enforcement's exploiting the media as the terrorists are said to do. He described a decision by the British Army to allow any of its troops in Northern Ireland to be interviewed by television reporters and said the policy "paid tremendous dividends." Clutterbuck claimed that the enlisted man, coming into the homes of the British viewers, refuted the image of the "fascist pigs," and the result was overwhelming British public support for the soldiers.

It should be noted that a broader point can be taken from this last observation. News that is not an act of God is an act of man. The media event has become a common tool, and everyone exploits the press: Politicians, businessmen, sports figures, and terrorists. But this exploitation should not be considered a justification for suppression. People in the press are aware of being used; sometimes they can do something about it, and sometimes they can't. Events are not less newsworthy because they are created: both a President's steamboat trip down the Mississippi and an airline hijacking are intended to gain media exposure; the press know it but are required by the unwritten rules of journalism to cover both.

The public-information function of the press cannot be minimized. In 1970 the *Columbia Journalism Review* studied a situation greatly analogous to an ongoing terrorist incident: the 1968 Detroit race riots. The *Review* argued that crisis situations greatly increase the need for news, particularly as people seek to confirm rumors and to clarify sketchy information. The Detroit case was an unusual one, because in the winter of 1968 the metropolitan newspapers were on strike and their absence "helped create a panic." The *Review* wrote:

> "★ ★ ★ there were rumors in the white community that blacks were planning to blow up the freeways, kill suburban white children, and destroy public buildings; in the black community, that white vigilantes were coming into the area to attack the residents. Gun clubs sprang up in the suburbs; black leaders urged preparation of survival kits."[4]

Finally, in a series of television appearances, the mayor calmed the situation down, at least temporarily. But the lack of adequate information contributed to tensions that wracked Detroit for several years.

The other side of this was the Hanafi Muslim takeover of several Washington, D.C., buildings in March 1977. Discussing the situation at a seminar on terrorism sponsored by the *Chicago Sun-Times* in April 1977, Leonard Downie, who managed the *Washington Post's* coverage, said:

> "It was our impression that once the first day was over and all of the media, broadcast and print, had given the public a rather full picture of what was going on that the city seemed to ease a great deal. The jams of traffic and gawkers were not that great around the three sites."[5]

He said that life in the city was back to normal and that people did not feel panicky because they knew what was going on. This, Downie concluded, contributed to an atmosphere in which the takeover could be more easily and peacefully resolved.

There is also an argument to be made for the ability of the media to stabilize a terrorist situation by acting as a check on the actions of both police and terrorists. At the Munich Olympics in 1972, when Black September gunmen held Israeli athletes hostage, there were more press assembled than at any terrorist incident in history. ABC alone had 400 staffers there. Yet there were few problems between press and police, and after the initial attack, there was no violence. In fact, it was when the drama moved to Fürstenfeldbrück Airbase, where no media were present, that the West German police made several serious tactical errors which led to the deaths of nine hostages, five terrorists, and one policeman. It would be naive to call these examples conclusive evidence of the value of the press, yet they are stronger than most evidence of the press' disrupting a situation.

More media coverage requires more cooperation by law enforcement officials, and some of the strongest arguments for more rather than less cooperation have come from law enforcement officials. Patrick V. Murphy, the former New York City police commissioner and now president of the Police Foundation, suggested at the *Sun-Times* seminar that "extreme caution" should be exercised in the formulation of any proposals to limit coverage of terrorist incidents. His reasoning was not based on the first amendment, but rather the practical consideration that "very possibly, where extraordinary violence is concerned, more and balanced coverage is better than less coverage."[6]

A number of Murphy's prominent colleagues, including former Washington, D.C., police chief Jerry Wilson, came to similar conclusions while studying the problem for the Task Force on Disorders and Terrorism of the National Advisory Committee on Criminal Justice Standards and Goals. Sitting on a panel which had no journalists, the high-ranking law officers found that the media had a greater ability to improve a terrorist situation than to disrupt it, and that law enforcement units should give them the fullest cooperation. The report told law enforcement officials to take great pains not to pressure the media or seem to be censoring them: "Civil authorities have everything to gain by working with the media rather than putting obstacles in the way of those whose task it is to convey the news to the public." The report approvingly quotes a Los Angeles police official: "We feel it is better to tell the truth. Even if the truth is not good, it's better than rumors, which are generally horrible."[7]

Most reporters realize—to stretch the analogy once more—that when the burning theater is down the street from their newspaper, *how* they shout "Fire!" becomes the critically important question. Most reporters will never have to cover a local terrorist incident, but when they do, they will be under intense scrutiny, and they must perform properly.

The press have been legitimately critized during hostage incidents because of concern over their physical presence and the possibility of their intervening in a delicate negotiation process. Expressed fears have to do with the media's revealing police movements and strategy and their becoming the "intelligence arm" of the hostage takers; annoying police or terrorists with questions; making the event appear overly dramatic and giving it undue significance; and publicizing the terrorists' propaganda demands.

In response, it must be noted that although some reporters have probably to some extent been guilty of doing these things, the media in the United States have not substantially disrupted any terrorist situation, nor done anything resulting in the loss of a life. For a reporter, the bottom line of responsibility would be to get as much accurate information as possible without endangering anyone's life.

For a journalist, a hostage story is a delicate situation that needs to be reported with caution. This means that an intelligent editor or news director will carefully review the information he is about to print or broadcast and that he will be in constant and clear communication with the police so he can quickly evaluate their requests and decide if he considers the requests legitimate. It means he will take care selecting the reporters he assigns to certain aspects of the story. He should keep his people physically out of the way of the police, and as in a fire, have them respect police lines. He should also show restraint in such matters as phoning terrorists and hostages.

There are many hypothetical considerations, but what they really come down to is common sense and good news judgment. There can be no absolutes, and each response has to be tailored to the event. A good example of this common sense approach was provided by the *Washington Post* in its coverage of the Hanafi takeover. It was a confusing and sometimes fast-moving situation. As Metro editor Downie explained, *Post* editors discovered early on that they were getting insufficient information from the authorities, so some of the textbook rules had to be scrapped. To assess what was happening in the early stages, they picked what Downie called a "calm" reporter to start phoning several of the occupied buildings. Downie said the calls were as brief and as infrequent as possible and that the *Post* told police when they were making them. Police were told they could cut the *Post* off any time they needed a line. Through the calls, the paper obtained valuable information, some of which the editors forwarded to the police, after they had made an independent decision regarding its importance. But soon after he started phoning, the reporter discovered that Hamaas Abdul Khaalis, the Hanafi leader, despised the *Post* because of several articles it had written on the Hanafis. The phone calls from the *Post* stopped.

There were other on-the-spot decisions that had to be made. Downie said *Post* editors realized that the Hanafis were picking up papers every morning, and so they made a decision not to publish any incendiary material that might set the Hanafis off. On several occasions, the paper found that the police were giving deliberate misinformation, such as a claim that the negotiations were not going well when, in fact, they were. Not wanting to embarrass the police at that point or to print false information, the paper's editors decided that in those cases nothing at all would be said on the subject. In an effort to swiftly squelch rumors, the *Post* kept reporters in close touch with a police command center where a great deal of information came informally from government officials. They also rotated street reporters among the occupied buildings so each reporter would be familiar with the entire scene. Downie said the *Post* carried out, on balance, about half the requests that the authorities made.[8]

Yet while the *Post's* coverage has generally been praised, the Hanafi siege featured a number of botched initiatives by the media. The first occurred when a TV newsman reported live that the police were sending supplies into one of the buildings where a group of people had evaded the gunmen. Police got the people out before the gunmen could react, but not before some tense moments. Another reporter, who worked for a local radio station, asked Khaalis during a live interview if he had set a deadline for executing the hostages. It was a question police feared could have prompted Khaalis to act, but they were relieved when the terrorist did not respond to it. A third reporter, a Washington TV anchorman, referred to Khaalis as a Black Muslim, when in fact it was the Black Muslims who had murdered Khaalis' family. Khaalis threatened to kill a hostage in retaliation unless the reporter apologized. There were also a number of non-journalists—disc jockeys and talk-show hosts—who tied up the lines by phoning Khaalis and increased the risk of inciting him.

Prior communication between law enforcement officials and the media would help both to prepare for hostage incidents. The key topic should be communications: to make sure that the police know what the media needs and that the media are aware of the capabilities and problems of the police.

Media and police communicate too little, and experience so far is that most of the blame belongs to the police. Even with a department as large and sophisticated as the Chicago Police Department, in two recent hostage incidents, the information situation was chaotic. During the takeover of the West German consulate by Croatians in 1978, it was almost impossible for reporters on the scene to find a police spokesman. There was nothing resembling an information center, and continuing rumors were unverifiable. Our reporters later told me that the worst chaos erupted when the takeover ended: police lines that had been strictly maintained all day suddenly broke down as the mayor and top police officials emerged from the consulate. Reporters had to scramble among hundreds of curious bystanders to catch a few phrases from the officials. Some news organizations managed to put the details and background of the incident together, but information came in bits and pieces from an array of confidential sources. The police added little. It was a similar situation during the recent hijacking of an American Airlines jet by a Serbian terrorist. Again the police told the press little and had no established lines of communication. The FBI proved only slightly more helpful.

The way to avoid such problems is to have police and media talk things out. Discussions should be on a technical level and might involve such things as the possibility of pooled coverage of extreme situations; the establishment of a news center; an expanded role for police public information officers; procedures for credentialing reporters; and sensitivity to problems that arise in phone contacts with terrorists. Police and press need to have some sense of the other's responsibilities. Neither the policeman nor the reporter is keeping a long, freezing vigil in front of an occupied building for laughs or to satisfy a voyeuristic impulse; both have sensitive jobs that are equally important, and each should understand that.

Police and press are two very different institutions and need to interact with care. Patrick Murphy said at the *Sun-Times* seminar that police should be as candid as possible when dealing with the press; he suggested that it would be wise for the police to make the media aware of the problems that some reporting can cause. But he cautioned that police keep requests for media self-regulation to a minimum: "That's not a very good role for the police to find themselves in, suggesting to news media executives how to control themselves."[9]

What this presumes, then, is a heavy burden on the media to act responsibly. It is legitimate to ask if they will. As far as terrorist incidents have shown, on balance, the press have acted responsibly. But there have been relatively few terrorist incidents, and what might be more instructive is to consider briefly how the media restrain themselves in general.

Two of the most important things a reporter must concern himself with in *any* story are balance and obtrusiveness. In both cases the press rates high marks for effort and fair grades for accomplishment. The average journalist really believes that a story should contain both sides and that he shouldn't be too far on one of those sides. He also understands that his presence can often have a drastic effect on the story, particularly if he is accompanied by $100,000 worth of television equipment. Beginning reporters are made aware of these dangers early on. Similarly, when he sees a judge hand down a particularly harsh sentence because the press is covering the case, the beginner learns that he can change the outcome of a story just by showing up. Sometimes the reporter can make himself less obtrusive, and sometimes he can't.

A VIEW FROM THE FOURTH ESTATE 101

Restraint becomes more important when the story involves potential violence. During the race riots of the late 1960s, television reporters realized that rioters were often playing to the cameras. Some TV people exploited this, but many reporters tried to minimize their own presence. Recent technological improvements have made cameras smaller and bright lights less necessary, and the reporters have been more successful. They have also realized the danger of live coverage of many kinds of violence, including terrorist violence, and have cut back their use of it.

TV journalists seem to have realized that live broadcasts deprive them of an important journalistic tool: the ability to edit. They seem to be willing to sacrifice drama for control. Yet such moves have their price, and not all television journalists are willing to pay it. Television is a competitive business, and journalists cringe at comments such as the following one from a viewer who wrote to an Indianapolis station that cut off live coverage of a hostage story: "You did the right thing. I switched the channel to find out what happened, but you did the right thing."

Far short of a hostage situation, there are many stories that the media have to be exceptionally careful in covering. Chicago had smoldering gang wars in the summer of 1978. The press, to an extent, cooperated with police requests to tone down some of their coverage and to provide a balanced picture of the communities where the gangs operated. This action did not stop the killings, but in some cases it may have eased the tension. Similar care had to be taken during recent school desegregation stories. In ongoing kidnapings, the press have cooperated with the FBI to keep from jeopardizing lives. Even in a story like the recent gasoline shortage, the media had to use caution not to create a panic.

All this does not precisely answer the question of whether the media will act responsibly; the realistic answer is that they will be responsible most of the time. But as these examples show, terrorism is just like a lot of other stories which, most journalists realize, must be covered with care. Mostly that care is evident; sometimes it's not. Also, the sort of loose guidelines that various people used to cover civil rights marches and gang wars did not evolve until those stories became ongoing and a policy was reached. If U.S. editors should find themselves covering terrorism on a routine basis, I suspect similar policies, whether written or not, will become more prevalent.

This is not to say that news organizations haven't already addressed the problem of terrorist coverage in some detail. A number of outlets, including the *Sun-Times*, have taken the step of establishing some broad policy guidelines. Other major organizations have discussed whether a formal policy was needed and have decided against it. A California State University study by Michael and Heidi Sommer⋆ in 1978 found that overall, 38 percent of newspaper and radio outlets had written guidelines while 52 percent had none. Those that did have guidelines tended to cite similar concerns. The first was that terrorism stories should be covered extensively, despite any risk of contagion, because suppression creates greater problems. The second was that they must be evaluated on a case-by-case basis and that normal news judgment should be the prevailing standard. The third was that terrorist incidents should not be sensationalized beyond their innate sensation but, rather, should be placed quickly in perspective. Finally, they were concerned that journalists respect the work of law enforcement officials and that they stay in constant communication with police for both information and possible guidance on coverage.

Those organizations that have not adopted guidelines argue that no guidelines could cover every situation and that the generalities come down to common sense and sound news judgment—and neither needs to be put on paper. They see written guides as curtailing their flexibility.

Here is a brief rundown of what a number of major news organizations have done on the subject:

- The National News Council, an independent media watch dog and research group consisting of media and non-media representatives, in 1977 rejected the idea of industry-wide guidelines with itself or a similar group as arbiter, and suggested that each news organization should consider certain self-restraints "in specific areas and in specific cases." The Council identified live television coverage and telephone calls to hostages as the two main areas that journalists should consider carefully.
- The *New York Times* does not have a written policy, and its executive editor, A. M. Rosenthal, has been among the most outspoken against guidelines. In a 1976 interview published in the *Los Angeles Times*, he said:

    "The last thing in the world I want is guidelines ⋆ ⋆ ⋆ from the government ⋆ ⋆ ⋆ from professional organizations or anyone else. The strength of the press is its diversity. As soon as you start imposing guidelines, they become peer group pressure then quasi-legal restrictions."[10]

- The *Times'* policy, according to managing editor Seymour Topping, is still to treat each event on its own merit: "We try to cover it with intelligence and a sense of balance covering the journalistic and human aspects of it."

⋆ The Sommer and Sommer study is included as Appendix B to this volume. - Ed.

A VIEW FROM THE FOURTH ESTATE

- The *Los Angeles Times*, the *Washington Post*, and the *Chicago Tribune* all say they use similar approaches. The basic philosophy is that there are no rules for a terrorist situation which do not apply to any other story.
- The Associated Press also does not have written guidelines, but managing editor Burl Osborne said that more care is exercised in a terrorist incident. He said reporters are told to keep the story in perspective and to quickly find out why the incident is taking place. He said that AP has tried to write guidelines but found it impossible to cover every case.
- Of the broadcast networks, ABC News also has not written formal guidelines. They found it impossible to write guidelines which covered all situations. A spokesman said that the main points ABC producers informally emphasize are to never put anyone's life in danger, to not interfere in the event, and to take a "back seat and let it happen." The network says it relies heavily on the experience and judgment of individual correspondents.
- NBC News relies on the section in its policy manual covering riots and civil disturbances. That section calls for correspondents and cameramen to act with care not to exacerbate an event and to avoid being used or manipulated by those involved. There is also a caution against sensationalizing the story beyond its already dramatic nature.
- CBS News has had broad guidelines for network correspondents since 1977. The guidelines emphasize that there can be no "specific, self-executing rule" for handling terrorism or hostage stories, but they call for "thoughtful, conscientious care and restraint" and "particular care in how we treat the terrorist/kidnapper." The standards call for the paraphrasing of terrorists demands unless the demands are free of rhetoric and propaganda; no live coverage of the terrorists "except in the most compelling circumstances," and only then with the permission of the president of CBS News; restricting telephone calls to the hostages or kidnapers; getting guidance from experts on what kind of reporting may exacerbate the situation; making sure law enforcement officers have easy access to CBS personnel if they need them; and keeping the story in balance so it does not crowd out other news of the day.★

    In all cases, network rules do not apply to affiliates, which make their own policy.
- Similar but more detailed standards have been given by the CBS Television Stations division to its owned-and-operated units, which tend to be the local outlets in big-city markets. These combine standards for covering terrorism with those for covering riots and civil demonstrations. They include a long list of specific policies reporters might consider, such as their using unmarked cars and smaller broadcast equipment, and their minimizing lights. Reporting guidelines include avoiding "coverage of i) self-designated 'leaders' if they appear to represent only themselves, and ii) any indviduals or groups who are clearly performing." They emphasize the avoidance of words and actions which might in any way influence the participants to do something differently.

★ These guidelines are included in this volume. - Ed.

- Among the print media, the *Louisville Courier-Journal* and *Louisville Times* have standards which call for the papers to make sure that experienced staff members are assigned to the story and that the paper's top news officials are involved in making decisions. The standards suggest that journalists contact law enforcement officials and that they avoid any action that would interfere with police reponsibilities. The guidelines conclude: "Although we cannot be responsible for the coverage by other news media, we can and will conduct a constant review of our own performance."★
- United Press International (UPI) has brief guidelines that call for coverage that is "thoughtful, conscientious and shows restraint." UPI reporters are told not to become a part of the story, not to provide a platform for the terrorists, not to jeopardize lives, and finally, that "[i]n all cases we will apply the rule of common sense."★
- The *Sun-Times*, too, has written guidelines, which begin: "Recognizing that circumstances vary in each story, the following standards are meant for general guidance." The guidelines state that the newspaper will publish regardless of the dangers of contagion, since the adverse effects of suppression are greater. Reporters are told to obey all instructions by police, but to quickly report to senior editors anything that seems like an attempt to manage or suppress news. Senior editors have the authority to withhold or defer what might be inflammatory information from the story, but they should consult with reporters and law enforcement authorities first. The last guideline sums up the newspaper's approach: "The constant objective should be to provide a credible report without hampering authorities or endangering life."★

What all the above comes down to is this:

- There should be coverage of terrorism without even the suggestion of censorship or voluntary suppression—both are far greater evils than terrorism. Coverage should be more rather than less extensive because the public is better served.
- There is room for improvement by both the media and law enforcement. Greater coverage will mean law enforcement officials will have to be more forthcoming with information and more cooperative with the press. For its own part, the press will have to be careful to act responsibly, and be more diligent in their pursuit of stories which, though not as provocative, may be equally as important.
- News organizations have to take care to balance stories and to place them in perspective; the plights of the victims and the authorities are as important as that of the terrorist. Followup stories cannot be neglected.
- Despite pronouncements by the press that terrorism should be treated on a case-by-case basis, a little advanced preparation could be in order. General standards, whether written or not, are often not communicated to front-line editors and reporters.

★ These guidelines are included in this volume. - Ed.

- But the most important aspect of prior planning involves communication between police and journalists. Each must have an understanding of the other's responsibilities and constraints. There should be informal, periodic sessions between a wide range of officers and reporters. Certainly, there should be conversation after a local incident has occurred and quite possibly after an incident in another locality. The police and the press have to talk.

FOOTNOTES

1. Carlos Marighella. *Urban Guerilla Minimanual.* Vancouver: Pulp Press, 1974.
2. Ben Bagdikian. *The effete conspiracy, and other crimes by the press.* New York: Harper and Rowe, 1972.
3. Richard Clutterbuck. *Guerillas and terrorists.* London: Faber & Faber, 1977, Preface, p.II.
4. Terry Ann Knopf. Media myths on violence. *Columbia Journalism Review,* Spring 1970, p.17.
5. Leonard Downie, Jr. The breaking story: How the Washington Post covered the siege. *The media and terrorism: A seminar sponsored by the Chicago Sun-Times and Chicago Daily News.* Chicago: Field Enterprises, c1977, 21–22.
6. Patrick V. Murphy. The police perspective. *The media and terrorism: A seminar sponsored by the Chicago Sun-Times and Chicago Daily News.* Chicago: Field Enterprises, c1977, p.11.
7. National Advisory Committee on Criminal Justice Standards and Goals. *Disorders and terrorism: Report of the Task Force on Disorders and terrorism.* Washington, D.C.: LEAA, 1976, Standard 4.10, p.66.
8. Leonard Downie, Jr. Op. cit, p.21.
9. Patrick V. Murphy. Op. cit, p.10.
10. A.M. Rosenthal, quoted in: David Shaw. Editors face terrorist demand dilemma. *Los Angeles Times,* September 15, 1976.

6. TERRORISM IN BRITAIN: ON THE LIMITS OF FREE EXPRESSION

Walter B. Jaehnig

Terrorism, wrote historian Walter Laqueur, occurs only in permissive democratic societies and in ineffective authoritarian regimes.[1] Laqueur's studies of terrorist activities over the past century indicate that violent protests do not appear where despotism is worst; terrorists seem to appreciate that there is no future in challenging effective dictatorships.[2]

But political terrorism remains a special burden of the industrialized democracies of Western Europe and North America. Figures produced by the Central Intelligence Agency show that between 1968 and 1978 about half of the world's *recorded* terrorist incidents occured in these regions.[3] The openness of these societies and the civil liberties enjoyed by their citizens seem to appeal to those who use violence as a form of political expression. There can be little doubt, however, that governments in the liberal democracies can act to preserve the stability of their civil societies when they feel threatened by terrorism. Ultimately, repressive legal measures can be adopted to protest the social order, and the might of modern, well-equipped police and military authorities can be unleashed against the terrorists.[4]

But this strategy is at base self-defeating: there is an inherent contradiction in restricting a society's civil liberties in the interests of preserving the liberal basis of the society. As a British commentator on terrorism has noted, "[o]ne of the reasons why terrorism is such a virulent poison is that the cure can damage society as much as the disease can."[5]

Central to this paradox are the roles of the news media in the democratic society. Modern terrorism and journalism have developed what has been referred to as a symbiotic relationship. Terrorists have recognized that the surest guarantee of publicity lies in a shocking appeal to traditional news values; journalists respond that members of the public can react to the terrorist threat only if they are informed fully about the terrorists' activities. Dr. Frederick Hacker, a Beverly Hills psychiatrist and a consultant on terrorism, said that the "mass media and terrorism are made for each other—if they didn't exist independently, they would have to invent each other."[6] Laqueur wrote on the same issue: "Terrorists and newspapermen share the naive assumption that those whose names make the headlines have power, that getting one's name on the front page is a major political achievement."[7]

It follows that questions have been raised as to whether restrictions on the press (including both newspapers and broadcast agencies) might not be a necessary part of the campaign against terrorism. Though a few American public officials have expressed this sentiment, for the most part more emphasis in this country has been placed upon developing greater cooperation and collaboration between public authorities and the news industry to ensure that reporters and their news organizations do not become the instruments of terrorists. Rather than legalistic solutions that would endanger press freedoms, affirmative steps by government and police authorities have been promoted. As the Federal Task Force on Disorders and Terrorism—composed mainly of police and public officials—concluded in December 1976,

> "[a] free and responsible news media is a most effective educative device and an indispensable bulwark against oppression. These potentials for good should be positively recognized by the civil authority; it should modify its policies sensibly and adapt its institutions and procedures to working with the media in the public interest."[8]

Numbered among the Task Force's specific recommendations for improving police/press relations during emergency situations were the proposal that police departments hold regular forums with the news media to discuss ground rules for the reporting of violence and terrorism, and the suggestion that police officials encourage attempts by the news media to develop self-regulating standards that would govern their reporting on terrorism. Measures of this sort—in particular those to be followed in kidnapings and in hostage cases—have been developed by the Federal Bureau of Investigation in cooperation with news organizations.[9]

These proposals have been based, however, upon the assumption that the press will assume greater responsibility for its actions. In a sense, the whole debate has been reminiscent of the Hutchins Commissions's pragmatic optimism of 1947: the press should be left free to control itself so long as it controls itself.[10] The federal Task Force noted, for example, that

> "★ ★ ★ these proposals may appear to contemplate a species of self-censorship alien to the traditions of the American free press; in fact, however, they are believed to represent examples of spontaneous accommodation to overriding public interest that are neither foreign to the standards of professional responsibility that now prevail in the news industry, nor without significant precedent in present news media practices."[11]

But the Task Force also recognized that for historical and economic reasons the news industry is highly competitive and that no self-regulatory policy can be expected to work unless news organizations cooperatively develop such a policy as well as the means to make it work. The news media's responses have been mixed: several major newsgathering organizations formulated terrorism-coverage guidelines though in fact these policies provide little more than restatements of their conventional operating practices. Others steadfastly resisted. As the executive editor of the *New York Times* explained his opposition,

> "I don't want guidelines from the government and I don't want any from professional organizations or anyone else. The strength of the press is its diversity. As soon as you start imposing guidelines, they become peer-group pressures and then group pressures and then quasi-legal restrictions."[12]

At this point the discussion has virtually ceased—perhaps because political terrorism *within* the United States has not been recognized as a sustained and pervasive problem. But where terrorism is an everyday occurrence, the news media's role is still problematic. This paper concentrates upon recent events in England, the site of continuing Ulster-related violence. Relations between press and Government there have been marked by similar appeals to the professional standards of journalists, and voluntary agreements governing the reporting of kidnaping, terrorism, and other police matters have been negotiated between the police and the news media. The British experience is unique, however, in one respect: in spite of attempts at cooperation between the authorities and news media, the Conservative government has threatened to apply antiterrorist legislation against the press itself.

THE BRITISH RESPONSES TO TERRORISM IN ENGLAND

Terrorist violence, Ulster-style, arrived in England in 1972 with an explosion near a British Army officers' mess in Aldershot that killed seven people.

A VIEW FROM THE FOURTH ESTATE

British authorities recorded 86 terrorist incidents in the next year which resulted in one death and 380 injuries.[13] The Irish Republican Army's terror campaign intensified in 1974: more people (45) were killed by political violence in England in that year than in all previous years of the 20th Century combined. The heaviest casualties occurred on November 21, 1974 when bombs placed in two crowded pubs in Birmingham killed 21 people.

The Government responded to the Birmingham bombings with the Prevention of Terrorism (Temporary Provisions) Act 1974—legislation which at its introduction by the Home Secretary was described as "draconian" and "unprecedented in peacetime." The law, among other things, proscribed the IRA and banned public displays of support for the IRA; empowered the Home Secretary to deport persons connected with terrorist acts in Great Britain, Northern Ireland, or elsewhere and to prohibit their entry; enlarged the police authorities' power of arrest and detention; and gave the police wide powers to carry out security checks on travelers entering or leaving Britain or Northern Ireland.

Though the Act was aimed at the IRA (the only organization proscribed under the law) and not at journalists, a number of its provisions could be construed to apply to reporters working on stories involving terrorism in Northern Ireland. Section 1 made it illegal for any person to solicit or invite "financial or other support for a proscribed organization." This would seem to prohibit "checkbook journalism," stories in which IRA sources were paid for their interviews, as well as raise questions as to when a news story "invites support" for its subject. Section 11 stipulated that a person who withholds information which might be of material assistance in preventing an act of terrorism or in securing the arrest of a terrorist would be liable under law. Other provisions made it an offense both to set up meetings of three or more persons that would be addressed by a person who was a member of the IRA and to assist persons to wear the IRA's insignia or wave a placard in its support. (Camera crews, for example, could not ask IRA members to wave their placards while the bright lights were on.)[15]

Until the summer of 1979, however, the antiterrorist legislation was not seen as a method of regulating the media's reporting of terrorism. In fact, a review of the Prevention of Terrorism Act in 1978 did not link the Act with news reporting in any way. Its author did describe Section 11 as having "an unpleasant ring about it in terms of civil liberties" and recommended that it be permitted to lapse, but apparently not because of its inhibiting effect upon the news industry.★[16]

★ The Government invoked Section 11 when it asked the Director of Public Prosecution to consider prosecuting the BBC for the broadcast at a Provisional IRA roadblock at Carrickpergus in 1980. The prosecution was declined by Attorney General Sir Michael Havers. - Ed.

Armed with the antiterrorist legislation, the Special Branch of the Metropolitan Police (New Scotland Yard) stepped up its campaign against Irish terrorists late in 1974. (Though the Metropolitan Police have jurisdiction only in the Greater London region, its Special Branch was established in the 19th Century to deal with Irish terrorism and still has national responsibilities with regard to Irish republicanism.) Senior Metropolitan Police officials simultaneously took the initiative in attempting to develop closer relations with the news media. While not strictly part of the Government's antiterrorist effort, this public relations campaign was based upon the idea that the police would retain public support for their activities—both those involved in ordinary policing and those used in combating terrorism—to the extent that they were able to obtain favorable news coverage.

Sir Robert Mark, then Metropolitan Police Commissioner, elaborated this strategy in a news policy statement he wrote for New Scotland Yard. (See Addendum B to this *chapter* for the entire statement). "There is no doubt that the operational effectiveness of the Force is to a very large extent dependent upon the goodwill, co-operation and support of members of the general public," he wrote. Because most members of the public have only infrequent contact with the police, their attitudes toward the police are filtered through the eyes of the news industry.

> "It is therefore of the utmost importance that every effort should be made to develop and maintain good relations with the news media representatives in order to render it more likely that their coverage will be full and fair."

Mark modified Yard procedures to ease the dissemination of news to media representatives and to make police facilities more available to reporters, and he clarified police regulations regarding the ranks of officers who would be permitted to disclose information to the news media.

Mark and his successor, Commissioner David McNee, also negotiated two "gentlemen's agreements" with the news industry that in varying degrees govern the media's reporting of police activities. The first provides for a voluntary blackout or reporting moratorium in cases involving either kidnapings or hostages; in return, the news media receive daily briefings from senior police officials and full disclosure of details of the case once the hostage or kidnaped person has been recovered. The voluntary blackout has been put into practice once; in 1975 a kidnaped girl was held in London for nine days without the incident even being mentioned in the press. The second agreement, signed in March 1979, attempts to clarify the relationship between New

A VIEW FROM THE FOURTH ESTATE 111

Scotland Yard and the British Broadcasting Corporation's news and current affairs department. (See Addendum A to this *chapter* for a copy of the agreement.) This agreement establishes the procedure BBC producers must follow when making programs on subjects which the Metropolitan Police consider to be "delicate" or "potentially sensitive."

Editors and police officials interviewed in London in the summer of 1979 generally considered the two agreements to be of some value in clarifying relations between institutions which often find themselves at odds. Because they are informal, voluntary statements of principal, they are seen as ways of providing for the news media's cooperation without sacrificing the independence of the press; the agreement could be broken by the press when it was felt that a given situation demanded publication. And certainly they were preferable to formal controls the Government might apply under the Prevention of Terrorism Act.

VOLUNTARY NEWS BLACKOUT ON KIDNAPINGS

The voluntary moratorium on news of kidnapings has its origins in a murder case in the English Midlands in January 1975. Shortly after a girl named Lesley Whittle was abducted, a freelance radio reporter heard of the kidnaping and asked the local police for details. The police refused to comment while the girl was missing, and the reporter broke the story over a local radio station. Two months later the girl's body was discovered.

Tense relations between press and police in the Whittle case led to a conference in September 1975 at New Scotland Yard between senior police officials and editors and senior executives of the national press and radio and television, representatives of the international press based in London, the provincial and suburban press, and local radio stations. Sir Robert Mark and his staff proposed that a broad "code of conduct" be adopted to govern the reporting of similar incidents, but no firm agreement was reached at the conference.

These initial negotiations were overtaken by events in November of that year, however, when a Greek Cypriot girl, Aloi Kaloghirou, was kidnaped in North London and a ransom was demanded from her family. The Yard's proposed moratorium was implemented with the agreement of London editors: news organizations were informed of the kidnap and the ransom demand, but were never provided with specific names, locations, or other details. Reporters assigned to the case received daily briefings from a senior police official. No mention of the kidnaping was made by the major national and London news organizations. Early on the 10th day the girl was released and her kidnapers were arrested. Reporters were summoned to New Scotland Yard for a complete briefing, and the embargo was lifted.

Police officials were pleased with the news media's cooperation and believed the moratorium had worked successfully. A Yard spokesman said that news reporters seemed to exhibit more anxiety about the behavior of their fellow journalists—and whether someone would break the blackout and scoop the opposition—than concern about whether the police would honor their part of the agreement.

Editors of several national newspapers and television organizations based in London agreed that the moratorium had worked—on this occasion. But this was no guarantee that the press would cooperate another time. "It would depend very much on the circumstances of each individual case—I wouldn't accept that every single time someone is kidnaped that we wouldn't publish anything until they've caught the kidnaper," said Derek Jameson, editor of the London *Daily Express*.[17] Most editors agreed with Don Horobin, deputy editor of Independent Television News (the commercial network's news agency), who said that the only justification for the agreement is "in the interests of saving lives. Protecting property is a different ballgame; if there is no threat to life, then it is a news event." Horobin also said that press cooperation is contingent upon the police maintaining their share of the bargain: "The Yard cooperation has been very good—it has been absolutely smack on. But they know damn well that if they let us down, future agreements would go through the window."[18] For it to work, the agreement requires total adherence from *all* members of the press as well. Said Mike Mulloy, editor of the London *Daily Mirror*: "What happens if someone gets a break on the story? If somebody breaks it then it all goes ★ ★ ★ we either all play the game, or★ ★ ★ ."[19]

British journalists also question whether the agreement could or should be extended to cover terrorist incidents. Peter Harland, a London journalist, has pointed out that political terrorism in Britain has been considerably defused by the Government's practice of treating any violent incident that does not constitute a direct threat to the state in the same manner as any other crime and not as a political offense. Therefore, the IRA has had to refuse to recognize the criminal courts and to go on hunger strikes in prison to "redress the publicity balance."[20] Mulloy, of the *Daily Mirror*, said that, in his estimation, the moratorium would not necessarily apply to incidents of a political nature but his newspaper might honor a request from the Government—not the police—for a temporary blackout if the crimes being committed were political.

A VIEW FROM THE FOURTH ESTATE

"If there was a wave of terrorist activities ★ ★ ★ I can't say that we wouldn't report it. The only way it would happen [a blackout] would be if we had a governmental approach." Other editors observed that the nature of the terrorist violence experienced in England in recent years and the high levels of activity by the IRA'S publicity wing have meant that news blackouts or moratoriums have not had to be considered.

The editors said that they had cooperated in the Kaloghirou case because police officials had been persuasive in making their case. Ultimately, however, the decision must remain in the hands of the news media. As Tony Crabbe, managing editor of BBC Television News, described his organization's attitude,

> "[t]he fact that we've done it once doesn't mean to say that we won't think very hard next time we're approached on something like that. Fine. It worked. It's every occasion on its merits. And what we must not have is any legal obligation on us not to publish. It's got to be up to us journalists to decide the merits of the argument the police are putting to us. And if we feel yes, on balance the public interest is better served by withholding information, we'll go along with it. But we retain the right ★ ★ ★ of publishing."[21]

In spite of these qualifications from representatives of the news industry, the Scotland Yard news blackout has been adopted by the Home Office as part of its campaign against terrorism. In a circular to Britain's 51 chief constables (chiefs of police) in August 1976, the Chief Officer of Police advised that

> "the increasing prevalence of terrorism and of the use of quasi-terrorist techniques in the pursuit of crime is likely to lead to situations in which the police find it necessary to ask press and broadcasting reporters not to publish information which comes into their possession, at any rate until the situation has been resolved."[22]

The police have no power to enforce such requests, the circular noted, and any such request represents "an encroachment upon freedom of the press." Because the print and broadcast organizations must be the judges of what use to make of information they obtain, the onus lies with the police to explain why such a request is being made. Where such requests are made, the Home Office suggests that these guidelines be followed:

(1) There is no general rule as to what constitutes a justification for such a request. In a hostage or kidnaping case, the request should be made only to protect the lives of innocent persons. The fact that disclosure might impede or prejudice police operations is not sufficient justification, unless the obstructions of these operations would put people's lives at risk.

(2) The Press Association (the domestic news agency of the United Kingdom and the Republic of Ireland) has agreed to circulate a request to withhold information from a chief constable to member news organizations if a person's life is at risk.

(3) The police official requesting a blackout should be prepared to answer off-the-record questions from journalists regarding his reasons for the request.

(4) The request not to publish should be strictly confined to information which is demonstrably likely to endanger the lives of innocent persons. Total blackouts should be requested only in highly exceptional circumstances.

(5) The period of press restraint should not exceed 48 hours; fresh requests should be made for extensions, if necessary.

(6) Reporters should be kept as fully informed as possible of the progress of police operations during the period restraint.

(7) If editors feel that they need a second opinion while considering the request to withhold information, they should consult the Director of Information Services at the Home Office.[23]

In May 1977, new Metropolitan Police Commissioner David McNee agreed to add an additional element to New Scotland Yard's blackout agreement. During a voluntary news moratorium, a Press Association news editor—acting as a "pool press person" on behalf of all cooperating news organizations—would be stationed at police headquarters and would be permitted to monitor the investigation. The editor would ensure that press briefings were complete and frank and would prepare a round-up report on the incident at its conclusion. This report would be available to cooperating news organizations and to subscribers to Press Association services.[24]

BBC-NEW SCOTLAND YARD AGREEMENT ON SENSITIVE PROGRAMING

The agreement reached in March 1979 between the Metropolitan Police and BBC grew out of a series of documentary and dramatic programs which police officials believed presented the police and their activities in an unsympathetic and unjust light. The BBC's broadcast in April 1978 of the realistic dramatic series "Law and Order"—which portrayed corruption in the judicial system, police, and prison service—led to a request from the Metropolitan Police for a formal, legally binding contract with the BBC which would have given New Scotland Yard the right to view in advance all material about it and, if necessary, the right to prevent transmission of the material.[25]

The BBC regarded the Yard's request as a form of censorship and resisted the idea of a legal contract. Nine months of negotiations—which at one stage involved top-level meetings between the director-general of the BBC and the Metropolitan Police Commissioner—resulted in the present, informal agreement, which is to govern the BBC's programing on "cases which the Metropolitan Police consider delicate, affecting privacy, 'sub judice,' national security and such areas." (See the Addenda to this *chapter.*) Straightforward news items and features on police work (such as the opening of new police stations and the introduction of new vehicles and equipment) are excluded from the agreement.

The guidelines establish the procedure BBC producers must follow when making programs in "potentially sensitive" areas that require the cooperation of the Metropolitan Police and the use of police facilities. The producer involved must meet with a representative of the Yard's "P" Department to describe the program and the subjects to be covered. The understanding reached at this conference must then be put in writing. The police must be informed of subsequent alterations to the producer's plans, and further meetings would be held to sort out any disagreements that arise. The police could complain to the BBC in advance of the program's transmission of any violations of the agreement and, if necessary, register a formal complaint with the director-general of the BBC.

Spokesmen for both the BBC and New Scotland Yard predicted that the agreement would not need to be used frequently. Richard Francis, the BBC's director of news and current affairs, was quoted as describing the agreement as merely a formal statement of the BBC's standard operating procedures, which did not involve any surrender of editorial responsibility.[26] However, another BBC news executive conceded in an interview that the police might interpret the guidelines more rigidly than the broadcasters, particularly in determining what is a "delicate" or "potentially sensitive" area and when "national security" is involved. In addition, publicity surrounding the agreement has led to the fear at the BBC that other organizations might follow the Yard's lead and seek their own informal "understandings" with the corporation.

Though the agreement applies only to the BBC-Metropolitan Police relationship, at the time of writing, the police were expecting to begin negotiations with commercial broadcasting's Independent Television (ITV) News agency with the aim of establishing a similar understanding.

ANTI-TERRORIST LEGISLATION AND THE NEWS MEDIA

The summer of 1979 marked the 10th anniversary of the period when the British Army had to assume responsibility for security in part of its own country. Journalists assigned to cover the Northern Ireland conflict and its spillover into England have had to confront a severe moral dilemma: How do reporters report the action of their nation's army when the army campaigns in its own land and occasionally commits acts of violence against some of the reporters' own people? How do journalists dispassionately explain the activities of a terrorist organization which is dedicated to driving the British from Ireland and has been proven capable of scoring its own set of successes? John Whale, an editorial writer for the *London Sunday Times*, described these dilemmas in distinguishing between reporters' roles as journalists and as citizens. As reporters, they do not have to make choices; they could report things as they found them. But as citizens, they had to recognize that their journalistic work could make one outcome of the conflict a little more likely than another:

> "For a journalist, there is a tension between the claims of his country and the claims of his work. It cannot be shrugged off with a word about allegiance owed only to humanity at large. A journalist is a member of the State he lives in, like it or not, and he accepts the obligations with the benefits of membership. The tension can never be entirely resolved."[27]

Others in Britain agree with Whale that the ultimate responsibility of journalists must be to their own society and its government. Conor Cruise O'Brien, editor of the *London Observer*, argues that there is no purely military or purely political solution to the problem of terrorism but supporters of the democratic system might fight terrorism by refusing to negotiate with terrorists and by depriving them of the publicity they seek.[28] O'Brien, a former Member of Parliament in the Republic of Ireland and the country's onetime Minister of Posts and Telegraphs, imposed a ban on the Irish state broadcasting service (RTE) prohibiting it from carrying interviews with IRA spokesmen and sympathizers on the grounds that the IRA was a terrorist organization and a danger to the state. "I accept it as the propaganda wing of a criminal organization: a public relations agency for a murder gang."[29]

A VIEW FROM THE FOURTH ESTATE 117

No such ban exists in Britain and Northern Ireland, though some argue that it should. Paul Wilkinson, a British political scientist, argues that his Government is "dragging its feet" on this aspect of antiterrorist policy:

> "It is surely crazy to allow spokesmen for terrorists out to destroy the state to enjoy all the advantages of broadcasting their message of hatred and fanaticism and to inspire their small cadre of militants to further outrages. That would not simply be an abuse of liberty: it would be the more irresponsible licence. Yet, under present British broadcasting practice, that is what is allowed to happen!
> "I believe that is not undemocratic in the least to ban murderers and apologists for terrorist crimes from the broadcasting services which reach into practically every home. For if there is an ultra-pornography of violence then they are its ultimate representatives. And I do not see that it does any service to our democracies or our cultural and intellectual life to indulge such evil."[30]

As a public service broadcasting agency dependent upon state financing, the BBC has guarded its independence zealously—but cautiously. It has been argued, for example, that the BBC has avoided Government controls of its coverage of the Northern Ireland conflict by adopting a "responsible" perspective on the war that is essentially the State's interpretation of the conflict.[31] While the BBC will not prohibit its journalists from presenting interviews with terrorists, such news items are shown only infrequently and only after permission has been obtained in advance from the director-general of the BBC. As a BBC news executive described the corporation's tradition of editorial freedom and responsibility:

> "We do often decide not to publish, but we retain the right to [publish]—we don't always publish everything, but we can publish everything. Because we *don't*, we *can*. Because we are able to point to times when we have used the medium responsibly, we then can say that, of course, we are ultimately the deciders, we can decide what can go out."[32]

However, the Conservative government of Mrs. Margaret Thatcher (elected in May 1979) has used the antiterrorist legislation to question the BBC's use of its editorial independence. On July 5, 1979, the BBC broadcast an interview with an anonymous member of the Irish National Liberation Army (INLA), a small terrorist organization that claimed responsibility for placing the bomb that in March had killed Airey Neave, M.P., then Opposition spokesman on Northern Ireland, at the House of Commons in London. The interview with the terrorist, who wore a wig, false mustache, and dark glasses, was filmed in Dublin. A week later Mrs. Thatcher strongly criticized the BBC's action:

> "Having seen a transcript of this programme, I am appalled it was ever transmitted. I believe it reflects gravely on the judgment of the BBC and those who were responsible for the decision."

The Prime Minister said that she had requested the Attorney-General to determine whether the BBC had broken any law with the interview and the broadcast.[33] Three days before the broadcast, the Government had announced that the INLA was being added to the list of political organizations outlawed in Britain and Northern Ireland under the Prevention of Terrorism Act. Prior to the broadcast of the INLA interview, the Act had not been suggested as a method of regulating the media's reporting of terrorism. In Northern Ireland itself, news reporters are in regular contact with members of banned organizations, but the antiterrorism legislation has not been used against them.[34]

Many others joined the Prime Minister in her rebuke of the BBC, however. Neave's widow said that the interview was "extraordinarily one-sided and unfair" and that she was grief-stricken that a terrorist was "given ample scope to besmirch the memory of my husband."[35] Merlyn Rees, a former Northern Ireland secretary in the Labour government, said in a letter to the BBC that

> "[i]n my view it was a grave error to show on TV a man claiming to be an organiser of a murder gang. I can only hope that details of the man and his activities have been passed to the Irish Garda [Police] and to the Special Branch."

The Lord Mayor of London said:

> "What a pity it is when an institution like the BBC puts someone who claims to have assisted in the murder of Airey Neave on the box and gives him a platform."

The Bishop of Chester asked in a letter to the *Daily Telegraph*:

> "What is the limit of responsibility, at law, of the investigations by able journalists and media-men and the publication of their work? If I am aware of the identity of a person who has committed a serious crime, am I not required as a citizen to inform the appropriate authorities? If I pay money to a self-confessed traitor and

A VIEW FROM THE FOURTH ESTATE

> murderer in order to gain a supposedly valuable news-story, am I not myself a traitor and guilty of 'aiding and comforting' the enemy?"[36]

Another critic of the BBC's ethics, Lord Chalfont, wrote in an article in the *Financial Weekly*:

> "As an example of perverse irresponsibility it would be difficult to match the spectacle of a state-sponsored broadcasting organisation transmitting a television interview with a terrorist who used the occasion to admit complicity in the recent murder of a Member of Parliament. The excuse that it was a 'newsworthy event' and, therefore, in some way excluded from the normal canons of human behaviour is symptomatic of the state of moral and intellectual confusion which the organs of public communication consistently display on the subject of terrorism."[37]

The BBC held firm in face of this public outcry, however. Sir Michael Swan, chairman of the BBC's board of governors, promised only that the corporation would review its guidelines regarding interviews with terrorists. At present the guidelines say that only on very rare occasions will the BBC show interviews with terrorists—when it is thought the interview will contribute to public understanding. Permission of the director-general must be obtained before the interview and before the film is broadcast.[38] Ian Trethowan, BBC director-general, summarized the BBC's position in a letter to the *Daily Telegraph* by pointing out that the BBC had televised only four such interviews in the previous 10 years, and none in the past five years.

> "We believe that the public has the common sense and stability to judge very accurately the character of the people they are seeing. They recognise a murderous thug for what he is ★ ★ ★ We do not believe that a BBC interview with the INLA will worsen by one iota the central problem of Northern Ireland: the inability of the two communities to reach rational settlement of their problems."[39]

At the time of writing, the Government had not announced whether it would proceed against the BBC for the INLA interview.★

The INLA interview was superseded, however, in November by Mrs. Thatcher's announcement in the House of Commons that the BBC would not

---

★ Interviews by the editor with Scotland Yard officials in August 1981 indicate that it is unlikely that the Government will follow through with its threat. - Ed.

be transmitting a "Panorama" television program that included footage shot at an IRA roadblock in the village of Carrickmore, County Tyrone, in Northern Ireland. New Scotland Yard was making an investigation into possible offenses under the Prevention of Terrorism Act in the incident.

Accounts of the incident varied; however, it appears that a four-man "Panorama" crew was in Ireland preparing a major project on the banned Provisional IRA. After receiving an anonymous telephone tip in Dublin, the crew drove 200 miles to Carrickmore and for about 12 minutes filmed several armed men stopping cars at an illegal roadblock.[40] Apparently both the Northern Ireland Police, the Royal Ulster Constabulary, and the British Army knew of the incident the day it happened, and the BBC crew informed "Panorama" editors that night.[41] Both the police and the army withdrew their cooperation from the project.

After complaints about the incident were filed with the BBC, the Corporation's board of governors made an internal inquiry and referred to the incident as "a relatively peripheral matter which was initially grossly exaggerated and misrepresented."[42] Though the governors were satisfied there was no collusion between the program's producer and the IRA, two BBC editors were reprimanded and the corporation's rules governing filming in Ireland were tightened still further.[43]

It is possible that no sanctions will be imposed against the BBC in either case. But as one British legal commentator noted, the involvement of the Government in the two cases can have a chilling effect on future reporting of Ulster terrorism:

> "Now every journalist preparing a programme on terrorism in Northern Ireland must reckon on at least the possibility of a Government-promoted police investigation into his conduct, his source and his researches."[44]

Reporters and television executives, of course, are not above the law and cannot be immune from prosecution for giving illegal assistance to terrorists.

> "But if referral by the Government becomes a matter of course for every programme which earns ministerial displeasure, it will begin to look suspiciously like a big stick to beat recalcitrant broadcasters whose house lacks that 'order' which the Government would like to impose. It may be that the authorities will come to regard the very act of filming terrorists or their activities as a good *prima facie* reason to despatch police on newsroom fishing expeditions: in which case, the *Prevention of Terrorism Act* could

provide a capacious back door for ministerial influence on programmes about Northern Ireland."[45]

Regardless of the outcome, the British experience seems to trace the limits of free expression in a society burdened by a long campaign against political terrorism. The state will place its highest priority upon protecting itself, despite its expressed concerns about both the professional responsibility of news media and the protection of civil liberties. Stretched to this extreme, the functions of informing a free society can be seen to be in direct conflict with those of protecting it. And this is the peculiar contribution of terrorism to our understanding of the mass media in a democratic society.

FOOTNOTES

1. The continuing failure of terrorism. *Harper's Magazine*, November 1976, p.71; The futility of terrorism. *Harper's Magazine*, March 1977, p.103.
2. Walter Laqueur. *Terrorism*, Boston: Little Brown & Company, 1977.
3. *International terrorism in 1978*. National Foreign Assessment Center, Central Intelligence Agency, March 1979, p.7.
4. For a useful review of legal responses to terrorism taken by governments around the world, see: Jordan J. Paust. International law and control of the media: Terror, repression and the alternatives. *Indiana Law Journal*, Summer 1978, 53(4), 621–78.
5. Richard Clutterbuck. *Living with Terrorism*, London: Faber & Faber, 1975, p.17.
6. David Haldane. Interview with Dr. Frederick J. Hacker. *Penthouse Magazine*, November 1977, p.141.
7. The futility of terrorism. *Harper's Magazine*, March 1977, p.99.
8. National Advisory Committee on Criminal Justice Standards and Goals. *Disorders and Terrorism: Report of the Task Force on Disorders and Terrorism*. Washington, D.C.: LEAA, 1976, Standard 4.10, p.65.
9. Stephen D. Gladis. The hostage/terrorist situation and the media. *FBI Law Enforcement Bulletin*, September 1979, 11–15.
10. Commission on Freedom of the Press. *A free and responsible press*. Chicago: University of Chicago, 1947. See, for example, the discussions on pp.18–19 and 125–128.
11. National Advisory Committee on Criminal Justice Standards and Goals. Op.cit, p.389.
12. David Shaw. Editors face terrorist demand dilemma. *Los Angeles Times*, September 15, 1976, p.14. For a longer discussion of the news industry's response to terrorism and the construction of news coverage guidelines, see: Walter B. Jaehnig. Journalists and terrorism: Captives of the libertarian tradition. *Indiana Law Journal*, Summer 1978, 53(4), 717–744.
13. *Review of the operation of the Prevention of Terrorism (Temporary Provisions) Acts 1974 and 1976 (Shackleton report)*. London: Home Office, August 1978, p.1.
14. Richard Clutterbuck. *Britain in agony: The growth of political violence*. London: Faber & Faber, 1978, p.146.
15. For a recent discussion of the effects of antiterrorist legislation on British journalism, see: Geoffrey Robertson. Panorama and Mrs. Thatcher. *Guardian Weekly*, November 18, 1979, p.5.
16. Shackleton Report, p.41.
17. Personal interview with the author, London, June 18, 1979.
18. Personal interview with the author, London, June 29, 1979.
19. Personal interview with the author, London, June 27, 1979.

20. Politics and greed: When lives are at stake, where is the difference? *IPI Report*, November 1977, p.7.
21. Personal interview with the author, London, July 2, 1979.
22. *Home Office Circular 128/1976*, August 18, 1976, p.1.
23. Ibid.
24. Information provided by Peter Freeman, chief news editor, the Press Association, London.
25. See stories in the *Guardian*, June 11 & 12, 1979, regarding the BBC/New Scotland Yard agreement.
26. Ibid.
27. John Whale. *The politics of the media*. London: Fontana, 1977, 127–128.
28. Conor Cruise O'Brien. Liberty and terrorism. *International Security*, Fall 1977, 2(2), 66–67.
29. Ibid.
30. Paul Wilkinson. *Terrorism and the liberal state*. New York: New York University Press, 1977, 168–169.
31. See: Philip Schlesinger. *Putting 'reality' together*. London: Constable, 1978, 205–243.
32. Personal interview with the author, London, July 2, 1979.
33. *Daily Telegraph*, July 13, 1979, p.1.
34. Observation by the author following interviews with journalists, army and police officials in Northern Ireland, July 1979.
35. *Daily Telegraph*, July 13, 1979, p.1.
36. Ibid.
37. There should be no free publicity for terrorists. *Financial Weekly*, July 13, 1979, p.9.
38. *Daily Telegraph*, July 14, 1979, p.9.
39. *Daily Telegraph*, July 14, 1979, p.14.
40. *Times* (London), November 16, 1979, p.4.
41. *Observer* (London), November 11, 1979, p.1.
42. *Times* (London), November 17, 1979, p.2.
43. *Times* (London), November 21, 1979, p.2.
44. Robertson. Op. cit.
45. Ibid.

ADDENDUM A

AGREEMENT ON PROGRAMMING IN SENSITIVE AREAS
METROPOLITAN POLICE (LONDON) AND
BRITISH BROADCASTING CORPORATION
(6 March 1979)

1. These points are only for cases which the Metropolitan Police consider delicate, affecting privacy, "sub judice", national security and such areas. They are not for news items or straightforward current affairs features on police—e.g. the opening of new police stations, the introduction of new vehicles and equipment, etc.
2. When embarking on a potentially sensitive programme, a BBC producer would meet with somebody from 'P' Department to talk over the subject and the area the BBC wished to portray, as well as the facilities they considered necessary to do this. The programme area would be defined as clearly as is possible at this stage. Afterwards, the BBC producer would send a letter to the Metropolitan Police setting out what had been agreed.
3. The Metropolitan Police would then agree to the letter's contents and acknowledge that it covered the necessary points.
4. The Metropolitan Police would be kept informed of any subsequent changes of plan and, if necessary, a further meeting would be convened to agree on any alterations. Similar talks would be held between the Police and the BBC to sort out any disagreement.
5. It would be open to the Metropolitan Police to write to the BBC outlining anything they thought went against an agreement between them. The BBC would then look into the matter and report their findings to the Metropolitan Police.
6. If the Police were not satisfied, they could register a formal complaint with the BBC's Director-General.

(signed)

Peter Neivens,
Deputy Assistant Commissioner
Director of Information,
Metropolitan Police

Richard Francis,
Director, News and Current Affairs
BBC

ADDENDUM B

METROPOLITAN POLICE (LONDON)
POLICY ON RELATIONS WITH THE NEWS MEDIA

1. There is no doubt that the operational effectiveness of the Force is to a very large extent dependent upon the goodwill, co-operation and support of members of the general public. There are two main ways in which public backing can be obtained or strengthened. The first is obviously by the adoption of a courteous and helpful attitude at all possible times by every member of the Force. The second, equally important, is by means of publicity given to the activities of the Force in the press and on television and radio.
2. Most members of the public come into direct contact with policemen infrequently and it follows that their image of the attitude towards the Force, when not dictated by hearsay, is largely governed by the approach adopted by the news media. It is therefore of the utmost importance that every effort should be made to develop and maintain good relations with news media representatives in order to render it the more likely that their coverage of police activities will be full and fair. Furthermore, if the Force as a public service is to be properly accountable for its actions the public has the right to the fullest possible knowledge of its activities.
3. In view of the fact that police sources supply a very large amount of important and interesting news material to the press, television and radio, it would seem that the maintenance of good relations should present no particular problem. Of course, the Force has to face certain restrictions on the disclosure of information which stand in the way of establishing a better relationship with the press. The most important of these restrictions arise from the judicial process, in both criminal and disciplinary cases; the special position of Metropolitan Police in relation to the Home Secretary as police authority, affecting the discussion of policy matters; the obligation to conform

to common policies agreed by chief constables with the Home Office; the need to maintain a substantial degree of uniformity of policy throughout the Metropolitan Police District; the requirement to be as fair as possible to all the news media; the need to observe the individual's right to privacy; and the paramount need to put the public interest before that of either the Force or the press.

4. However, relations with the news media are not as good as they could be; there is in particular a reluctance to accept that the role of the news media is to obtain and disclose to the public as much information as possible and that in pursuance of this role they are of course properly concerned with the affairs of the Metropolitan Police. The police have made unnecessary difficulties for themselves by tending to withhold information which could safely be made public, and the flow of information to the Press Bureau at Scotland Yard has not been sufficient to enable the Bureau to serve effectively the Force and the news media. This tendency has been encouraged because at times openness with the news media has resulted in incorrect or unfairly critical reporting to which the natural reaction is to be less forthcoming in the future. But I have no doubt that it is in the interests of the Force to seek a better working relationship with the press, television and radio. It is my firm belief that the Metropolitan Police have a great deal more to be proud of than the public know and that a little more openness with the news media, heightening trust, confidence and co-operation, is all that is required to correct that ignorance. In particular, there is convinving evidence that given an opportunity to do so the press, both as individuals and collectively, will give a great deal of support to the Force. I have therefore decided, with the full support of the Deputy and Assistant Commissioners, to introduce various changes in policy and practice with the aim of bringing about, over a period of time, a better relationship with the news media and consequently a better understanding on their part and that of the public of the Force's problems and policies.

DISCLOSURE OF INFORMATION DIRECT TO THE NEWS MEDIA

5. The aim should be to provide for the supply to the news media of factual information within officers' knowledge about incidents at as low a level as possible. Provided an embargo has not been imposed at higher level and disclosure would not compromise judicial processes in either criminal or disciplinary cases factual information may be so supplied by any officer of the rank of inspector or above, or by any officer of lower rank who has the prior authority of an officer of the rank of inspector or above. It will be for

commanders, detective chief superintendents and chief superintendents in charge of sub-divisions to ensure that officers under their command are fully briefed on the levels at which and extent to which factual information may be supplied. Statements on matters of policy, however, must continue to be referred to the senior departmental officers concerned.

6. Where the necessary confidence and trust has developed between the Force and the press there may be occasions when senior officers will feel able to talk to reporters on an "off-the-record" basis, dealing with matters not for public disclosure, explaining reasons for maintaining confidentiality and specifying what might be published at that stage. It will be for commanders to decide at what levels within their areas of responsibility of supplying information to the press the advice of the News Branch or Divisional Press Liaison Officer should be sought or enquiries referred to the Press Bureau. When this is done all relevant details should be supplied immediately.

7. In all dealings with the news media a sympathetic and flexible attitude is to be adopted. So far as possible I wish the Force to speak for itself and the result will be to place more authority and responsibility upon all officers. The new approach to dealings with the news media will of course involve risks, disappointments and anxieties; but officers who act and speak in good faith may be assured of my support even if they made errors of judgement when deciding what information to disclose and what information to withhold. I fully accept that if the new measures are to succeed in their objective some mistakes will be made in the process.

SUPPLY OF INFORMATION TO THE PRESS BUREAU

8. If the new policy is to succeed the flow of information to the News Branch through the Press Bureau must be increased and speeded up so that all news items which may be of interest to the media can be made available to them at the earliest possible moment. It is equally important that there should be a helpful, prompt and flexible response to requests from the Bureau for information needed to answer enquiries and it should not always be necessary for the divisional commander or the investigating officer in a case to be contacted when the Press Bureau are seeking information to answer enquiries or clarify facts: on many occasions points of fact could be dealt with at a lower level. The Bureau should be told of any reasons why publicity would be helpful. The Bureau, and indeed the News Branch as a whole, cannot operate effectively without the close co-operation and support of all members of the Force.

9. If good relations with all the news media are to be established and maintained it is vital that any information given direct to one or more representatives should be passed on immediately to the Press Bureau who will decide whether in fact it should be regarded as exclusive information or whether it can be made generally available. Editors and senior executives of the news media are in general opposed to any kind of "lobby" system whereby certain reporters are given preferential treatment as regards disclosure of information.

NEW PRESS IDENTIFICATION CARD AND FACILITIES TO BE MADE AVAILABLE

10. Following a review carried out in conjunction with senior representatives of the news media, it has been decided to introduce a re-designed and re-worded press card. The revised card, which will continue to indentify the holder and to bear his or her photograph will be brought into use in the near future. Facsimiles will be provided for display at stations and all officers are to make themselves completely familiar with the form of the card. It is crucial to the success of the altered approach to relations with the news media that in future holders of the press identification card should find it of real value in day-to-day dealings with the Metropolitan Police, carrying a significance which is readily recognised and accepted by all members of the Force. To this end the wording of the new card will lay emphasis on the facilities available to news media representatives rather than the penalties which may be invoked in the event of misuse and will declare that holders should be given all reasonable police assistance to perform their duties. The press card will not carry an automatic right of access to the scene of an incident or convey authority to pass police lines since these must remain matters for the judgement of the senior police officer at the scene. However, in normal circumstances card-holders are to be provided with all such information and opportunities for access as can be made available.

11. Although special facilities cannot be accorded to non-holders of Metropolitan and City Police press cards, wherever possible I wish the Force to endeavour to meet the reasonable needs of bona fide representatives of the news media★,who are not Metropolitan and City Police press card holders but who may have to undertake, from time to time or in an emergency, an

---

★ Members of the Press, such as those holding membership cards of the NUJ, the IOJ or appropriate unions and associations. - Ed.

assignment in which police assistance is needed, for example at a major incident. However, where regular enquiries are received from non-card holders the matter is to be brought to the attention of the Press Bureau.

LIAISON WITH THE LOCAL PRESS

12. The more open approach to the news media and the increased supply of information, either direct or via the Press Bureau, is intended to apply to all spheres of the press, television and radio— national, regional and local. So far as the local press is concerned, officers in charge of stations have previously been authorised to give representatives of local newspapers items of purely local news which come to their knowledge. As a further step to improve the supply of information the practice which is already widespread whereby a designated officer is responsible for liaison with the local press on a day-to-day basis is to be extended to every station. Commanders or nominated senior officers would hold briefing meetings once or twice a year for all officers so designated at which the Divisional Press Liaison Officer and a senior 'P' Department representative should be present. It would also be helpful if local press reporters could have the opportunity for regular contact, say at weekly or fortnightly intervals, with an officer of chief inspector or inspector rank at their local station. I am sure there is a great deal more news of purely local interest which could be made available without transgressing any of the principles of confidentiality that the Force is required to observe. It must be remembered, however, that any items of news which may be of wider interest should also be made generally available via the Press Bureau.

TRAINING

13. The new policy will depend for its success on the growing understanding by police officers at every level of the need for a good relationship with the news media. The achievement of this depends to some extent upon those responsible for training. Basic training should therefore touch on the general concept of the new policy and intermediate and higher training should stress the advantages to be derived from the avoidance of unnecessary secrecy and from the achievement of mutual trust between the Force and the news media. A growing confidence, not likely to be impaired by inevitable occasional criticism of each other, should prove of great benefit to the police and the news media and thus to society itself.

IV   RECOMMENDATIONS FOR COVERING TERRORISM

7. PAPER ON TERRORISM

The National News Council★

Washington had returned to normal after the Hanafi Muslim siege when the National News Council met at Drake University in Des Moines, Iowa, in March 1977. News coverage of the event, however, was still receiving widespread attention.

The Hanafi Muslim episode had become "a media event," in the words of Charles Seib of the *Washington Post*. "The media," Seib declared, "were as much a part of it as the terrorists, the victims and the authorities. The news business did what it always does when it deals with violence, bloodshed and suspense: It covered it excessively."[1]

Even President Carter was drawn into the discussion when U.N. Ambassador Andrew Young criticized the media for glorifying such events. "The First Amendment has got to be clarified by the Supreme Court in the light of the power of the mass media," Young said. "I don't know if it protects the right of people literally to destroy the things we believe in." Young also said the news media should censor themselves.[2]

When the President was called upon to respond to Young's suggestion, Press Secretary Jody Powell issued this statement:

"★ ★ ★ The President does feel that the manner of coverage of these situations does merit discussion and sober consideration. He recognized the complexity of the problem and frankly has no easy solution in mind. He sees this as a problem that should be

---

★ This paper is not a report *by* the National News Council but a report *to* the Council. It was never acted upon by the Council but was used as a means to generate some discussion concerning the coverage of terrorist activities. An official statement was issued by the Council on March 22, 1977 and is reprinted in this paper. - Ed.

addressed by the news media as a powerful and responsible institution in our society. He has no desire to seek legislation or to otherwise impose a solution and hopes those who make news decisions will themselves determine definable boundaries of legitimate coverage."[3]

With this in mind, the Council examined the coverage, the issues surrounding it, and suggestions for the establishment of guidelines for the news media. Electing neither to write guidelines nor to advocate them, the Council issued this statement:

> "The National News Council has considered the question of news coverage of terrorist action—and the controversy which has arisen about the appropriate limits of such coverage.
> "At the threshold, the Council rejects as unthinkable any notion that such activities should not be reported because they are perceived as "contagious." The dangers of suppression should be self-evident: doubts over what the media have withheld and the motives for such a blackout; questions about other types of news which might also have been withheld ostensibly in the public interest; and the greater possible risks involved in wild and reckless rumors and exaggerated, provocative word-of-mouth reports.
> "Nevertheless, the Council suggests that each news organization consider certain self-restraints in specific areas and in specific cases. First, the Council urges a re-examination on a case-by-case basis of the dangers in the practice of live coverage which precludes full context or judicious editing.
> "Second, the Council asks all news media to consider the dangers in the practice of telephoning for interviews with the terrorists or hostages during the event. Such telephone interviews can tie up telephone communication between negotiators and terrorists, and can incite the terrorists to ultimate violence. The Council therefore urges appropriate discussion with authorities before any such calls are made either by electronic or print media reporters.
> "Some news organizations already are developing internal guidelines to deal with such situations. The Council offers to become a repository for such guidelines or internal memoranda and to circulate them to all interested news organizations."

Since then, at least two conferences on the coverage of terrorism have been held—one by the Washington chapter of the Radio-Television News Directors Association (RTNDA) and the other by the *Chicago Sun-Times* and *Daily News*. These conferences drew together professionals from various fields with an interest in terrorist acts: journalists, law officials, psychologists,

RECOMMENDATIONS FOR COVERING TERRORISM 135

and legal authorities. Four news organizations are known to have adopted guidelines; some other organizations have said they plan to follow. Still others have vetoed the idea of guidelines, choosing instead to decide how to cover each event as it happens.

Following the intentions put forth in its statement, the Council has collected information on terrorism, the pros and cons of guidelines, and the guidelines themselves. That information is assembled in this paper without judgment on the wisdom or acceptability of the suggestions. They are simply stated for the consideration of journalists who are concerned with improving the quality of coverage given to these events.

Perhaps it is necessary first to understand the terrorists and what motivates them. Several persons have defined categories of terrorists, but the most complete categories seem to be those of Cherif Bassiouni, professor of law at DePaul University in Chicago. Bassiouni's first category covers terrorists involved in separatists movements resulting from indigenous conflicts based on race, religion, ethnicity, or language. The second type of terrorist aims to alter the economic, social, and political structures of the state. A third type of terrorist engages in violence in order to propagandize a claim or to redress an individual grievance. Terrorists of this category are the most prevalent in the U.S.

Within the third category are three subdivisions. The terrorist may be out for personal gain, perhaps hijacking a plane for ransom. In this subdivision may fall the person who is trapped in the commisssion of a crime and takes hostages in an attempt to go free. Then there is the psychopath, an unbalanced personality who seeks recognition more than anything else. Within the third subdivision falls the person who is out to vindicate a personal claim; Anthony Kiritsis, who in Indianapolis held a shotgun to a bank president's* neck because the bank had refused him credit, may be an example of this. Bassiouni, however, qualifies this last category. It is difficult, he says, to separate this person from the psychopath.[5]

The fourth category, which may be the most difficult to deal with, is the ideologically motivated terrorist. This person wants to make a point, to gain power. Compromise may be unacceptable, and killing to help the cause, a trivial matter.[6]

What all of these types have in common, most experts agree, is a desire for publicity. This seems clear in the United States, where terrorists seldom, if ever, escape. Brian Jenkins, a Rand Corporation expert on terrorism, explained the terrorists' motives this way:

---

* Kiritsis' victim was, in fact, manager of the Meridian Mortgage Company. This mortgage company had refused Kiritsis credit. - Ed.

"While terrorists may kill, sometimes wantonly, the primary objective of terrorism is *not* mass murder. Terrorists want a lot of people watching and a lot of people listening, not a lot of dead people. I see terrorism as violence for effect. Terrorists choreograph dramatic incidents to achieve maximum publicity, and in that sense, terrorism is theater."[7]

So where does this leave the journalists? One television news director in Cleveland says his station may no longer cover terrorists at all:

"We feel that the coverage we give such incidents is partly to blame, for we are glorifying lawbreakers, we are making heroes out of non-heroes. In effect, we are losing control over our news departments. We are being used."[8]

Most news organizations, however, seek a more moderate position. "I'm torn," says Richard Wald, president of NBC News. "I want to report, but I don't want to help to overdramatize or dramatize."[9]

Guidelines are discussed as one way to prevent excesses of coverage. But to some journalists, guidelines suggest censorship and inflexibility. They worry that guidelines would result in the suppression of vital information that may be embarrassing to authorities or contrary to community standards. The civil rights struggle in the South would never have been fully publicized under guidelines, they say. Besides, they argue, full coverage does more to calm than to inflame the community.

"The last thing in the world I want is guidelines," says A. M. Rosenthal, executive editor of the *New York Times*. "I don't want guidelines from the government and I don't want any from professional organizations or anyone else. The strength of the press is its diversity. As soon as you start imposing guidelines, they become peer-group pressures and then quasi-legal restrictions. I'm just viscerally against it. Besides, you have to judge each situation individually, on a case-by-case basis. You have to weigh the human dangers and then journalistic values of each case as it comes up. No policy could possibly cover every case."[10]

The Chicago *Tribune* uses a similar case-by-case approach with the highest authority available in the organization making the decisions.[11] The Gannett newspapers policy has been stated by John C. Quinn, senior vice president of news and information:

"The issue is not whether such outrages against society should be covered; of course they must be. The crucial question is how that job must be done. The need and the ability to grab the reader with aggressive, exciting news coverage must be matched with cool, professional news judgment that recognizes in every story the specific significance at hand and its potential for serious repercussions. The news coverage performance that reflects the full meaning of a highly charged story in the tone as well as in the detail will indeed communicate to the community what the readers want and need to know without risking any temptation for anyone, including journalists, to get caught up in the emotion of the moment."[12]

Discussing a few do's and don'ts for the coverage of terrorism, Wald, of NBC News, says:

"I don't know any really good rules to guide us in those situations, but what we do is this: We hire sensible people, promote smart bosses, tell them to be careful, and generally it works. They wind up being sensible and smart, and they don't do terrible things, and it works out okay. Every once in a while, it doesn't. It's the price we pay for the system we have."[13]

Although the Associated Press has not adopted guidelines, Executive Editor and Vice President Louise D. Boccardi says they are being considered:

"We feel we have a responsibility to not contribute to or inflame a dangerous situation in which lives are at stake. Given the nature of the journalists' work, it may be that such a credo is the only suitable guideline. Perhaps there is a need for more specifics. That's what we're looking at."[14]

Other organizations, while not adopting formal guidelines, have established temporary rules for covering specific acts of terrorism. WMAL TV[15] and the *Washington Post*[16] did that during the Hanafi Muslim siege in Washington.

Persons who favor guidelines seem to feel they are a way of establishing acceptable professional standards that can be flexible enough to cover any situation. Norval Morris, dean of the University of Chicago Law School, says the press and police should be able to reach agreement on extreme cases.[17]

Some persons not representing news organizations have suggested guidelines, both general and specific. Psychologist★ Bassiouni makes two suggestions—to use pool coverage, and to create a council to formulate and

---

★ Professor of Law. - Ed.

supervise voluntary restraints on media activities. Pool coverage is to prevent the problems created by a mass of reporters descending on a locality and to eliminate the competitiveness that sometimes leads to oneupmanship in the news media.[18]

Charles Fenyvesi, editor of the *National Jewish Monthly* and a hostage during the Hanafi Muslim Siege, agrees with the idea of a media council. A committee of editors could agree on "declaring and enforcing what might be called a news media emergency," he says. "A media emergency would mean the suspension of some of the rules of the profession. For instance, instead of aggressively gathering news and scooping competition, protecting or at least not endangering lives should be our top priority. And whoever violates this rule would be held accountable and subject to disciplinary action by his employer."[19]

Temporary delays in reporting have been suggested. "Nothing would be lost if the public didn't get information for 30 minutes, an hour or even a couple of days," says George Gerbner of the Annenberg School of Communications in Philadelphia.[20]

Dr. Preston Horstman, a psychologist with the Prince George's County (Md.) police department, participated in the RTNDA conference in Washington. He made six recommendations for coverage:[21]

1. Do not name the individual (terrorist); naming gives credit and strengthens what he/she is doing. Do not print the methods; this prevents imitation. Do not print anything the terrorists say. This takes away what they want to accomplish.
2. If media coverage is part of the demands, it should be done in as limited a manner as possible with as few people involved as possible. Take care not to be manipulated.
3. The act itself should be shown as a despicable act by losers.
4. The point should be made that no hostage situation has been successful.
5. No direct calls should ever be made to the terrorists: that draws out the process.
6. Continuing onsite coverage should not be used: it gives away intelligence to the terrorists.

In a two-part article entitled "Terrorism and Television," *TV Guide* listed proposals for television coverage gathered from experts on violence. They were essentially the same as Horstman's with two additions:

> Keep air time in proportion to the objective news value of the terrorist act.

— Give documentaries and analyses on the problems facing the country or community "and even access to the airways for the voices of reason among dissident groups, thereby reducing the likelihood of their resorting to violence to have their grievance heard."[22]

Perhaps the most comprehensive study and guidelines around come from the 661-page report of the U.S. Government's Task Force on Disorders and Terrorism.[23] That report was published in December 1976, by the National Advisory Committee on Criminal Justice Standards and Goals, an arm of the Law Enforcement Assistance Administration.* Throughout the report, the Task Force exhorts Government and law enforcement officials to maintain open and honest relations with the press. Although the other guidelines discussed here have dealt only with coverage during the commission of the act of terrorism, the committee has three sets of guidelines—one each for ongoing coverage, for contemporaneous coverage, and for follow-up reporting.[24]

NATIONAL ADVISORY COMMITTEE ON CRIMINAL JUSTICE STANDARDS AND GOALS, REPORT OF THE TASK FORCE ON DISORDERS AND TERRORISM

News and Entertainment Media Responsibility for the Prevention of Extraordinary Violence

Factual and fictional depictions of incidents of extraordinary violence in the mass media are an important part of the background against which individual choices whether or not to participate in crimes of this nature are made. They also are a significant influence on public fears and expectations. So long as extraordinary violence is a fact of social life, the special responsibility of the mass media in the prevention of extraordinary violence should dictate some guiding principles to govern the presentation of this material. In particular:

1. Factual journalistic coverage of extraordinary violence in the mass media should be as accurate and complete as the availability of information permits. Such coverage should:
    a. Give appropriate emphasis to the immediate and long-term consequences of extraordinary violence, for both victims and perpetrators;
    b. Include reliable information on the capacity of law enforcement agencies to deal with extraordinary violence; and

---

* The National Advisory Committee on Criminal Justice Standards and Goals was not "an arm" of LEAA. It did, however, receive LEAA support. - Ed.

c. Avoid unnecessary glamorization of persons who engage in crimes of extraordinary violence.

2. Editorials, features, and journalistic background pieces concerning extraordinary violence should attempt to place the phenomenon in total context, by reference to other problems of law enforcement and to related political and social issues.

3. Particular fictional presentations of extraordinary violence in the entertainment media, and the variety of mass entertainment that has criminal violence as its subject matter, should be crafted so as to:

a. Avoid giving any general impression that participation in extraordinary violence is a common, glamorous, or effective means of resolving personal or political problems;

b. Avoid conveying the impression that law enforcement responses to extraordinary violence are generally either incompetent or marked by the use of extreme force; and

c. Present affirmative portrayals of private individuals and officials coping effectively with extraordinary violence and its consequences.

News Media Self-Regulation in Contemporaneous Coverage of Terrorism and Disorder

When an incident involving a confrontation between law enforcement officers and participants in mass disorder, terrorism, or quasi-terrorism is in progress, the role of the news media is an important and controversial one. The manner in which information about the incident is collected, and the form of its presentation to the public, will necessarily affect the conduct of the agencies and persons involved. In addition, these factors will be critical influences on the growth or spread, if any, of the incident. Finally, the approach taken by the media to news gathering and reporting on an incident-by-incident basis will have an important cumulative effect on public attitudes toward the phenomenon of extraordinary violence, the groups and persons who participate in it, and the official measures taken against it.

No hard rules can be prescribed to govern media performance during incidents of extraordinary violence. Whatever principles are adopted must be generated by the media themselves, out of a recognition of special public responsibility. But in general, the essence of an appropriate approach to news gathering is summarized in the principle of minimum intrusiveness: Representatives of the media should avoid creating any obvious media presence at an incident scene that is greater than that required to collect full, accurate, and balanced information on the actions of participants and the official response to them. Similarly, the essence of an appropriate approach to contemporaneous reporting of extraordinary violence lies in the principle of complete, noninflammatory coverage; the public is best served by reporting that omits no important detail and that attempts to place all details in context.

Putting these general principles into practice, however, requires hard choices for the media, both at the organizational policy level and by the working reporter. In particular:

1. News media organizations and representatives wishing to adopt the principle of minimum intrusiveness in their gathering of news relating to incidents of extraordinary violence should consider the following devices, among others:

    a. Use of pool reporters to cover activities at incident scenes or within police lines;

    b. Self-imposed limitations on the use of high-intensity television lighting, obtrusive camera equipment, and other special newsgathering technologies at incident scenes;

    c. Limitations on media solicitation of interviews with barricaded or hostage-holding suspects and other incident participants;

    d. Primary reliance on officially designated spokesmen as sources of information concerning law enforcement operations and plans; and

    e. Avoidance of inquiries designed to yield tactical information that would prejudice law enforcement operations if subsequently disclosed.

2. News media organizations and representatives wishing to follow the principle of complete, noninflammatory coverage in contemporaneous reporting of incidents of extraordinary violence should consider the following devices, among others:

    a. Delayed reporting of details believed to have a potential for inflammation or aggravation of an incident that significantly outweighs the interest to the general public;

    b. Delayed disclosure of information relating to incident location, when that information is not likely to become public knowledge otherwise and when the potential for incident growth or spread is obviously high;

    c. Delayed disclosure of information concerning official tactical planning that, if known to incident participants, would seriously compromise law enforcement efforts;

    d. Balancing of reports incorporating self-serving statements by incident participants with contrasting information from official sources and with data reflecting the risks that the incident has created to noninvolved persons;

    e. Systematic predisclosure verification of all information concerning incident-related injuries, deaths, and property destruction; and

    f. Avoidance, to the extent possible, of coverage that tends to emphasize the spectacular qualities of an incident or the presence of spectators at an incident scene.

Followup Reporting of Extraordinary Violence by News Media

Although contemporaneous news-gathering and reporting practices can have great impact on the course of an incident of extraordinary violence and the shape of its eventual resolution, the coverage that the phenomena of extraordinary violence receive during nonemergency periods is ultimately even more significant. From the followup reporting of particular incidents and their aftermaths, as well as from general and background reporting, the public at large receives the bulk of its information about disorder, terrorism, and quasi-terrorism and about official response to these law enforcement problems. What constitutes responsible selection of objectives and means for ongoing, nonemergency coverage is difficult to define with precision. But it is clear that a media policy that emphasizes reporting an emergency to the near exclusion of followup coverage constitutes a disservice to the public. Bearing in mind the interests and characteristics of its audience, every news organ should make a serious, complete and noninflammatory presentation of information that will serve to put extraordinary violence in context, including:

1. Factual material documenting the aftermath of particular incidents, and emphasizing:

    a. Effects of extraordinary violence on individual victims and the community at large;

    b. Apprehension, trial, and sentencing of persons participating in extraordinary violence;

    c. Community reactions to law enforcement efforts in incident handling; and

    d. Official and nonofficial efforts to identify and address underlying grievances and precipitating social conditions.

2. Factual material not specifically tied to particular incidents, emphasizing such topics as:

    a. Local and national trends and tendencies in extraordinary violence;

    b. Available preventive security and law enforcement techniques applicable to extraordinary violence.

    c. Comparison of foreign and domestic experiences with extraordinary violence;

    d. Aims, characteristics, and records of terrorist groups;

    e. Background and recent history of quasi-terrorism and related forms of extraordinary violence; and

    f. Recent history and causative factors of mass disorder.

3. Editorial material analyzing options in public policy and private conduct, and where appropriate, recommending courses of action, in such topic areas as:

    a. Kinds and levels of preventive security;

b. Law enforcement techniques;
c. Community roles and responsibilities in emergencies; and
d. Elimination of causes of extraordinary violence.

The four news organizations that have submitted copies of their guidelines to the National News Council are CBS News, the *Louisville Times* and *Courier-Journal*, the *Chicago Daily News* and *Sun-Times*, and United Press International. Those guidelines, which follow, have in common a flexible approach and standards that might be considered simple professionalism. In general, they say:

1. The judgment of the newsworthiness of the event should be made on a case-by-case basis, using normal news judgment.
2. Coverage should be full, accurate, and balanced, with no attempt made to sensationalize.
3. Journalists should stay out of the way of law enforcement officials but stay in touch with those officials for information and guidance on coverage.

The News Council again states its interest in receiving copies of guidelines adopted by news organizations or other information pertinent to the coverage of terrorism. Such material would be made available on request to other journalists and news organizations interested in responsible news coverage of terroristic acts when such occur.

CBS NEWS PRODUCTION STANDARDS

Coverage of Terrorists (4/7/77)

Because the facts and circumstances of each case vary, there can be no specific self-executing rules for the handling of terrorist/hostage stories. CBS News will continue to apply the normal tests of news judgment and if, as so often they are, these stories are newsworthy, we must continue to give them coverage despite the dangers of "contagion." The disadvantages of suppression are, among [other] things, (1) [its] adversely affecting our credibility ("What else are the news people keeping from us?"); (2) [its] giving free rein to sensationalized and erroneous word of mouth rumors; and (3) [its] distorting our news judgments for some extraneous judgmental purpose. These disadvantages compel us to continue to provide coverage.

Nevertheless, in providing for such coverage there must be thoughtful, conscientious care and restraint. Obviously, the story should not be sensationalized beyond the actual fact of its being sensational. We should exercise particular care in how we treat the terrorist/kidnaper.

More specifically:

1. An essential component of the story is the demands of the terrorist/kidnaper, and we must report those demands. But we should avoid providing an excessive platform for the terrorist/kidnaper. Thus, unless such demands are succinctly stated and free of rhetoric and propaganda, it may be better to paraphrase the demands instead of presenting them directly through the voice or picture of the terrorist/kidnaper.

2. Except in the most compelling circumstances, and then only with the approval of the President of CBS News, or in his absence, the Senior Vice President of News, there should be no live coverage of the terrorist/kidnaper since we may fall into the trap of providing an unedited platform for him. (This does *not* limit live on-the-spot reporting by CBS News reporters, but care should be exercised to assure restraint and context.)

3. News personnel should be mindful of the probable need by the authorities who are dealing with the terrorist for communication by telephone and hence should endeavor to ascertain, wherever feasible, whether our own use of such lines would be likely to interfere with the authorities' communications.

4. Responsible CBS News representatives should endeavor to contact experts dealing with the hostage situation to determine whether they have any guidance on such questions as phraseology to be avoided, what kinds of questions or reports might tend to exacerbate the situation, etc. Any such recommendations by established authorities on the scene should be carefully considered as guidance (but not as instruction) by CBS News personnel.

5. Local authorities should also be given the name or names of CBS personnel whom they can contact should they have further guidance or wish to deal with such delicate questions as a newsman's call to the terrorists or other matters which might interfere with authorities dealing with the terrorists.

6. Guidelines affecting our coverage of civil disturbances are also applicable here, especially those which relate to avoiding the use of inflammatory catchwords or phrases, the reporting of rumors, etc. As in the case of policy dealing with civil disturbances, in dealing with a hostage story reporters should obey all police instructions but report immediately to their superiors any such instructions that seem to be intended to manage or suppress the news.

7. Coverage of this kind of story should be in such overall balance as to length, that it does not unduly crowd out other important news of the hour/day.

RECOMMENDATIONS FOR COVERING TERRORISM

THE COURIER-JOURNAL AND THE LOUISVILLE TIMES

May 18, 1977

The following are guidelines for the newspapers' coverage in the event terrorists take and hold hostages in our area.

It will be our policy to cover the story fully and accurately. To do otherwise—to withhold information—could destroy our credibility and give life to reckless and exaggerated rumors in the community.

At the same time, our approach will be one of care and restraint. We will avoid sensationalism in what we write and how we display it, taking care not to play the story beyond its real significance.

We will make every effort not to become participants in the event. We will resist being used by the terrorists to provide a platform for their propaganda.

If terrorists demand that we publish specific information, we will agree to do so only if we are convinced that not to publish it would further endanger the life of a hostage. Our decision on whether to publish will be made only after consultation with the most senior editor available and, when possible, top police officials.

We will always be mindful of the dangers in telephoning terrorists or hostages for interviews during the event, realizing that such action could interrupt vital negotiations or incite the terrorists to violence.

We will assign experienced staff members to the story. We will involve the papers' top news officials when making decisions.

Insofar as possible, we will maintain contact with the resposible law enforcement officials dealing with the situation. It will always be our aim to avoid taking any action that would interfere with the proper execution of duties by police or other officials.

Although we cannot be responsible for the coverage by other news media, we can and will conduct a constant review of our own performance.

THE SUN-TIMES AND DAILY NEWS (CHICAGO) STANDARDS FOR COVERAGE OF TERRORISM

Recognizing that circumstances vary in each story, the following standards are meant for general guidance:
1. Normal tests of news judgment will determine what to publish despite the dangers of contagion, since the adverse effects of suppression are greater.

2. Coverage should be thoughtful and restrained and not sensationalized beyond the innate sensation of the story itself. Inflammatory catchwords, phrases and rumors should be avoided.
3. Demands of terrorists and kidnapers should be reported as an essential point of the story but paraphrased when necessary to avoid unbalanced propaganda.
4. Reporters should avoid actions that would further jeopardize the lives of hostages or police.
5. Reporters should obey all police instructions but report immediately to their supervisors any such instructions that seem to manage or suppress the news.
6. Supervising editors and reporters should contact authorities to seek guidance—not instructions—on the use of telephones or other facilities, the reporting of negotiations of police strategies.
7. Editors, reporters, and photographers should not become part of the story, should not participate in negotiations and should not ask terrorists about deadlines.
8. The senior supervisory editor should determine what—if any—information should be withheld or deferred after consultation with reporters and appropriate authorities.
9. The constant objective should be to provide a credible report without hampering authorities or endangering life.

GUIDELINES OF UNITED PRESS INTERNATIONAL

Genuine concern has been expressed by the news media. There is concern that spectacles such as the Hanafi siege in Washington may turn into a media event. There is concern that the media is being used as a forum for terrorists and kidnapers to express their views. There is concern about the definition, degree, and perspective of the news coverage.

Most editors agree that these happenings must be reported. Editorials have pointed to the Constitution, the credibility of a free press, and the public's right to know.

Then where do we draw the line between legitimate news coverage and being exploited? The answer seems to be in individual news judgment and sense of responsibility.

There can be no clearly defined policy for terrorist and kidnaping stories. The circumstances vary in each case. UPI has established a set of guidelines which we feel are workable in most circumstances.

- We will judge each story on its own and if a story is newsworthy cover it despite the dangers of contagion.
- Our coverage will be thoughtful, conscientious, and show restraint.

RECOMMENDATIONS FOR COVERING TERRORISM

- We will not sensationalize a story beyond the fact of it being sensational.
- We will report the demands of terrorists and kidnapers as an essential point of the story but not provide an excessive platform for their demands.
- We will do nothing to jeopardize lives.
- We will not become a part of the story.
- If we do talk to a kidnaper or a terrorist, we will not become a part of the negotiations.
- If there has been no mention of a deadline we will not ask the kidnaper or terrorist if there is one.
- In all cases we will apply the rule of common sense.

FOOTNOTES

1. Charles B. Sieb. The Hanafi episode: A media event. *Washington Post*, March 18, 1977.
2. John Herbers. Carter says coverage of sieges is a problem for the news media. *New York Times*, March 15, 1977.
3. Ibid.
4. *The media and terrorism: A seminar sponsored by the Chicago Sun-Times and Chicago Daily News*. Chicago: Field Enterprises Inc.: c1977, p.6.
5. Ibid.
6. Ibid.
7. Neil Hickey. Terrorism and television, Part I. *TV Guide*, July 31, 1976, p.4.
8. Philip Revzin. A reporter looks at media role in terror threats. *Wall Street Journal*, March 14, 1977.
9. Richard Wald. Lecture at University of California - Riverside, March 21, 1977.
10. Quoted in: David Shaw. Editors face terrorist demand dilemma. *Los Angeles Times*, September 15, 1976.
11. Clayton Kirkpatrick, editor of the *Chicago Tribune*. Letter to the National News Council. (Dated)July 11, 1977.
12. Ina Meyers. Terrorism in the News. *Daily Times* (Marmaroneck, N.Y.).
13. Richard Wald. Op. cit.
14. Louis D. Boccardi, executive editor and vice president of the Associated Press. Letter to the National News Council, (Dated) March 31, 1977.
15. Sam Belman, executive director of news for WMAL TV. Letter to the National News Council. (Dated) May 31, 1977.
16. *The media and terrorism*, 17–22.
17. Ibid., p.32.
18. Ibid., p.9.
19. Ibid., p.30.
20. Terrorism and censorship. *Time*, March 28, 1977, p.57.
21. Preston Horstman speaking in a debate sponsored by the Radio-Television Directors Association (RTNDA), Washington Chapter, March 1977.
22. Terrorism and television, Part II. *TV Guide*, August 7, 1976, 12–13.
23. National Advisory Committee on Criminal Justice Standards and Goals. *Disorders and terrorism: Report of the Task Force on Disorders and Terrorism*. Washington, D.C.: LEAA, 1976.
24. Ibid. Standard 10.2, p.366; Standard 10.8, p.387; and Standard 10.12, p.401.

8. GUIDELINES FOR UNITED STATES GOVERNMENT SPOKESPERSONS DURING TERRORIST INCIDENTS

U.S. Department of State

In a terrorist situation, the ultimate responsibility of the USG [U.S. Government] to protect the security and well-being of this country and its citizens must often be weighed against another equally important tenet, the public's right to know. The public's interest in being kept informed of fast-breaking events is encouraged and responded to by the media whose chief objective is to obtain and provide as much information as possible as quickly as possible. In a terrorist situation, acts of violence naturally attract media coverage and the attention of the public. As a consequence, the USG is faced with the difficult and sensitive task of dealing responsibly with these events and their impact in a highly charged atmosphere.

It is with this recognition of the differing roles of the media and the USG that we must find an appropriate balance for USG spokespersons dealing with the press during a terrorist event. Press officers both in Washington and at posts abroad should always be as helpful, direct, and forthcoming with the media as possible, recognizing that

> "under the First Amendment, the U.S. Government has no right to prohibit or limit coverage of a newsworthy event. However, it is appropriate to seek voluntary media cooperation in minimizing risks to life and to point out that certain media actions might exacerbate a dangerous situation." (Deputy Attorney General Civiletti before Congress, August 1978).

With these considerations in mind, the following guidelines have been prepared by the Public Information Committee of the NSC/SCC [National

RECOMMENDATIONS FOR COVERING TERRORISM

Security Council/Special Coordinating Committee] Inter-Agency Working Group to Combat Terrorism. These instructions have been approved by all concerned USG agencies and are to be followed by USG spokespersons both at home and abroad during a terrorist crisis.

General Instructions

Both at the scene of the incident and in Washington, complete coordination is necessary between spokespersons so that the USG speaks with one voice. In addition, prior coordination of press comments with relevant local or foreign authorities is also a necessary step. Abroad, host governments have primary responsibility for managing terrorist incidents involving American citizens or property, including possible attacks on USG installations. U.S. diplomats or military spokespersons, therefore, must, if at all possible, clear press statements or comments in advance with Washington and coordinate them with the host government as well. When this is not possible, both Washington and the host government should be fully informed as to the statements that are being made by the USG spokesperson on the scene.

In the United States, official press officers should respect the jurisdictions and interests of all concerned USG agencies, both at the national as well as the State and local levels. Appropriate and reasonable clearance procedures should be followed. The Department of Justice and the Federal Bureau of Investigation have responsibility for coordinating most press statements on domestic acts of terrorism; the Federal Aviation Administration has responsibility for aircraft hijackings in flight; the Department of State and, in certain instances, the Department of Defense, acts of terrorism abroad. Releases concerning incidents involving officials or property of foreign governments or organizations in the United States are to be coordinated with the Department of State.

Another important and difficult aspect of USG-press relations during terrorist incidents are those involving the people or property of private American business firms, foundations, religious associations, or other groups. The needs, requirements, and objectives of private American businesses or associations involved in a hostage or other terrorist incident often may be different from those of the USG. Terrorists may demand not only ransom, but also the purchase of newspaper space or radio/television time to publicize their existence or viewpoints. USG spokespersons cannot become involved in these activities, but they should not prevent or hinder private Americans from acting in what they may believe are their own or the hostage(s)' best interests.

It is the responsibility of USG spokespersons to be fully conversant with U.S. policy considerations regarding terrorist situations. Priority must be given to the safe return of any hostages and to the apprehension of the terrorists. For posts abroad, Department of State guidance should be requested on any policy considerations or interpretations. The Department of Justice and the FBI have similar responsibility in domestic terrorist situations.

Before a Terrorist Incident

- Maintain good contacts with local press.
  Arrange background discussions with the local press so that the lines of communication are open and they are aware of some of the basic scenarios, expectations, and ground rules that will be maintained by the USG during a terrorist event. Also, this will be a good way to assess the mood, requirements, and suggestions of the press most immediately involved.
- Maintain contact with other USG and foreign spokespersons.
  In Washington, press officers for the NSC/SCC Working Group agencies should maintain current lists of their counterparts in other member agencies for use during an incident.
  Abroad, Foreign Service, military and other official USG spokespersons should be acquainted with those officials in host-government press offices who would act as government spokespersons during a terrorist incident.
  It is important that in the case of a foreign incident, contact be maintained with the Department of State so that up-to-date information is available by noon for the daily press briefing.
- Participate in simulation exercises.
  Practice makes, if not perfect, at least for greater familiarity with the heightened demands of a terrorist situation. Include simulated coordination with other press offices in all Post Terrorism Contingency Plans and terrorism-related exercises. Make certain that any simulated situation being undertaken includes the USG press spokesperson and consideration of the public and press component as part of the dry run.
- Special accreditation.
  Prepare a plan for special accreditation of the press during a terrorist incident of duration since both additional foreign and domestic press will very likely be arriving from other locations.

During A Terrorist Incident

- Seek to provide essential, factual information to the press during the course of an incident. Maintain accuracy. Discourage and dispel rumors

RECOMMENDATIONS FOR COVERING TERRORISM 151

by issuing as frequently as possible as much correct and factual information as you can. Be alert to the "contagion" of rumors and curb them quickly. Try to avoid premature publicity which could be dangerous, particularly in hostage situations.
- Do not overdramatize or sensationalize the situation. Be calm, responsive, and accurate in your dealings with the press and convey the Government's condemnation of lawless violence.
- Give frequent press briefings at specified times. Be accessible. Have a designated area for briefings *away* from the incident scene, at or near the command center, depending on the command center location, size and availability of facilities, and security requirements.
- Designate one press spokesperson who will be at or have expeditious communication with the command center and who will be the official communicator to the press during the incident. This person should have full and up-to-date information and should have a designated deputy at the scene with the press at all times. Communication should be accurate and complete between the spokesperson and other officials involved in the handling of the terrorist situation.
- Make certain the spokesperson has a fully informed and available deputy so that if the incident goes on for many hours or days, the thread, continuity, familiarity, and accessibility are not lost with the press or with the circumstances of the incident. Gaps in communication because of exhaustion or improper backup can open up the possibility of misinformation or lack of information flow between the spokesperson and the press.
- Provide a designated press area as near to the scene of the incident as possible.
- Verify press bona fides. USG spokespersons should deal only with accredited news people. Be prepared for an influx of out-of-town or foreign press.
- Explain our concern regarding the possible hazards of direct contact or phone calls with, or live coverage of, the terrorists or the incident scene. Discourage live interviews with participants and the use of mini-cameras at or near the incident site.
- As spokesperson, don't act as terrorist(s)' "messenger" to the public. Coordinate closely with the command center as to your instructions in this regard, which may vary in degree as the needs of the specific situation require.
- Provide access to other officials and experts, as appropriate, who can background the press on aspects of the specific event.
- Urge caution with press interviews or unknown or amateur "experts" on terrorist motivation or background.
- Underline counterproductive aspects of reporting on any operational activities of the police, military, or other counterterrorism forces.
- Use appropriate phraseology; for example, encourage the downplaying of inflammatory words (and pictures). Keep in mind that terrorists most

often have access to radios and/or television, and will monitor what is being shown or said publicly.

After a Terrorist Incident

- Hold a background debriefing session with the media to exchange views, give some perspective to the situation, provide USG comment on media reporting and analysis, get media reaction, and improve, where necessary, planning for future incidents.

APPENDIX A

MEDIA GUIDELINE DOCUMENTS

From: NATIONAL ADVISORY COMMITTEE ON CRIMINAL JUSTICE STANDARDS AND GOALS, REPORT OF THE TASK FORCE ON DISORDERS AND TERRORISM, 1976.

Standard 10.2: *News and Entertainment Media Responsibility for the Prevention of Extraordinary Violence*

Factual and fictional depictions of incidents of extraordinary violence in the mass media are an important part of the background against which individual choices whether or not to participate in crimes of this nature are made. They also are a significant influence on public fears and expectations. So long as extraordinary violence is a fact of social life, the media cannot and should not avoid portraying and discussing it. But the special responsibility of the mass media in the prevention of extraordinary violence should dictate some guiding principles to govern the presentation of this material. In particular:

1. Factual journalistic coverage of extraordinary violence in the mass media should be as accurate and complete as the availability of information permits. Such coverage should:

    a. Give appropriate emphasis to the immediate and long-term consequences of extraordinary violence, for both victims and perpetrators;

    b. Include reliable information on the capacity of law enforcement agencies to deal with extraordinary violence; and

    c. Avoid unnecessary glamorization of persons who engage in crimes of extraordinary violence.

2. Editorials, features, and journalistic background pieces concerning extraordinary violence should attempt to place the phenomenon in total context,

by reference to other problems of law enforcement and to related political and social issues.

3. Particular fictional presentations of extraordinary violence in the entertainment media, and the variety of mass entertainment that has criminal violence as its subject matter, should be crafted so as to:

    a. Avoid giving any general impression that participation in extraordinary violence is a common, glamorous, or effective means of resolving personal or political problems;

    b. Avoid conveying the impression that law enforcement responses to extraordinary violence are generally either incompetent or marked by the use of extreme force; and

    c. Present affirmative portrayals of private individuals and officials coping effectively with extraordinary violence and its consequences.

Standard 10.8: *News Media Self-Regulation in Contemporaneous Coverage of Terrorism and Disorder*

When an incident involving a confrontation between law enforcement officers and participants in mass disorder, terrorism, or quasi-terrorism is in progress, the role of the news media is an important and controversial one. The manner in which information about the incident is collected, and the form of its presentation to the public, will necessarily affect the conduct of the agencies and persons involved. In addition, these factors will be critical influences on the growth or spread, if any, of the incident. Finally, the approach taken by the media to news gathering and reporting on an incident-by-incident basis will have an important cumulative effect on public attitudes toward the phenomenon of extraordinary violence, the groups and persons who participate in it, and the official measures taken against it.

No hard rules can be prescribed to govern media performance during incidents of extraordinary violence. Whatever principles are adopted must be generated by the media themselves, out of a recognition of special public responsibility. But in general, the essence of an appropriate approach to news gathering is summarized in the principle of minimum intrusiveness: Representatives of the media should avoid creating any obvious media presence at an incident scene that is greater than that required to collect full, accurate, and balanced information on the actions of participants and the official response to them. Similarly, the essence of an appropriate approach to contemporaneous reporting of extraordinary violence lies in the principle of complete, noninflammatory coverage; the public is best served by reporting that omits no important detail and that attempts to place all details in context.

APPENDIX A: MEDIA GUIDELINE DOCUMENTS

Putting these general principles into practice, however, requires hard choices for the media, both at the organizational policy level and by the working reporter. In particular:

1. News media organizations and representatives wishing to adopt the principle of minimum intrusiveness in their gathering of news relating to incidents of extraordinary violence should consider the following devices, among others:

    a. Use of pool reporters to cover activities at incident scenes or within police lines;

    b. Self-imposed limitations on the use of high-intensity television lighting, obtrusive camera equipment, and other special newsgathering technologies at incident scenes;

    c. Limitations on media solicitation of interviews with barricaded or hostage-holding suspects and other incident participants;

    d. Primary reliance on officially designated spokesmen as sources of information concerning law enforcement operations and plans; and

    e. Avoidance of inquiries designed to yield tactical information that would prejudice law enforcement operations if subsequently disclosed.

2. News media organizations and representatives wishing to follow the principle of complete, noninflammatory coverage in contemporaneous reporting of incidents of extraordinary violence should consider the following devices, among others:

    a. Delayed reporting of details believed to have a potential for inflammation or aggravation of an incident that significantly outweighs their interest to the general public;

    b. Delayed disclosure of information relating to incident location, when that information is not likely to become public knowledge otherwise and when the potential for incident growth or spread is obviously high;

    c. Delayed disclosure of information concerning official tactical planning that, if known to incident participants, would seriously compromise law enforcement efforts;

    d. Balancing of reports incorporating self-serving statements by incident participants with contrasting information from official sources and with data reflecting the risks that the incident has created to noninvolved persons;

    e. Systematic predisclosure verification of all information concerning incident-related injuries, deaths, and property destruction; and

    f. Avoidance, to the extent possible, of coverage that tends to emphasize the spectacular qualities of an incident or the presence of spectators at an incident scene.

Standard 10.12: *Followup Reporting of Extraordinary Violence by News Media*

Although contemporaneous news-gathering and reporting practices can have great impact on the course of an incident of extraordinary violence and the shape of its eventual resolution, the coverage that the phenomena of extraordinary violence receive during nonemergency periods is ultimately even more significant. From the followup reporting of particular incidents and their aftermaths, as well as from general and background reporting, the public at large receives the bulk of its information about disorder, terrorism, and quasi-terrorism and about official response to these law enforcement problems. What constitutes responsible selection of objectives and means for ongoing, nonemergency coverage is difficult to define with precision. But it is clear that a media policy that emphasizes reporting an emergency to the near exclusion of followup coverage constitutes a disservice to the public. Bearing in mind the interests and characteristics of its audience, every news organ should make a serious, complete and noninflammatory presentation of information that will serve to put extraordinary violence in context, including:

1. Factual material documenting the aftermath of particular incidents, and emphasizing:

    a. Effects of extraordinary violence on individual victims and the community at large;

    b. Apprehension, trial, and sentencing of persons participating in extraordinary violence;

    c. Community reactions to law enforcement efforts in incident handling; and

    d. Official and nonofficial efforts to identify and address underlying grievances and precipitating social conditions.

2. Factual material not specifically tied to particular incidents, emphasizing such topics as:

    a. Local and national trends and tendencies in extraordinary violence;

    b. Available preventive security and law enforcement techniques applicable to extraordinary violence.

    c. Comparison of foreign and domestic experiences with extraordinary violence;

    d. Aims, characteristics, and records of terrorist groups;

    e. Background and recent history of quasi-terrorism and related forms of extraordinary violence; and

    f. Recent history and causative factors of mass disorder.

3. Editorial material analyzing options in public policy and private conduct, and where appropriate, recommending courses of action, in such topic areas as:

    a. Kinds and levels of preventive security;

APPENDIX A: MEDIA GUIDELINE DOCUMENTS 157

    b. Law enforcement techniques;
    c. Community roles and responsibilities in emergencies; and
    d. Elimination of causes of extraordinary violence.

CBS NEWS PRODUCTION STANDARDS

Coverage of Terrorists (4/7/77)

Because the facts and circumstances of each case vary, there can be no specific self-executing rules for the handling of terrorist/hostage stories. CBS News will continue to apply the normal tests of news judgment and if, as so often they are, these stories are newsworthy, we must continue to give them coverage despite the dangers of "contagion." The disadvantages of suppression are, among [other] things, (1) [its] adversely affecting our credibility ("What else are the news people keeping from us?"); (2) [its] giving free rein to sensationalized and erroneous word of mouth rumors; and (3) [its] distorting our news judgments for some extraneous judgmental purpose. These disadvantages compel us to continue to provide coverage.

Nevertheless, in providing for such coverage there must be thoughtful, conscientious care and restraint. Obviously, the story should not be sensationalized beyond the actual fact of its being sensational. We should exercise particular care in how we treat the terrorist/kidnaper.

More specifically:

1. An essential component of the story is the demands of the terrorist/kidnaper, and we must report those demands. But we should avoid providing an excessive platform for the terrorist/kidnaper. Thus, unless such demands are succinctly stated and free of rhetoric and propaganda, it may be better to paraphrase the demands instead of presenting them directly through the voice or picture of the terrorist/kidnaper.

2. Except in the most compelling circumstances, and then only with the approval of the President of CBS News, or in his absence, the Senior Vice President of News, there should be no live coverage of the terrorist/kidnaper since we may fall into the trap of providing an unedited platform for him. (This does *not* limit live on-the-spot reporting by CBS News reporters, but care should be exercised to assure restraint and context.)

3. News personnel should be mindful of the probable need by the authorities who are dealing with the terrorist for communication by telephone and hence should endeavor to ascertain, wherever feasible, whether our own use of such lines would be likely to interfere with the authorities' communications.

4. Responsible CBS News representatives should endeavor to contact experts dealing with the hostage situation to determine whether they have any guidance on such questions as phraseology to be avoided, what kinds of questions or reports might tend to exacerbate the situation, etc. Any such recommendations by established authorities on the scene should be carefully considered as guidance (but not as instruction) by CBS News personnel.

5. Local authorities should also be given the name or names of CBS personnel whom they can contact should they have further guidance or wish to deal with such delicate questions as a newsman's call to the terrorists or other matters which might interfere with authorities dealing with the terrorists.

6. Guidelines affecting our coverage of civil disturbances are also applicable here, especially those which relate to avoiding the use of inflammatory catchwords or phrases, the reporting of rumors, etc. As in the case of policy dealing with civil disturbances, in dealing with a hostage story reports should obey all police instructions by reporting immediately to their superiors any such instructions that seem to be intended to manage or suppress the news.

7. Coverage of this kind of story should be in such overall balance as to length, that it does not unduly crowd out other important news of the hour/day.

THE COURIER-JOURNAL AND THE LOUISVILLE TIMES

May 18, 1977

The following are guidelines for the newspapers' coverage in the event terrorists take and hold hostages in our area.

It will be our policy to cover the story fully and accurately. To do otherwise—to withhold information—could destroy our credibility and give life to reckless and exaggerated rumors in the community.

At the same time, our approach will be one of care and restraint. We will avoid sensationalism in what we write and how we display it, taking care not to play the story beyond its real significance.

We will make every effort not to become participants in the event. We will resist being used by the terrorists to provide a platform for their propaganda.

If terrorists demand that we publish specific information, we will agree to do so only if we are convinced that not to publish it would further endanger the life of a hostage. Our decision on whether to publish will be made only after consultation with the most senior editor available and, when possible, top police officials.

APPENDIX A: MEDIA GUIDELINE DOCUMENTS

We will always be mindful of the dangers in telephoning terrorists or hostages for interviews during the event, realizing that such action could interrupt vital negotiations or incite the terrorists to violence.

We will assign experienced staff members to the story. We will involve the papers' top news officials when making decisions.

Insofar as possible, we will maintain contact with the responsible law enforcement officials dealing with the situation. It will always be our aim to avoid taking any action that would interfere with the proper execution of duties by police or other officials.

Although we cannot be responsible for the coverage by other news media, we can and will conduct a constant review of our own performance.

THE SUN-TIMES AND DAILY NEWS [CHICAGO] STANDARDS FOR COVERAGE OF TERRORISM

Recognizing that circumstances vary in each story, the following standards are meant for general guidance:
1. Normal tests of news judgment will determine what to publish despite the dangers of contagion, since the adverse effects of suppression are greater.
2. Coverage should be thoughtful and restrained and not sensationalized beyond the innate sensation of the story itself. Inflammatory catchwords, phrases and rumors should be avoided.
3. Demands of terrorists and kipnapers should be reported as an essential point of the story but paraphrased when necessary to avoid unbridled propaganda.
4. Reporters should avoid actions that would further jeopardize the lives of hostages or police.
5. Reporters should obey all police instructions but report immediately to their supervisors any such instructions that seem to manage or suppress the news.
6. Supervising editors and reporters should contact authorities to seek guidance—not instructions—on the use of telephones or other facilities, the reporting of negotiations or police strategies.
7. Editors, reporters, and photographers should not become part of the story, should not participate in negotiations, and should not ask terrorists about deadlines.
8. The senior supervisory editor should determine what—if any—information should be withheld or deferred after consultation with reporters and appropriate authorities.
9. The constant objective should be to provide a credible report without hampering authorities or endangering life.

UNITED PRESS INTERNATIONAL

Terrorism/Kidnaping Coverage Guidelines

The United Press International National Broadcast Advisory Board recommends posting in your newsroom the following guidelines to help broadcast news operations deal with the dilemma of covering acts of kidnaping and terrorism:
1. Each station should have established procedures for coverage of such events, which should include prompt notification of management.
2. Judge each story on its own, and if the story is newsworthy, cover it.
3. Coverage should be thoughtful, conscientious and show restraint, and be carried out with an awareness of the potential danger to life and person.
4. Report demands made as an essential point of the story, but do not provide an excessive platform for those demands.
5. Reporters should avoid deliberately injecting themselves into the story as intermediaries or negotiators.
6. If there has been no mention of a deadline, no one should ask the terrorist-kidnapers if there is one.
7. Above all, apply the rules of common sense.

APPENDIX B

THE PROJECT ON MEDIA COVERAGE OF TERRORISM: A SUMMARY OF NATIONAL SURVEYS AND OTHER INVESTIGATIONS, 1977–79.

Michael Sommer, Ph.D.
and
Heidi Sommer, Ph.D.

The Irvine Company (California)

ACKNOWLEDGEMENTS

The authors are extremely grateful for the insights provided by many research pioneers on terrorism, including Bassiouni, Hacker, Hubbard, Jenkins, and Laqueur, among others.
Great special thanks is due Kenneth Devol, chairman, Department of Journalism, California State University, Northridge, and former president Association for Education and Journalism, for his continued encouragement and untiring support of the Project on Media Coverage of Terrorism.
The authors wish to express their appreciation to the following persons who took part in the gathering and analysis of data: Kazuo Abiko, Ann Bethel, Susan Castledine, Jacqueline Cartier, Mulakh Dua, Judy Elias, Janice Feldstein, Harry Gilbert, Kathleen Goldman, Anita Klaz, Dongchin Lee, Greg Lewis, Charles Mayes, John Michaeli, and Marva Washington.

CONTENTS

Summary of Findings, POMCT (The Project on Media Coverage of Terrorism) Project #1, Data Released August 17, 1977. 166

Summary of Findings, POMCT Project #2, Data Released October 31, 1977. 169

Summary of Findings, POMCT Project #3, Data Released August 17, 1978. 177

Implications and Recommendations, 1979. 185

POMCT PROJECT #1, DATA RELEASED AUGUST 17, 1977

SUMMARY

This study of the police chiefs of the Nations's 30 most populated cities indicated the chiefs believed television reporters have generally not done a good job of covering terrorism and that live television coverage of terrorism encourages it.

More than half of the chiefs replied to a questionnaire about television coverage of terrorism mailed in May 1977.

In April 1977, the Gallup Poll found that Americans were divided about whether the media should give complete, detailed coverage to acts of terrorism. This survey sought to investigate "how the guys on the firing line, the police chiefs, felt." As expected, the police chiefs were not favorable in their reactions to television coverage of terrorist activities or about TV reporters who cover terrorism. Many had deep feelings about it and welcomed the chance to express them.

Among the major results of the survey reported in 1977:

- Ninety-three percent of the police chiefs believed live TV coverage of terrorist acts encourages terrorism.
- None of the big-city police chiefs surveyed believed that coverage of terrorist acts should be televised live. Sixty percent thought such TV coverage should be delayed or video taped, and 27 percent believed terrorist acts should not be covered by television.
- Forty-six percent of the police chiefs considered live television coverage of terrorist acts "a great threat" to hostage safety, and 33 percent considered it "a moderate threat." Only 7 percent considered it a minimal threat.
- More than half of the police chiefs had generally unfavorable judgments of on-the-scene television reporters covering terrorists. Twenty percent of the police chiefs believed TV reporters covering terrorist acts were "poor," and 33 percent believed they were "average." Only 20 percent believed that TV journalists covering terrorists were good.
- Sixty-seven percent of the police chiefs said TV journalists should only communicate with terrorists with official consent. Another 33 percent believed that under no circumstances should TV journalists communicate with terrorists while they are engaged in criminal activity.

Many police chiefs felt quite deeply about the necessary relationship be-

APPENDIX B

tween the media and police agencies in a democracy and wrote extensive comments.

Wrote one police chief: "It is very important for the police agencies to realize the press also has a duty to perform and a right to perform that duty." "The media must report a breaking news story but it must be put in perspective," added another.

"It is a delicate subject of critical concern to the safety of the community. Mature self-governing guidelines by the media and understanding of media by law enforcement is needed," added another.

"Widespread publication of details of incidents can foster future incidents or be utilized to improve future attempts. Also, details of how officials successfully concluded an incident can be utilized by those inclined to perpetrate a future incident," wrote one police chief.

Another wrote: "We are of the opinion that televising terrorist acts only seeks to instill increased aggressive demeanor in the terrorist(s) and promotes hostile behavior in individuals monitoring such coverage who advocate deviant conduct."

Another said: "It appears to be a case of monkey see, monkey do. There are times when police outwit the hostage taker, sometimes lie to him, or trick him. Some of these tactics lessen police credibility, and it becomes more challenging for the police negotiators to come up with new ways and means."

"On-scene liaison between police and media in keeping with a policy of department-wide openness and a program of ongoing liaison promotes a climate of mutual trust and understanding wherein the police and the media can fulfill their respective obligations to the public," stated a police chief.

Asked whether live TV coverage of terrorist acts encourages terrorism, one police chief commented, "It's probably a necessary evil." Another believed that television coverage encourages terrorism, "especially live coverage of terrorists' statements and demands which are calculated to exacerbate and expand the incident." Another added: "I would like to see a study done on this."

Asked whether they believed on-the-scene television reporters covering terrorists generally are excellent, good, average, or poor, the police chiefs commented:
- "It's generally good, but you certainly have both extremes."
- "The range perhaps runs from excellent to poor. All too often the 'spirit' of competition outweigh sound judgment or thought of the results."
- "The majority of the reporters ★ ★ ★ use good judgment and cooperate with the authorities, however when the mood of the reporters becomes competitive, their judgment decreases to a much lower level."

- "Hanafi terrorists in Washington, D.C. had the media furnishing intelligence from all TV angles, up to the minute. Phone lines used by media and conversations were highly dangerous. General opinion of police was that media was at its worst."

Should TV journalists communicate with terrorists while they are engaged in criminal activity? "No," said the police chiefs, "or at least not without official consent." And they added:

- "It gives an unnecessary power base and exposure to ne'er do wells."
- "It might be deemed appropriate for some situations. Without official consent, they might unknowingly work at odds or cross purposes with official action or non-action."
- "With official consent it is possible that the reporters might act in best interests of all or most of the parties."
- "Consent (should) only be given when this contact is neogtiated by the terrorist or when other positive benefits would result from this contact."

APPENDIX B

POMCT PROJECT #2, DATA RELEASED OCTOBER 31, 1977

SUMMARY

The second POMCT study, this one of police chiefs and television news directors in the country's largest cities, indicated both groups agreed with the then newly written CBS News guidelines for coverage of terrorist and hostage stories.

A questionnaire was mailed to police chiefs and television news directors in the Nation's 30 most populated cities regarding their attitudes toward the CBS News guidelines.

More than half of the police chiefs replied to the questionnaire about guidelines mailed in May 1977. Thirty-five percent of the television news directors in the same cities replied to an identical questionnaire mailed in August 1977.

Both the police chiefs and the television news directors appeared to agree with the CBS News guideline against live television coverage of the terrorist act "except in the most compelling circumstances."

According to the National News Council, at the time, four news organizations were known to have adopted guidelines for coverage of terrorism, and some were considering their adoption. The survey indicated that on the one hand, some journalists disagreed about the wisdom of adopting guidelines and on the other hand, there appeared to be some sentiment to adopt them, especially in view of the frequency of terrorist acts then being reported by the Nation's media.

The survey sought to establish, first, how the police chiefs, "the guys on the firing line," felt about guidelines on television coverage of terrorism and, in particular, about those of CBS News, the first broadcast news organization to propose them. It also sought to find out how television news directors, the persons who would implement these or similar guidelines, felt about them.

The survey indicated that both groups strongly agreed with the guidelines. But what remained to be seen was whether, despite their favoring the guidelines, significant numbers of television news organizations would actually adopt these or similar ones.

CBS News presented its seven guidelines in April 1977.

In the Project's survey, police chiefs and television news directors were asked to comment about them if they wished to do so.

Among the major results of the survey reported in 1977:

1. Seventy-three percent of the police chiefs and 87 percent of the television news directors agreed with the first CBS guideline which recommends that journalists should avoid providing excessive platforms for terrorists and, unless succinctly stated, paraphrase their demands.

The first CBS News guideline specifically states:

"An essential component of the story is the demands of the terrorist/kidnaper and we must report those demands. But we should avoid providing an excessive platform for the terrorist/kidnaper. Thus, unless such demands are succinctly stated and free of rhetoric and propaganda, it may be better to paraphrase the demands instead of presenting them directly through the voice or picture of the terrorist/kidnaper."

The survey revealed these attitudes toward this guideline:

	Agree	*Disagree*	*No Opinion*	*Other*
Police Chiefs	73%	7%	20%	0%
TV News Directors	87	5	5	3

Nearly half of the police chiefs expressed comments about the first CBS News guideline. One police chief stated: "The media should not report the specific demands but only the fact that demands have been made and that they are being negotiated. When demands are made public before resolution of the situation, the terrorists may change their position because the demands may make them lose 'face.' The public is entitled to the facts after the situation has been resolved." Another police chief stated: "I think CBS would assume the reporter does not read more into a terrorist's statement than is actually discernible." One police chief wrote extensive comments about a terrorist incident in Beilen, Holland. He said: "The terrorists demanded publicity regarding 'A Free and Independent South Mulucca' and prisoner release, else 1 person would die every 30 minutes. Three hostages were killed. The burden is on newspapers to do their wish or live with themselves afterwards."

Commenting on the same guideline, one television news director stated: "I don't think you can set firm guidelines for the news." Another indicated his disagreement with the guidelines, remarking, "Sometimes yes, sometimes

APPENDIX B

no." Yet another said, "Each situation is unique."

2. Ninety-three percent of the police chiefs and 81 percent of the television news directors agreed with the second CBS News guideline proposing no live coverage of a terrorist act. Significantly, this guideline was among two receiving the most agreement from police chiefs but also receiving the greatest percentage of disagreement from television news directors.

The second guideline states:

"Except in the most compelling circumstances, and then only with the approval of the President of CBS News, or in his absence, the Senior Vice President of News, there should be no live coverage of the terrorist/kidnaper, since we may fall into the trap of providing an unedited platform for him. (This does not limit live, on-the-spot reporting by CBS News reporters, but care should be exercised to assure restraint and context.)"

The survey revealed these attitudes toward this guideline:

	Agree	Disagree	No Opinion	Other
Police Chiefs	93%	7%	0%	0%
TV News Directors	81	13	3	3

The comments of police chiefs on the second CBS News guideline included: "It's the best of a bad bargain. I would prefer coverage afterwards, but realistically one cannot expect the media to censor and delay news." One police chief stated: "The authorities should have the final say on live coverage. If the media does decide to have live coverage, then the authorities should be advised." While this guideline was the one about which the most television news directors, 13 percent disagreed, few had comments to make about it. One stated: "I agree, but this sounds like double-talk."

3. Eighty-six percent of the police chiefs and 84 percent of the television news directors agreed with the third CBS guideline recommending that reporters be mindful of the need of authorities to communicate with terrorists by telephone and urging that reporters find out whether their use of such

lines would interfere with the communications of the authorities.

The third CBS News guideline states:

"News personnel should be mindful of the probable need by the authorities who are dealing with the terrorists for communication by telephone and hence should endeavor to ascertain, wherever feasible, whether our own use of such lines would be likely to interfere with the authorities' communications."

The survey revealed these attitudes toward this guideline:

	Agree	Disagree	No Opinion	Other
Police Chiefs	86%	7%	7%	0%
TV News Directors	84	5	3	8

One police chief commenting on the third CBS News guideline stated: "Newspersons should never communicate with terrorists unless requested to do so by authorities. Untrained persons, newspersons or others, should not talk to hostage takers." Another police chief stated: "The media should not try to contact terrorists. It's a police matter." Still another wrote: " 'Are you really going to kill all those people if your demands are not met?' Such questions gear up the hostage taker, and he might be goaded into action to prove himself. The situation would worsen by the spotlight of attention. The terrorist might want to look big."

The comments of television news directors on the guideline include: "We should not be trying to call the terrorist in the first place." One wrote: "We must not tie up phones into places where hostages are being held." Another television news director wrote: "I agree with the guideline, but it remains the option of news judgment."

4. Ninety percent of the television news directors and 86 percent of the police chiefs agreed with the fourth CBS News guideline which recommends that CBS News representatives contact experts dealing with the hostage situation to determine whether they have any guidance, but advises that such recommendations should be carefully considered as guidance and not as instruction.

APPENDIX B

The fourth CBS News guideline specifically states:

"Responsible CBS News representatives should endeavor to contact experts dealing with the hostage situation to determine whether they have any guidance on such questions as phraseology to be avoided, what kinds of questions or reports might tend to exacerbate the situation, etc. Any such recommendations by established authorities on the scene should be carefully considered as guidance (but not as instruction) by CBS News personnel."

The survey revealed these attitudes toward this guideline:

	Agree	Disagree	No Opinion
Police Chiefs	86%	7%	7%
TV News Directors	90	5	5

Several police chiefs commented on the fourth CBS News guideline. One stated: "Any recommendation given by the authorities should be considered as an instruction and it should be carried out to the letter. The decision of the authorities is based on all available facts known at the time." Another police chief wrote: "Consultation with public safety authorities on the scene should be included if the 'expert' consulted is not the police authority in charge." Yet another police chief commented: "This is a good idea. There are 'no-no's' and areas of sensitivity. Police have certain skills in negotiating with and understanding the criminal. We study, we learn, we do. A crash course is better than none."

One television news director, in commenting on this guideline, stressed, "The information should be instructional."

5. Ninety-three percent of the police chiefs and 90 percent of the television news directors agreed with the fifth CBS News guideline recommending that local authorities be given the names of CBS personnel whom they can contact should they have further guidance about newsperson's calls to terrorists or matters which might interfere with the authorities dealing with the terrorists.

The fifth CBS News guideline specifically states:

"Local authorities should also be given the name or names of CBS personnel whom they can contact should they have further guidance or wish to deal with such delicate questions as a newsman's call to the terrorists or other matters which might interfere with authorities dealing with the terrorists."

The survey revealed these attitudes toward this guideline:

	Agree	*Disagree*	*No Opinion*
Police Chiefs	93%	7%	0%
TV News Directors	90	5	5

One police chief commented on this guideline: "There should be no calls to the terrorists." Another police chief stated: "This might prevent a reporter from going the limit to make a scoop. We experienced this in the riots of 1967. National network television crews incited young people to perform to obtain live action film."

Commenting on the guideline, one television news director stated: "There are no firm rules here." Another stated: "It should be the other way around. Local authorities are too busy to contact the media in such a situation."

6. Ninety-four percent of the television news directors and 86 percent of the police chiefs agreed with the CBS News guideline recommending that reporters covering terrorist acts should avoid the use of inflammatory language and the reporting of rumors and obey all police instructions, reporting those instructions to their superiors, however, which seem intended to manage or suppress the news.

The sixth CBS News guideline specifically states:

"Guidelines affecting our coverage of civil disturbances are also applicable here, especially those which relate to avoiding the use of inflammatory catchwords or phrases, the reporting of rumors, etc. As in the case of policy dealing with civil disturbances, in dealing with a hostage story reporters should obey

APPENDIX B   175

all police instructions but report immediately to their superiors any such instructions that seem to be intended to manage or suppress the news."

The survey revealed these attitudes toward this guideline:

	Agree	Disagree	No Opinion	Other
Police Chiefs	86%	7%	7%	0%
TV News Directors	94	0	3	3

One police chief commented on this guideline: "Media superiors should then discuss these instructions with the police authorities, particularly if they do not feel the instructions should continue to be honored. It is hoped that these discussions would occur prior to the publication of any report that would be contrary to the police instructions." Another police chief stated: "There is a thin line between supression of news and completing the police mission." Yet another police chief wrote: "What is interpreted by the reporters as supression may not be the case at hand, merely a matter of semantics." One police chief said: "If we want cooperation, we must give cooperation. It is a two-way street. Common sense and good judgment work toward the best interests of the public and private sectors."

Several television news directors also commented on this guideline. One stated: "This gives flexibility to ignore authorities' wishes, and so is needed." Another wrote: "I agree, except that often such police orders are simply self-serving or designed to keep the story from being covered." Another television news director said: "I believe reporters should use their judgment at the scene, but should also report police actions to their superiors." Echoing this sentiment, another television news director remarked: "I agree in part. Qualified reporters should use their own discretion. In this situation, there may not be time to hold a conference."

7. Eighty-six percent of the police chiefs and 87 percent of the television news directors agreed with the CBS News guideline recommending that coverage of terrorist acts should be in such overall balance as to length that it does not unduly crowd out other important news.

The seventh CBS News guideline specifically states:

"Coverage of this kind of story should be in such overall balance as to length, that it does not unduly crowd out other important news of the hour/day."

The survey revealed these attitudes toward the guideline:

	Agree	Disagree	No Opinion	Other
Police Chiefs	86%	0%	14%	0%
TV News Directors	87	5	3	5

Commenting on this guideline, one police chief wrote: "The magnitude of the story will dictate this."

A television news director, commenting on this guideline, said: "Sometimes special open-ended coverage is justified." Another television news director stated: "I think the nature of this story would force it to get greater length than a normal news story." Yet another wrote: "This is double-talk. The story should get the play it demands based on existing circumstances."

One television news director, who had extensive experience with a hostage situation, wrote several comments on his experience and decried the need for guidelines.

He wrote: "No answers are really possible. It seems to me circumstances will dictate answers to these questions and the answers in any one case may be totally different from another. If one, for instance, laid down an unbreakable rule that no terrorist would appear live, what happens when said terrorist says he'll kill hostages unless he gets coverage? This happened in Indianapolis and Cleveland."

"No set of rules are reliable in these situations. Decisions must be made on the spot, and news executives will not be able to rely on many guidelines to bail them out."

"The CBS rules read well, but my argument holds here, too."

"We have, however, found a couple of standards which seem to cover the situations.

1. Reporters are to avoid making themselves part of the story.
2. No calls will be placed into the hostages, terrorists, or 'holed up.'
3. The most important rule of all is we will do nothing to further endanger life. If this means losing competitive advantage, so be it."

"These are rather simple rules, obviously, but in my opinion, the more specific and complex ones don't work."

APPENDIX B

POMCT PROJECT #3, DATA RELEASED AUGUST 17, 1978

SUMMARY

The third POMCT study indicated that the Nation's police chiefs and media differ about the coverage of terrorism and disagree about whether media coverage encourages terrorism, whether it is a threat to hostage safety, and whether journalists should communicate with terrorists.

This study surveyed the attitudes toward terrorism coverage held by police chiefs, television and radio news directors, and newspaper editors in the Nation's 30 most populated cities and involved comparing the results of 4 national surveys.

The research appeared to show that police were concerned about the effects of media coverage on hostage and public safety and on imitation. On the other hand, the media were concerned about the people's right to know, press freedom, and responsible coverage. Three phrases commonly used by both groups, though they differed on how best to cover terrorism, were "common sense, responsibility, and caution." There appeared to be no easy answers to the coverage of terrorism.

Media and police indicated the necessity of proceeding forward with responsibility, taking care to endanger neither lives nor the people's right to know where knowledge is vital. Attitudes indicated the coverage of terrorism to be at best an excruciating business, exacting great pressures on public authorities and the media alike. Neither censorship nor scoop-happy reporting got high marks. Many respondents believed terrorist coverage called for difficult decisions under difficult circumstances from able minds. On balance, both the police and the media appeared to be aware of coverage problems and appeared to be trying to be as responsible and cooperative as they could.

Among the highlights of the research reported in 1978:

1. *The nation's police chiefs and some of the media agreed that live television coverage of terrorist acts encourages terrorism.* Nearly all of the police chiefs (93 percent) believed it does. Forth-three percent of newspaper editors also believed that it does, but one third (33 percent) did not, and 24 percent said it depended on the circumstances. Television news directors were evenly divided on the question, with 35 percent believing that live television coverage of terrorist acts encouraged terrorism and 35 percent believing it did not.

Nearly a quarter of the television news directors, or 24 percent, believed that it depended on the circumstances.

QUESTION: Do you believe live television coverage of terrorist acts encourages terrorism?

	No	Other	Don't Know or No Answer
Police Chiefs	0%	7%	0%
TV News Directors	35	24	6
Newspaper Editors	33	24	0

2. *The media and police chiefs differed sharply about to what extent live television coverage of terrorist acts constituted a threat to hostage safety.* As reported by the project in August 1977, nearly one-half (46 percent) of the police chiefs considered live television coverage of terrorists acts a "great threat" to hostage safety, one-third (33 percent) considered it a "moderate threat," and 7 percent considered it a "minimal threat." Only 3 percent of the television news directors and none of the newspaper editors considered live TV coverage a "great threat." However, twice as many newspaper editors considered live television coverage of terrorist acts a "minimal threat" as did television news directors. Television news directors were divided and appeared somewhat unsure about to what extent live TV coverage of terrorism is a threat to hostage safety, with nearly one-third (32 percent) considering it a "minimal threat," another 32 percent considering it a "moderate threat" and 27 percent indicating that it depended on the circumstances. Nearly a third of all 3 groups considered live TV coverage a "moderate threat."

QUESTION: To what extent do you consider live television coverage terrorists acts a threat to hostage safety?

	Minimal Threat	Moderate Threat	Great Threat	Other	Don't Know
Police Chiefs	7%	33%	46%	7%	7%
TV News Directors	32	32	3	27	6
Newspaper Editors	67	29	0	4	0

3. *The Nation's police chiefs differed sharply with television news directors about whether television news reporters should communicate with terrorists while the terrorists are engaged in criminal activity.* One-third of the police chiefs (33 percent) believed that under no circumstances should TV journalists communicate with terrorists and more than two-thirds of the chiefs (67 percent) believed that TV journalists should communicate with terrorists only with official consent. However, only 13 percent of the television news directors believed that under no circumstances should a TV journalist communicate with a terrorist, and more than one-third (38 percent) believed communication should take place with official consent. More than a quarter (27 percent) of the TV news directors believed that communication with terrorists should take place at the media's own discretion, and more than one-fifth (22 percent) believed communication with terrorists should depend on the circumstances.

QUESTION: Should TV journalists communicate with terrorists while the terrorists are engaged in criminal activity?

Circumstances

	Under No Circumstances	With Official Consent	At Media's Own Discretion	Other/ Depends on Circumstances
Police Chiefs	33%	67%	0%	0%
TV New Directors	13	38	27	22

4. *A plurality of all 3 media groups (38 percent of the TV news directors, 33 percent of the radio news directors, and 38 percent of the newspaper editors) believed that communication with terrorists engaged in terrorist activity should take place with official consent, but more than a quarter of all 3 groups (27 percent of the TV news directors, 26 percent of the radio news directors, and 33 percent of the newspaper editors) believed that communication with terrorists engaged in criminal activity could take place at the media's own discretion. Conversely, only a minority of all 3 media groups (13 percent of the TV news directors, 20 percent of the radio news directors, and 10 percent of the newspaper editors) believed that no communication should take place with terrorists engaged in criminal activity under any circumstances.*

QUESTION: Should journalists communicate with terrorists while the terrorists are engaged in criminal activity?

	Under No Circumstances	With Official Consent	At Media's Own Discretion	Other
TV News Directors	13%	38%	27%	22%
Radio News Directors	20	33	26	21
Newspaper Editors	10	38	33	19

5. As reported by the project in August 1977, *more than half of the police chiefs (53 percent) believed the judgments of on-the-scene television reporters covering terrorist stories were "average" or "poor."* One-fifth (20 percent) of the police chiefs believed television reporters covering terrorist acts were "poor," and one-third (33 percent) believed they were "average." Only 20 percent believed that TV journalists covering terrorists were "good." Television news directors to some degree agreed with police chiefs in assessing the performance of TV reporters but gave them slightly better marks. Less than half as many television news directors as police chiefs (8 percent to 20 percent) believed that TV reporters covering terrorists acts were "poor."

APPENDIX B

QUESTION: Do you believe the judgment of on-the-scene television reporters covering terrorists generally is:

	Excellent	Good	Average	Poor	Don't Know	No Answer	Other
Police Chiefs	13%	20%	33%	20%	0%	14%	0%
TV News Directors	13	30	35	8	3	3	8

6. *Radio news directors gave radio news reporters covering terrorist acts slightly higher marks than did television news directors for television journalists.* More than half of the radio news directors (54 percent) believed the judgment of on-the-scene radio reporters covering terrorist stories generally was "excellent" or "good" while 43 percent of the television news directors gave television reporters similar ratings.

QUESTION: Do you believe the judgment of on-the-scene television/radio reporters covering terrorists generally is:

	Excellent	Good	Average	Poor	Don't Know	No Answer	Other
TV News Directors	13%	30%	35%	8%	3%	13%	8%
Radio News Directors	10	44	25	8	1	0	12

7. *Newspaper editors, by nearly a two-to-one majority (57 percent to 29 percent), did not believe newspaper coverage of terrorist acts encourages terrorism.* However, radio news directors were nearly evenly divided with 42 percent believing live radio coverage of terrorist acts does not encourage terrorism, but 36 percent saying it does.

QUESTION OF NEWSPAPER EDITORS: Do you believe newspaper coverage of terrorist acts encourages terrorism?

	Yes	No	Other
Newspaper Editors	29%	57%	14%

QUESTION OF RADIO NEWS DIRECTORS: Do you believe live radio coverage of terrorist acts encourages terrorism?

	Yes	No	Other	Don't Know
Radio News Directors	36%	42%	21%	1%

8. *The Nation's police chiefs and television news directors differed sharply on whether television coverage of terrorist acts should be broadcast live, delayed, or blacked out.* As reported by the project in August 1977, none of the big-city police chiefs surveyed believed that coverage of terrorist acts should be televised live. Sixty percent thought such TV coverage should be delayed or video taped, and 27 percent believed terrorist acts should not be covered by television. However, while 8 percent of the television news directors believed TV coverage of terrorist acts should be carried live, only 19 percent believed it should be delayed or video taped for later broadcast. Nearly two-thirds (65 percent) of the TV news directors believed the decision should be based on the circumstances. Only 5 percent of the television news directors believed in blacking out TV coverage altogether.

QUESTION: Do you believe radio coverage of terrorist acts should be:

	Live	Delayed—(Taped)	Blacked Out	Other	Don't Know
Police Chiefs	0%	60%	27%	13%	0%
Radio News Directors	8	19	5	65	3

APPENDIX B

9. *A plurality of radio news directors (36 percent) favored live radio coverage of terrorist acts, however, nearly an equal number (35 percent) said live radio coverage depends on the circumstances.* Nearly one-quarter (24 percent) favored delayed or taped coverage. Only 5 percent of the radio news directors favored blacked-out coverage.

QUESTION: Do you believe radio coverage of terrorist acts should be:

	Live	Delayed—(Taped)	Blacked Out	Other
Radio News Directors	36%	24%	5%	35%

10. *When TV news directors, radio news directors, and newspaper editors were asked what extent they considerd their own media's live or immediate coverage terrorist acts a threat to hostage safety, all three appeared to agree that immediacy of coverage, using their own media, constitutes only a minimal threat. However, newspaper editors and radio news directors appeared more certain than television news directors who are in charge of a live, visual medium.*

QUESTION: To what extent do you consider live/immediate coverage of terrorist acts a threat to hostage safety?

	Minimal Threat	Moderate Threat	Great Threat	Other	Don't Know
TV News Directors	32%	32%	3%	27%	6%
Radio News Directors	47	19	14	17	3
Newspaper Editors	76	19	0	5	0

Moreover, all three media groups agreed that live or immediate coverage of terrorist acts does not constitute a "great threat" to hostage safety.

11. *While nearly two-thirds of radio stations (65 percent) had a policy concerning the coverage of terrorist acts, one-third (33 percent) did not, and more than half (52 percent) of the newspapers also did not have such a policy.*

QUESTION: Do you have a policy concerning coverage of terrorist acts?

	Yes	No	Other	No Answer
Radio News Directors	65%	33%	1%	1%
Newspaper Editors	38	52	10	0

12. *Overwhelmingly, newspaper editors believed in normal coverage of terrorist acts and would resort neither to censorship nor to printing special editions in reporting such activities.*

QUESTION: Do you believe newspaper coverage of terrorist acts should be:

	Printed in a Special Edition	Printed in the Next Regular Edition	Held, until . . .
Newspaper Editors	0%	100%	0%

APPENDIX B

IMPLICATIONS AND RECOMMENDATIONS, 1979

We view the foregoing surveys as very modest research in a decidedly needed area of inquiry. At best, the research, limited by inadequacies of design and funds, points to the need for more and better research.

This research, as all scholarship, also reflects the backgrounds, insights, and, no doubt, the biases of the authors. Our backgrounds are in journalism, law, psychology, sociology, and politics, with whatever merits and demerits these fields bring to an inquiry of this kind. Our backgrounds also reflect experience in police reporting, although our deficiencies in criminology and some other fields were painful to us.

These inadequacies, however, ironically allowed us to opine that research in terrorism needs either Renaissance persons or very skilled teams specializing in a variety of areas. Furthermore, in our view, any useful approach to understanding the complexities of media coverage of terrorism needs an understanding of the unique problems of journalism, police science, politics, psychology, and a host of other disciplines.

Our initial review of the literature, undertaken in 1977, indicated not only a paucity of knowledge about media coverage of terrorism, but also a lack of meaningful interdisciplinary approaches to the topic. The latter, in our view, has hurt useful inquiry into this occasionally and lately alarming political and social phenomenon. Bluntly, we found too many times to our liking that some journalists, police, psychiatrists, and others were mistaken or talking through their hats. Often they simply did not have, or did not care to have, sufficient, qualitative background or experience in the problems of other disciplines involved in terrorism that they were analyzing.

We have discussed the results of our research with some European journalists and government officials, particularly in West Germany, England, France, Austria, and Sweden. We found these spirited discussions mainly that: spirited. Often they were limited in value for an American investigator's inquiry into the special problems of media coverage of terrorism that we face in this country. European terrorism, thankfully, is different from our own variety in kind and intensity, and our Constitution and political and journalistic traditions are decidedly different. For good or bad, we are carriers of the libertarian banner.

We should warn against being trapped by some European research approaches and philosophical concepts in approaching this inquiry. But we would at the same time also warn against not heeding some of the lessons the Europeans have to offer.

Our major problem, however, was not with our European friends, but with some American peers.

A major criticism of journalists, police, and academics working the vineyards of this field could well be that too many tend to pluck self-fulfilling sour grapes. From journalists, we hear too many well-intentioned but curiously pious statements about "the right to know" and real or imagined threats to first-amendment freedoms and the need for better self-regulation when occasionally unintelligent, inexperienced, and unthinking if not irresponsible reporting is the real problem. From police, we hear too many misplaced notions of the media as sensationalistic, leftwing deadbeats. And one even hears a psychologist or two arguing that: "I'm the guy you really want to listen to."

Nonsense. No one discipline or profession yet has a good handle on the multiple and complex problems of media coverage of terrorism. We urge all parties in good faith to open their eyes, ears, minds, and hearts, to learn from each other, and, above all, to cooperate with each other. Now.

Journalists are expected to find out and report whatever they can, within the bounds of law and ethics. Police should not expect anything less from them. They will seldom get it, not if the journalist is a good professional. Most journalists, overwhelmingly so, are responsible professionals. And, when you come right down to it, it's to the police' advantage to have them there, provided they do not cause injury to life, limb, or property, for two reasons: First, by informing, they allay public suspicion, fear, and panic. Second, many police find it advantageous to have the media present "to set the record straight" for the public constituency that both groups serve, though both have been known to forget that.

Of course, police will also find unintelligent, inexperienced, unthinking and, quite occasionally, irresponsible journalists. But, thankfully, there are not many of them and, when they are found out, most are unceremoniously disengaged by a profession that surely does not want or need them around. Responsible police officials are mandated to follow the same credo with respect to their undesirables.

Most police must be admired and respected for putting their lives on the line every day. They and their families suffer the myriad psychological scars that no journalist could adequately portray.

Some of the authors' best friends happen to be policemen, and we are second to none in our appreciation and awe of them. We would not want their jobs. We lack their devotion, courage, and willingness to serve every second of every day in tense public service at insufficient pay. And were the

APPENDIX B

pay sufficient, it would never be enough.

However, these same police friends, as we have told them, would do well to better understand the unique place of the media in the history and daily survival of this country. Without the media we might have police, but not a democracy, not America.

Therefore, a real, not cursory understanding of the media, not just by superior officers but by policemen and policewomen "down the line" is essential toward the betterment of police and media relations in general and the coverage of terrorism in particular.

The reverse, of course, holds true for journalists.

Let there be constant seminars, interchanges, communication and, above all, reasoned understanding between police and journalists. In the absence of it, we will pay for our pettiness and pride.

And, let Government, foundations, news organizations, police organizations, indeed any suitable group interested in the betterment of this precious country open up its treasuries to spur research and meaningful interaction between journalists, police, psychologists, and other parties in the pursuit of knowledge, not self-serving biases.

And let us pursue both research and cooperation with all deliberate speed. Because for all journalists, police, and psychologists alike know about the problems, complexities, and results of media coverage of terrorism, they really don't know very much.

We continue to muddle along, pretending we know some truths, talking through our hats, trumpeting our biases, or we can take a better approach: we can get at some truths.

The truth, He said, shall make us free. It will also help us to understand the complex and difficult problems and results of the American media's coverage of terrorism, allowing for both the people to be adequately informed and the police to protect the public safety.

If these are indeed our goals, and let us first agree that they are, then let us get on with realizing them. Now.

BIBLIOGRAPHY

TERRORISM AND THE MASS MEDIA: A RESEARCHER'S BIBLIOGRAPHY

Richard L. Moreland
and
Michael L. Berbaum

Modern-day terrorism makes the issue of a possible relationship between exposure to the mass media and subsequent violent behavior more urgent than ever before. Unfortunately, while many people have strong opinions about the relationship between terrorism and the mass media, few have actually performed any research on it. Our bibliography is intended to aid anyone who might be planning such research. We have attempted to include a wide selection of relevant materials from such fields as psychology, sociology, communications, journalism, and law that might help to answer some of the questions that must arise in any investigation of the relationship between terrorism and the mass media. Inevitably, some interesting work has been omitted because of space limitations or has been simply overlooked. Nevertheless, we feel that we have been able to collect most of the major references in this topic area.

Entries in the bibliography are all presented according to A.P.A. style. Journal articles include title, journal, year, volume, and pages in that order. Dates are given for magazine articles; book references are standard. Order numbers, where known, are given for materials available through the National Criminal Justice Reference Service (NCJRS).

Akers, R. *Deviant behavior: A social learning approach.* Belmont, Calif.: Wadsworth, 1973.
Alexander, Y. *The role of communications in the Middle East conflict: Ideological and religious perspectives.* New York: Praeger, 1973.

Alexander, Y. Some perspectives on international terrorism. *International Problems*, 1975, *14*(3–4), 24–29.
Alexander, Y. (Ed.). *International terrorism: National, regional, and global perspectives*. New York: Praeger, 1976.
Alexander, Y. Communications aspects of international terrorism. *International Problems*. 1977, *16*, 55–60.
Alexander, Y. Terrorism and the media in the Middle East. In Y. Alexander & S.M. Finger (Eds.), *Terrorism: Interdisciplinary perspectives*. New York: John Jay, 1977.
Alexander, Y. Terrorism, the media, and the police. *Journal of International Affairs*, 1978, *32*, 101–113.
Alexander, Y. Terrorism and the media: Some considerations. In Y. Alexander, D. Carlton & P. Wilkinson (Eds.), *Terrorism: Theory and practice*. Boulder, Colo.: Westview Press, 1979.
Alexander, Y., Carlton D., & Wilkinson, P. (Eds.). *Terrorism: Theory and practice*. Boulder, Colo.: Westview Press, 1979.
Alexander, Y., & Finger, S.M. (Eds.). *Terrorism: Interdisciplinary perspectives*. New York: John Jay, 1977.
Alexander, Y., & Finger, S.M. Terrorism and the media. *Terrorism*, 1979, *2*, 55–137.
Allen, T., & Piland, R.M. Bungling assassins rate page one. *Journal of Communication*, 1976, *26*(4), 98–101.
Allport, G.W., & Postman, L. *The psychology of rumor*. New York: Holt, 1947.
Altheide, D.L. *Creating reality: How TV news distorts events*. Beverly Hills, Calif.: Sage Publications, 1976.
Andel, W.M. von. Media in gijzeling [Media and the taking of hostages]. *Algemeen Politieblad*, 1975, *124*(16), 384–386. (NCJRS 28281)
Andison, F.S. TV violence and viewer aggression: A cumulation of study results, 1956–1976. *Public Opinion Quarterly*, 1977, *41*, 314–331.
Arendt, H. *On violence*. New York: Harcourt, Brace & World, 1969.
Armor, D.J. Measuring the effects of television on aggressive behavior. Santa Monica, Calif.: Rand Corporation, 1976.
Arnold, M. Assassination attempts spark controversy over news media. *New York Times*, September 28, 1975, p.52.
Australian Broadcasting Tribunal. *Self-regulation for broadcasting*? Canberra: Australian Government Publishing Service, 1977.
Bailey, N.T. *The mathematical theory of epidemics* New York: Hafner, 1957.
Baker, R.K., & Ball, S.J. (Eds.). *Violence and the media: A staff report to the National Commission on the Causes and Prevention of Violence*. Washington, D.C.: U.S. Government Printing Office, 1969.
Baldwin, T.F., & Lewis, C. Violence in television: The industry looks at itself. In G.A. Comstock & E.A. Rubinstein (Eds.), *Television and social behavior* (Vol. 1). Washington, D.C.: U.S. Government Printing Office, 1971.
Ball, S. Methodological problems in assessing the impact of television programs. *Journal of Social Issues*, 1976, *32*, 8–17.

BIBLIOGRAPHY

Ball-Pokeach, S.J., & DeFleur, M.L. A dependency model of mass-media effects. *Communication Research*, 1976, *3*, 3–21.

Bandura, A. *Aggression: A social learning analysis.* Englewood Cliffs, N.J.: Prentice-Hall, 1973.

Baraclough, B., Shepard, D., & Jennings, C. Do newspaper reports of coroners' inquests incite people to commit suicide? *British Journal of Psychiatry*, 1977, *131*, 528–532.

Bassiouni, M.C. (Ed.). *International terrorism and political crimes.* Springfield, Ill.: Charles Thomas, 1975.

Bauer, R.A., & Bauer, A.H. America, mass society, and mass media. *Journal of Social Issues*, 1960, *16*, 3–66.

Bedell, S. Is TV exploiting tragedy? *TV Guide*, June 16, 1979, 4–8.

Bell, J.B. *Transnational terror.* Washington, D.C.: American Enterprise Institute for Public Policy Research, 1975.

Bell, J.B. Trends on terror: The analysis of political violence. *World Politics*, 1977, *29*, 476–488.

Bell, J.B. *A time of terror: How democratic societies respond to revolutionary violence*, New York: Basic Books, 1978.

Belson, W.A. A technique for studying the effects of a television broadcast. *Applied Statistics*, 1956, *5*, 195–202.

Belson, W.A. Measuring the effects of television: A description of method. *Public Opinion Quarterly*, 1958, *22*, 11–18

Belson. W.A. *The impact of television.* Melbourne: Cheshire, 1967.

Berelson, B. Events as an influence on public opinion. *Journalism Quarterly*, 1949, 26, 145–148.

Berger, S. Conditioning through vicarious instigation. *Psychological Review*, 1962, *69*, 405–456.

Berkowitz, L. *Aggression: A social psychological analysis.* New York: McGraw-Hill, 1962.

Berkowitz, L. The contagion of violence: An S-R mediational analysis of some effect of observed aggression. In W.J. Arnold & M.M. Page (Eds.), *Nebraska Symposium on Motivation* (Vol. 18). Lincoln, Nebr.: University of Nebraska Press, 1970.

Berkowitz, L., & Edfeldt, A.W. *Report from a media violence symposium in Stockholm.* Stockholm: University of Stockholm, 1974.

Berkowitz, L., & Macauley, J. The contagion of criminal violence. *Sociometry*, 1971, *34*, 238–260.

Biller, O.A. Suicide related to the assassination of President John F. Kennedy. *Suicide and Life-Threatening Behavior*, 1977, *7*(1), 40–44.

Blumenthal, S., & Bergner, L. Suicide and newspapers: A replicated study. *American Journal of Psychiatry*, 1973, *130*(4), 471–491.

Blumer, H. *Movies and conduct.* New York: MacMillan, 1933.

Blumer, H. Suggestions for the study of mass-media effects. In E. Burdick & A.J. Brodbeck (Eds.), *American voting behavior.* Glencoe, Ill.: The Free Press, 1959.

Blumer, H., & Hauser, R.M. *Movies, delinquency, and crime.* New York:

MacMillan, 1933.
Blumler, J., & Katz, E. *The uses of mass communications.* Beverly Hills: Sage Publications, 1973.
Bogart, L. American television: A brief survey of research findings. *Journal of Social Issues,* 1962, *18,* 36–42.
Bogart, L. How the public gets its news. *Newspaper Readership Report,* 1978, *2,* 1–3.
Bortz, J., & Braune, P. The effects of daily newspapers on their readers: Exemplary presentation of a study and its results. *European Journal of Social Psychology,* 1980, *10,* 165–193.
Boston, G.D. *Terrorism: Supplement to the second edition. A selected bibliography.* Washington, D.C.: National Institute of Law Enforcement and Criminal Justice, Law Enforcement Assistance Administration, U.S. Department of Justice, 1977.
Boston, G.D., O'Brian, K., & Palumbo, J. *Terrorism: A selected bibliography* (2nd Ed.). Washington, D.C.: National Institute of Law Enforcement and Criminal Justice, Law Enforcement Assistance Administration, U.S. Department of Justice, 1977.
Bower, R.T. *Television and the public.* New York: Holt, Rinehart, & Winston, 1973.
Boyanowsky, E.O., Newtson, D., & Walster, E. Film preferences following a murder. *Communications Research,* 1974, *1,* 32–43.
Brandenburg v. Ohio, 395 U.S. 444 (1969).
Branzburg v. Hayes, 408 U.S. 665 (1972).
Brown, R.W. Mass phenomena. In G. Lindzey (Ed.), *Handbook of social psychology* (Vol. 2). Cambridge, Mass.: Addison-Wesley, 1954.
Browne, M., & Nanes, A.S. *International terrorism.* Washington, D.C.: Library of Congress, 1978.
Buckalew, J.K. News elements and selection by television news editors. *Journal of Broadcasting,* 1969–70, *14,* 47–54.
Buckley, A.D. (Ed.) International terrorism. *Journal of International Affairs,* 1978, *32,* 1–147.
Burnet, M. *The mass media in a violent world.* New York: UNESCO Workshops, 1971.
Burton, A.M. *Urban terrorism: Theory, practice and response.* New York: Free Press, 1976.
Buss, A.H. *The psychology of aggression.* New York: Wiley, 1961.
Cantor, M. *Prime-time television: Content and control.* Beverly Hills, Calif.: Sage, 1980.
Cantril, H. *The psychology of social movements.* New York: Wiley, 1941.
Carlton, D., & Schaerf, C. (Eds.). *International terrorism and world security.* New York: John Wiley, 1975.
Carter, D., & Adler, R. (Eds.). *Television as a social force: New approaches to TV criticism.* New York: Praeger, 1975.
Carter, D., & Strickland, S. *TV violence and the child: The evolution and fate*

of the Surgeon General's Report. New York: Russell Sage Foundation, 1975.

Carter, R.E. Newspaper gatekeepers and the sources of news. *Public Opinion Quarterly,* 1958, *22,* 133–144.

Carter, R.F., & Greenberg, B.S. Newspapers or television: Which do you believe? *Journalism Quarterly,* 1965, *42,* 29–34.

Catton, W.R. Militants and the media: Partners in terrorism? *Indiana Law Journal,* 1978, *53,* 703–715.

Causes of suicide: A mentally infectious disease. *Times* (London), March 28, 1931, p.8.

Central Intelligence Agency. *Annotated bibliography on transnational and international terrorism.* Washington, D.C., 1976

Central Intelligence Agency, National Foreign Assessment Center. *International and transnational terrorism: Diagnosis and prognosis.* (RP 76-10030, April 1976)

Central Intelligence Agency, National Foreign Assessment Center. *International terrorism in 1976.* (RP 77-100034U, July 1977)

Central Intelligence Agency, National Foreign Assessment Center. *International terrorism in 1977.* (RP 78-10255U, August 1978)

Central Intelligence Agency, National Foreign Assessment Center. *International terrorism in 1978.* (RP 79-10149, March 1979)

Chaffee, S.H. Television and adolescent aggressiveness. In G.A. Comstock & E.A. Rubinstein (Eds.), *Television and social behavior* (Vol. 3). Washington, D.C.: U.S. Government Printing Office, 1971.

Chaffee, S.H. The interpersonal context of mass communication. In F.G. Kline & P.J. Tichenon (Eds.), *Current perspectives in mass communication.* Beverly Hills, Calif.: Sage Publications, 1972.

Chaffee, S.H., Ward, L.S., & Tipton, L. Mass communication and political socialization. *Journalism Quarterly,* 1970, *47,* 647–659.

Clark, D., & Blankenburg, W. Trends in violent content in selected mass media. In G. Comstock & E. Rubinstein (Eds.), *Television and social behavior (Vol. 1).* Washington, D.C.: U.S. Government Printing Office, 1970.

Clark, D.G., & Hutchison, E.R. (Eds.). *Mass media and the law.* New York: Wiley, 1970.

Clarke, P., & Ruggels, L. Preferences among news media for coverage of public affairs. *Journalism Quarterly,* 1970, *47,* 464–471.

Clinard, M. *Sociology of deviant behavior.* New York: Holt, Rinehart, & Winston, 1968.

Clutterbuck, R.L. *Protest and the urban guerrilla.* New York: Abelard-Schuman, 1974.

Clutterbuck, R.L. *Living with terrorism.* New York: Arlington House, 1975.

Clutterbuck, R.L. *Guerillas and terrorists.* London: Faber and Faber, 1977.

Clutterbuck, R.L. *Britain in agony: The growth of political violence.* London: Faber & Faber, 1978.

Clutterbuck, R.L. *Kidnap and ransom: The response.* London & Boston: Faber, 1978.
Coffin, T.E. Television's impact on society. *American Psychologist,* 1955, *10,* 630–641.
Cohen, S. The evidence so far. *Journal of Communication,* 1975, *25,* 14–24.
Coleman, J.S., Katz, E., & Menzel, H. The diffusion of an innovation among physicians. *Sociometry,* 1957, *20,* 253–270.
Collier, D., & Messick, R.E. Prerequisites versus diffusion: Testing alternative explanations of social security adoption. *American Political Science Review,* 1975, *69,* 1299–1315.
Comay, M. Political terrorism. *Mental Health and Society,* 1976, *3*(5–6), 249–261.
Comstock, G. *Television and human behavior: The key studies.* Santa Monica, Calif.: Rand Corporation, 1976.
Comstock, G. *The evidence on television violence.* Santa Monica, Calif.: Rand Corporation, 1976.
Comstock, G. The role of social and behavioral science in policymaking for television. *Journal of Social Issues,* 1976, *32*(4), 157–178.
Comstock, G. *Television in America.* Beverly Hills, Calif.: Sage, 1980.
Comstock, G., Chaffee, S., Katzman, N., McCombs, M., & Roberts, D. *Television and human behavior.* New York: Columbia University Press, 1978.
Comstock, G., & Fisher, M. *Television and human behavior: A guide to the pertinent scientific literature.* Santa Monica, Calif.: Rand Corporation, 1975.
Comstock, G., Lindsey, G., & Fisher, M. *Television and human behavior.* Santa Monica, Calif.: Rand Corporation, 1975.
Comstock, G.A., & Rubinstein, E.A. (Eds.). *Television and social behavior, Volume 1: Content and controls.* Washington, D.C.: U.S. Government Printing Office, 1971.
Comstock, G.A., & Rubinstein, E.A. *Television and social behavior, Volume 3: Television and adolescent aggressiveness.* Washington, D.C.: U.S. Government Printing Office, 1971.
Comstock, G.A., Rubinstein, E.A. & Murray, J.P. *Television and social behavior, Volume 5: Television's effects: Further explorations.* Washington, D.C.: U.S. Government Printing Office, 1971.
Cooper, H.H.A. Terrorism and the media. In Y. Alexander & S.M. Finger (Eds.), *Terrorism: Interdisciplinary perspectives.* New York: John Jay Press, 1977.
Coxe, B. *Terrorism.* Air Force Academy, Colo.: Air Force Academy Library, 1977.
Crelinsten, R.D., Laberge, A., & Szabo, D. *Terrorism and criminal justice: An international perspective.* Lexington, Mass.: D.C. Heath, 1978.
Crime and the cinema in the United States. *International Review of Education Cinematography,* 1929, *!,* 303–314.
Czerniejewski, H.J. Guidelines for the coverage of terrorism. *Quill,* 1977,

July-August, 21–23.
Daley, C.U. (Ed.). *The media and the cities.* Chicago: University of Chicago Press, 1968.
Davies, J.C. Toward a theory of revolution. *American Sociological Review*, 1962, *27*, 5–14.
Davis, F. Crime news in Colorado newspapers. *American Journal of Sociology*, 1951, *57*, 325–330.
Davison, J. The triggered, the obsessed, and the schemers. *TV Guide*, February 2, 1974, 4–6.
Davison, W.P. *Mass communication and conflict resolution.* New York: Praeger, 1974.
DeFleur, M.L. Mass communication and the study of rumor. *Sociological Inquiry*, 1962, *32*, 51–70.
Demant, V.A. The unintentional influences of TV. *Cross-Currents*, 1955, *5*, 220–225.
Demaris, O. *Brothers in blood: The international terrorist network.* New York: Scribners, 1977.
Deutschmann, P.J., & Danielson, W.A. Diffusion of knowledge of the major news story. *Journalism Quarterly*, 1960, *37*, 345–355.
Diamond, E. *The tin kazoo: Television, politics, and the news.* New York: New York Times Books, 1975.
Dickens, M., & Williams, F. Mass communications. *Review of Educational Research*, 1964, *34*(2), 211–221.
Dominick, J.R. Television and political socialization. *Educational Broadcasting Review*, 1972, *6*, 48–56.
Dominick, J.R. Crime and law enforcement on prime-time television. *Public Opinion Quarterly*, 1973, *37*, 241–250.
Dominick, J.R. Crime and law enforcement in the mass media. In C. Winick (Ed.), *Deviance and the mass media.* Beverly Hills, Calif.: Sage Publications, 1978.
Doyle, E.J. Propaganda by deed: The media response to terrorism. *Police Chief*, June 1979, 40–41.
Drummond, W.J., & Zycher, A. Arafat's press agents. *Harper's*, March 1976, 24–30.
Easson, W.E. De-glamorize the rapist. *Journal of Clinical Psychiatry*, 1978, *39*(3), p.180.
Edgar, R.M., & Edgar, D.E. Television violence and socialization theory. *Public Opinion Quarterly*, 1971–72, *35*(4), 608–612.
Ekman, P. *Long-term behavioral effects of TV programs.* Final report, NIMH grant MH-24513, 1976.
Ekman, P. *Affect, altruism, aggression and TV violence.* Final report, NIMH grant MH-24099, 1977.
Elliott, J.D., & Gibson, L.K. (Eds.). *Contemporary terrorism: Selected readings.* Gaithersburg, MD.: Bureau of Operations and Research, International Association of Chiefs of Police, 1978.
Elliot, W.Y. (Ed.). *Television's impact on American culture.* East Lansing,

Mich.: Michigan State University Press, 1965.
Emery, W.B. *Broadcasting and government: Responsibilities and regulations.* East Lansing, Mich.: Michigan State University Press, 1971.
Emmett, B.P. A brief history of broadcasting research in the United Kingdom, 1936–1955. In Y. Kumugai & S. Takashima (Eds.), *Studies of broadcasting.* Radio and TV Culture Research Institute, Japan Broadcasting Corporation, 1966.
Epstein, E.C. The uses of "terrorism": A study in media bias. *Stanford Journal of International Studies,* 1977, *12,* 67–78.
Evans, A.E., & Murphy, J.F. (Eds.). *Legal aspects of international terrorism.* Lexington, Mass.: D.C. Heath & Co., 1978.
Evans, E. *Calling a truce to terror: the American response to international terrorism.* Westport, Conn.: Greenwood Press, 1979.
Fearing, F. Social impact of the mass media of communication. In N.B. Henry (Ed.), *Mass media and education.* Chicago: University of Chicago Press, 1954.
Federal Bureau of Investigation Academy. *Terrorist Activities-Bibliography.* Quantico, Virginia, 1975.
Feingold, M., & Johnson, G.T. Television violence—reactions from physicians, advertisers, and the networks. *New England Journal of Medicine,* 1977, *296*(8), 424–427.
Felsenfeld, L., & Jenkins, B. *International terrorism: An annotated bibliography.* Santa Monica, Calif.: Rand Corporation, 1973.
Fenton, F. The press and crimes against the person. *Bulletin of the American Academy of Medicine,* 1911, *12,* 307–315.
Fenyvesi, C. Looking into the muzzle of terrorists. *Quill,* 1977, July-August, 16–18.
Feshbach, S., & Singer, R.D. *Television and aggression.* San Francisco: Jossey-Bass, 1971.
Fischer, G.H. Measurement model for the effects of mass media. *Acta Psychologica,* 1972, *36,* 207–220.
Flanders, J.P. A review of research on imitative behavior. *Psychological Bulletin,* 1968, *69,* 316–337.
Francois, W.E. *Mass media law and regulation.* Columbus, Ohio: Grid, Inc., 1978.
Frank, R.E., & Greenberg, M.G. *The public's use of television.* Beverly Hills, Calif.: Sage, 1980.
Frazier, S.H. Mass media and psychiatric disturbance. *Psychiatric Journal of the University of Ottawa,* 1976, *1*(40), 171–173.
Freidson, E. The relation of the social situation of contact to the media in mass communication. *Public Opinion Quarterly,* 1953, *17,* 230–238.
Friedlander, R. A. Sowing the wind: Rebellion and violence in theory and practice. *Denver Journal of International Law and Policy,* 1976, *6,* 83–93.
Friedlander, R.A. Terrorism and political violence: Do the ends justify the means? *Chitty's Law Journal,* 1976, *24,* 240–245.
Friedlander, R. A. Terrorism and international law: What is being done?

Rutgers Camden Law Journal, 1977, *8*, 383–392.
Friedlander, R.A. Coping with terrorism: What is to be done? *Ohio Northern University Law Review*, 1978, *5*, 432–443.
Friedlander, R.A. *Terrorism: Documents of international and local control.* Dobbs Ferry, N.Y.: Oceana Publications, 1979.
Friedman, H.L., & Johnson, R.L. Mass media use and aggression: A pilot study. In G.A. Comstock & E.A. Rubenstein (Eds.), *Television and social behavior (Vol. 3)*. Washington, D.C.: U.S. Government Printing Office, 1971.
Friendly, F.W. *The good guys, the bad guys, and the first amendment.* New York: Random House, 1976.
Fromkin, D. The strategy of terrorism. *Foreign Affairs*, 1975, *53*, 683–698.
Funkhouser, G.R. Trends in media coverage of the issues of the 60's. *Journalism Quarterly*, 1973, *50*, 533–538.
Galloway, J. The agenda setting function of mass media. In T. Mohen (Ed.), *Proceedings of a conference and mass communication.* Sydney: New South Wales Institute of Technology, 1977.
Gallup poll: News of terrorism gets good, bad views. *Indianapolis Star*, April 28, 1977, p.37.
Garner, H.G. An adolescent suicide, the mass media and the educator. *Adolescence*, 1975, *10*(38), 241–146.
Garvey, R., Loye, D., & Steele, G. Impact of dramatized television entertainment on adult males. *American Journal of Psychiatry*, 1977, *134*(2), 170–174.
Gaucher, R. *The terrorists: From tsarist Russia to the O.A.S.* London: Secker & Warburg, 1968.
Geen, R.G., & O'Neal, E.C. *Perspectives on aggression.* New York: Academic Press, 1976.
Geis, G. The case of rape: Legal restrictions on media coverage of deviance in England and America. In C. Winick (Ed.), *Deviance and the mass media.* Beverly Hills, Calif.: Sage Publications, 1978.
Gerbner, G. Violence in television drama: Trends and symbolic functions, In G.A. Comstock & E.A. Rubinstein (Eds.), *Television and social behavior* (Vol. 1). Washington, D.C.: U.S. Government Printing Office, 1971.
Gerbner, G. Proliferating violence [Violence Profile no. 8]. *Society*, 1977, *14*, 10–14.
Gerbner, G., & Gross, L. Living with television: The violence profile. *Journal of Communication*, 1976, *26*, 172–199.
Gerbner, G., & Gross, L. The scary world of TV's heavy viewer. *Psychology Today*, 1976, *9*, 41–45.
Gerbner, G., Gross, L., Eleey, M.F., Jackson-Beeck, M., Jeffries-Fox, S., & Signorielli, N. TV violence profile no. 8: The highlights. *Journal of Communication*, 1977, *27*, 171–180.
Gerbner, G., Gross, L., Eleey, M.F., Jackson-Beeck, M., Jeffries-Fox, S., & Signorielli, N. Cultural indicators: Violence profile no. 9. *Journal of Communication*, 1978, *28*, 176–207.

Gleason, J.M. A Poisson model of incidents of international terrorism in the United States. *Terrorism: An International Journal*, 1980, *4*, 259–265.

Goin, J. Terrorism, the other guy's problem: Impact of terrorist violence on U.S. society. *National Sheriff*, 1977, *29*, 27.

Goldstein, M.J., & Kant, H.S. *Pornography and sexual deviance: A report of the Legal and Behavioral Institute.* Berkeley, Calif.: University of California Press, 1973.

Goranson, R.E. A review of recent literature on psychological effects of media portrayals of violence. In R.K. Baker and S.J. Ball (Eds.), *Violence and the media: A staff report to the National Commission on the Causes and Prevention of Violence.* Washington, D.C.: U.S. Government Printing Office, 1969.

Goranson, R.E. Media violence and aggressive behavior: A review of the experimental research. In L. Berkowitz (Ed.), *Advances in experimental social psychology* (Vol. 5). New York: Academic Press, 1970.

Gordon, T.F., & Verna, M.E. *Effects and processes of mass communication: A comprehensive bibliography, 1950–1975.* Beverly Hills, Calif.: Sage Publications, 1978.

Gorney, R., Loye, D., & Steele, G. Impact of dramatized television entertainment on adult males. *American Journal of Psychiatry*, 1977, *134*, 170–174.

Graham, H.D., & Gurr,T.R. *The history of violence in America: A report to the National Commission on the Causes and Prevention of Violence*, New York: Bantam, 1969.

Green, L.C. *Nature and control of international terrorism.* Alberta, Canada: University of Alberta, 1974.

Green, L.C. *The Tehran Embassy incident and international law.* Toronto: Canadian Institute of International Affairs, 1980.

Greenberg B. The content and context of violence in the media. In R. Baker & S. Ball (Eds.), *Violence and the media.* Washington, D.C.: U.S. Government Printing Office, 1969.

Greenberg, B.S. Person-to-person communication in the diffusion of news events. *Journalism Quarterly*, 1964, *41*, 489–494.

Greenberg, B.S. & Gordon, T.F. *Critics and public perceptions of violence in TV programs.* East Lansing, Mich.: Michigan State University, 1970.

Greenberg, B.S. & Roloff, M.E. *Mass media credibility: Research results and critical issues.* News Research Bulletin Number 6, American Newspaper Publications Association, 1974.

Gross, F. *Violence in politics: Terror and political assassination in Eastern Europe and Russia.* The Hague: Mouton, 1972.

Hacker, F.J. *Crusaders, criminals, crazies: Terror and terrorism in our time.* New York: W.W. Norton, 1976.

Hacker, F.J. *Terror and terrorism.* New York: Bantam, 1976.

Halloran, J.D. *Mass media and socialization.* Leeds, England: International Association for Mass Communication Research, 1976.

Halloran, J.D. Studying violence and the media: A sociological approach. In

BIBLIOGRAPHY

C. Winick (Ed.), *Deviance and the mass media.* Beverly Hills, Calif.: Sage Publications, 1978.

Hartley, R. *The impact of viewing aggression: Studies and problems of extrapolation.* Office of Social Research: CBS, 1964.

Hartmann, P., & Husband, C. The mass media and racial conflict. *Race,* 1970–71, *12,* 267–282.

Hartnagel, T.F., Teevan, J.L., & McIntyre, J.J. Television violence and violent behavior. *Social Forces,* 1975, *54,* 341–351.

Haskins, J. The effects of violence in the printed media. In R.K. Baker & S.J. Ball (Eds.), *Violence and the media.* Washington, D.C.: U.S. Government Printing Office, 1969.

Havens, M.C. *Assassination and terrorism: Their modern dimensions.* Manchacha, Tex.: S. Swift Publishing Co., 1975.

Heller, M.S., & Polsky, S. *Studies in violence and television.* New York: American Broadcasting Co., 1976.

Helmreich, R. Media-specific learning effects: An empirical study of the effects of television and radio. *Communications Research,* 1976, *3*(1), 53–63.

Hemenway, H. To what extent are suicide and crimes against the person due to suggestion from the press? *Bulletin of the American Academy of Medicine,* 1911, *12,* 253–263.

Hendrick, G. H. When television is a school for criminals. *TV Guide,* January 29, 1977, 4–8.

Heyman, E., & Mickolus, E. *Imitation by terrorists: Quantitative approaches to the study of diffusion patterns in transnational terrorism.* Paper presented to the Joint National Meeting of the Operations Research Society of America, New York City, 1978.

Hibbs, D.A. *Mass political violence: A cross-national causal analysis.* New York: John Wiley, 1973.

Hickey, N. Terrorism and television, Part I. *TV Guide,* July 31 - August 6, 1976, 2–6.

Hickey, N. Terrorism and television: The medium in the middle, Part II. *TV Guide,* August 7–13, 1976, 10–13.

Hill, R.J., & Bonjean, C.M. News diffusion: A test of the regularity hypothesis. *Journalism Quarterly,* 1964, *41,* 336–342.

Himmelweit, H.T. A theoretical framework for the consideration of the effects of television: A British report. *Journal of Social Issues,* 1962, *18,* 16–28.

Hirsh, P.M., Miller, P.V., & Kline, F.G. *Strategies for communication research.* Beverly Hills, Calif.: Sage Publications, 1977.

Hobsbaum, E.J. *The revolutionaries.* New York: New American Library, 1975.

Holaday, P.W., & Wohl, R. *Getting ideas from the movies.* New York: Macmillan, 1933.

Holz, R. Television violence: A paper tiger? *CRC Report,* 1971, *57.*

Horowitz, I.L. Can democracy cope with terrorism? *Civil Liberties Review,* 1977, *4,* 29–37.

Houchins v. KQED, Inc. 438 U.S. 1, 13 (1978).

Hovland, C. Effects of the mass media of communication. In G. Lindzey (Ed.),

The handbook of social psychology. Reading, Mass.: Addison-Wesley, 1954.
Hovland, C.I., Lumsdaine, A.A., & Sheffield, F.D. *Experiments on mass communication.* Princeton, N.J.: Princeton University Press, 1949.
Howitt, D. Attitudes towards violence and mass media exposure. *Gazette* (Netherlands), 1972, *18*, 208–234.
Howitt, D., & Cumberbatch, G. *Mass media violence and society.* London: Elek, 1975. New York: Wiley, 1975.
Howitt, D., & Dembo, R. A subcultural account of media effects. *Human Relations*, 1974, *27*, 24–41.
Hubbard, D.G. *The skyjacker: His flights of fantasy.* New York: Macmillan, 1971; Collier Books, 1973.
Hughes, M. The fruits of cultivation analysis: A reexamination of some effects of television watching. *Public Opinion Quarterly*, 1980, *44*, 287–302.
Hutchinson, M.P. The concept of revolutionary terrorism. *Journal of Conflict Resolution*, 1972, *16*, 383–396.
Hyams, E.S. *Terrorists and terrorism.* New York: St. Martin's Press, 1975.
Hyman, H.H., & Singer, E. (Eds.), *Readings in reference group theory and research.* New York: The Free Press, 1968.
Ingelfinger, F.J. Violence on TV: An unchecked environmental hazard. *New England Journal of Medicine*, 1976, *294*, 837–838.
Institute of Public Affairs, University of Iowa, *Terrorism* (Part I). Iowa City, Iowa: n.d., 21p. (NCJRS 32698)
Institute of Public Affairs, University of Iowa, *The problem* (Part II). *The question of control.* Iowa City, Iowa: n.d. 21p. (NCJRS 32698)
Institute for the Study of Conflict. Terrorism can be stopped. *Skeptic*, 1976, *11*, 44–49.
International terrorism. *Stanford Journal of International Studies*, 1977, *12*, 1-192.
Israel, H., & Robinson, J.P. Demographic characteristics of viewers of television violence and news programs. In E.A. Rubinstein, G.A. Comstock, & J.P. Murray (Eds.), *Television and social behavior* (Vol. 4). Washington, D.C.: U.S. Government Printing Office, 1971.
Jaehnig, W.B. Journalists and terrorism: Captives of the libertarian tradition. *Indiana Law Journal*, 1978, *53*, 717–744.
Jenkins, B.M. *The five stages of urban guerrilla warfare: The challenge of the 1970's.* Santa Monica, Calif.: Rand Corporation, 1971.
Jenkins, B.M. International terrorism: A balance sheet. *Survival*, 1975, *17*, 158–164.
Jenkins, B.M. *International terrorism: A new mode of conflict.* Los Angeles, Calif.: Crescent Publications, 1975.
Johnpoll, B. Terrorism and the mass media in the United States. In Y. Alexander & S.M. Finger (Eds.), *Terrorism: Interdisciplinary perspectives.* New York: John Jay, 1977.
Johnson, C. Terror. *Society*, 1977, *15*, 48–52.
Jones, E.T. The press as metropolitan monitor. *Public Opinion Quarterly*,

1976, *40*, 239-244.

Jones, J., & Miller, A. The media and terrorist activity: Resolving the First Amendment dilemma. *Ohio Northern University Law Review*, 1979, *6*, 70-81.

Kaplan, R.M., & Singer, R.D. Television violence and viewer aggression: A reexamination of the evidence. *Journal of Social Issues*, 1976, *32*, 35-70.

Karber, P.A. Urban terrorism: Baseline data and a conceptual framework. *Social Science Quarterly*, 1971, *52*, 521-533.

Karmen, A. How much heat, how much light: Coverage of New York City's blackout and looting in the print media. In C. Winick (Ed.), *Deviance and the mass media*. Beverly Hills, Calif.: Sage Publications, 1978.

Katz, E. *Social research on broadcasting: Proposals for further development*. London: British Broadcasting Corporation, 1977.

Katz, E., Gurevitch, M., & Haas, H. On the use of the mass media for important things. *American Sociological Review*, 1973, *38*, 164-181.

Kent, I., & Nicholls, W. The psychodynamics of terrorism. *Mental Health and Society* (Basel), 1977, *4*, 1-8,

Kittrie, N.N. New look at political offenses and terrorism. In S.F. Landau (Ed.), *Criminology in perspective: Essays in honor of Israel Drapkin*. Lexington, Mass.: Lexington Books, 1977.

Klapper, J.T. *The effects of mass communication*. New York: The Free Press, 1960.

Klapper, J.T. The social effects of mass communication. In W. Schramm (Ed.), *The science of human communication*. New York Basic Books, 1963.

Klapper, J.T. The impact of viewing "aggression": Studies and problems of extrapolation. In O.N. Larson (Ed.), *Violence in the mass media*. New York: Harper, 1968.

Knight, J., Friedman, T., & Suliant, J. Epidemic hysteria: A field study. *American Journal of Public Health*, 1965, *55*, 858-865.

Krattenmaker, T.G., & Powe, L.A. Televised violence: First amendment principles and social science theory. *Virginia Law Review*, 1978, *64*, 1123-1297.

Kraus, S. Mass communication and political socialization: A re-assessment of two decades of research. *Quarterly Journal of Speech*, 1973, *59*, 390-400.

Kupperman, R.H., & Trent, D.M. *Terrorism: Threat, reality, response*. Stanford, Calif.: Hoover Institution Press, Stanford University, 1979.

Kutchinsky, B. The effects of easy availability of pornography on the incidence of sex crimes: The Danish experience. *Journal of Social Issues*, 1973, *29*, 163-181.

Lador-Lederer, J.J. A legal approach to international terrorism. *Israel Law Review*, 1974, *9*, 194-220.

Lang, G.E., & Lang, K. Some pertinent questions on collective violence and the news media. *Journal of Social Issues*, 1972, *28*, 93-110.

Lang, D.K., Baker, R.K., & Ball, S.J. *Mass media and violence*. Volume 9 of the Report of the U.S. Commission on the Causes and Prevention of Violence. Washington, D.C.: U.S. Government Printing Office, 1969.

Laqueur, W. Interpretations of terrorism: Fact, fiction, and political science. *Journal of Contemporary History*, 1977, *12*, 1–42.

Laqueur, W. *Terrorism*. Boston: Little Brown, 1977.

Laqueur, W. (Ed.). *The terrorism reader*. Philadelphia: Temple University Press, 1978.

Larsen, O.N. Social effects of mass communication. In R.E. Faris (Ed.), *Handbook of modern sociology*. New York: Rand McNally, 1964.

Larsen, O.N. *Violence in the mass media*. New York: Harper & Row, 1968.

Larsen, O.N., & Hill, R. Mass media and interpersonal communication in the diffusion of a news event. *American Sociological Review*, 1954, *19*, 426–433.

Lazarsfeld, P.F., & Field, H. *The people look at radio*. Chapel Hill, N.C.: University of North Carolina Press, 1946.

Lazarsfeld, P.F., & Kendall, P.L. *Radio listening in America*. New York: Prentice Hall, 1948.

Leach, E.R. *Custom, law, and terrorist violence*. Edinburgh: University Press, 1977.

Leibstone, L. Rules of terrorism for the victim, terrorist, and media. *Louisville Courier Journal*, April 17, 1977, p. 3.

Levin, H.J. Competition among mass media and the public interest. *Public Opinion Quarterly*, 1954, *18*, 62–79.

Lewels, F.J. *The uses of the media by the Chicano movement: A study in minority access*. New York: Praeger, 1974.

Leyens, J.P., Camino, L., Parke, R.D., & Berkowitz, L. Effects of movie violence on aggression in a field setting as a function of group dominance and cohesion. *Journal of Personality and Social Psychology*, 1975, *32*, 346–360.

Li, R., & Thompson, W.R. The "coup contagion" hypothesis. *Journal of Conflict Resolution*, 1975, *19*, 63–88.

Liebert, R.M., & Schwartzberg, N.S. Effects of mass media. *Annual Review of Psychology*, 1977, *28*, 141–173.

Linde, P. Fair trials and press freedom: Two rights against the state. *Willamette Law Journal*, 1977, *13*, 211, 216–217.

Lineberry. W. *The struggle against terrorism*. New York: H.W. Wilson, 1977.

Liston, R.A. *Terrorism*. Nashville & New York: Thomas Nelson, Inc., 1977.

Livingston, M.H., Kress, L.B., & Wanek, K.G. (Eds.). *International terrorism in the contemporary world*. Westport, Conn.: Greenwood Press, 1978.

Loffert, D.W. The effects of television and its effect on social upheaval. In R.S. Parker, (Ed.), *The emotional stress of war, violence, and peace*. Pittsburgh, Penn.: Stanwix House, 1972.

Lowry, D. Gresham's law and network TV news selection. *Journal of Broadcasting*, 1971, *15*, 397–408.

Lucas, W.A., & Possner, K.B. *Television news and local awareness: A retrospective look*. Santa Monica, Calif.: Rand Corporation, 1975.

Lupsha, P. Explanation of political violence: Some psychological theories. *Politics and Society*, 1971, *2*, 88–104.
Maccoby, E.E. Effects of mass media. In M.L. Hoffman & L.W. Hoffman (Eds.), *Review of child development research*. New York: Russel Sage Foundation, 1964.
Miahofer, W. The strategy of terrorism. *Polizei* (Cologne), 1977, *68*, 16.
Mallin, J. *Terror and urban guerillas—A study of tactics and documents*. Coral Gables, Fla.: University of Miami Press, 1971.
Mander, J. *Four arguments for the elimination of television*. New York: Morrow, 1978.
Margolin, J. Psychological perspectives on terrorism. In Y. Alexander & S.M. Finger (Eds.), *Terrorism: Interdisciplinary perspectives*. New York: John Jay, 1977.
Marx, H.L. *Television and radio in American life*. New York: H.H. Wilson, 1953.
McCormack, T. Machismo in media research: A critical review of research on violence and pornography. *Social Problems*, 1978, *25*, 544–555.
McCormick, J.M., & Coveyou, M.R. Mass political imagery and the salience of international affairs. *American Politics Quarterly*, 1978, *6*, 498–509.
McEwen, M.T., & Sloan, S. Terrorism: Police and press problems. *Terrorism*, 1979, *2*, 1–54.
McGrath, W.B. Hysteria. *Arizona Medicine*, 1976, *33*, p.309.
McIntyre, J.J., & Teevan, J.J. Television violence and deviant behavior. In G.A. Comstock & E.A. Rubinstein (Eds.), *Television and social behavior* (Vol.3). Washington, D.C.: U.S. Government Printing Office, 1971.
McKnight, G. *The terrorist mind*. Indianapolis, Ind.: Bobbs-Merrill, 1975.
McPhee, W.N. *News strategies for research in the mass media*. New York: Columbia University Press, 1953.
The Media and terrorism: A seminar sponsored by the Chicago Sun-Times and the Chicago Daily News. Chicago: Field Enterprises. c1977, 21–22.
Mendelsohn, H. Socio-psychological perspectives on the mass media and public anxiety. *Journalism Quarterly*, 1963, *40*, 511–516.
Menzies, E. Preferences in television content among violent prisoners. *FCI Research Reports*, 1971, *3*, 1–29.
Merton, R.K., & Rossi, A.S. Contributions to the theory of reference group behavior. In R.K. Merton (Ed.), *Social theory and social structure*. New York: The Free Press, 1967.
Meyer, J.C. Newspaper reporting of crime and justice. *Journalism Quarterly*, 1975, *52*, 731–734.
Meyer, T.P. Some effects of real newsfilm violence on the behavior of viewers. *Journal of Broadcasting*, 1971, *15*, 275–285.
Meyers, I. Terrorism in the news. *Daily Times* (Mamaroneck, N.Y.), April 2, 1977.
Meyersohn, R.B. Social research in television. In B. Rosenberg & D.M. White (Eds.), *Mass culture: The popular arts in America*. Glencoe, Ill.: The Free Press, 1956.

Mickolus, E.F. *Annotated bibliography on transnational and international terrorism.* Washington, D.C.: Central Intelligence Agency, 1976.
Midlarsky, M.I. Mathematical models of instability and a theory of diffusion. *International Studies Quarterly*, 1970, *14*, 690–84.
Midlarsky, M.I. Analyzing diffusion and contagion effects: The urban disorders of the 1960's. *American Political Science Review*, 1978, *72*, 996-1008.
Midlarsky, M.I., & Hutchinson, M.G. *Why violence spreads: The contagion of international terrorism.* Paper presented at the Annual meeting of the International Studies Association, March 21–24, 1979, Toronto.
Milbank, D.L. *International and transnational terrorism: Diagnosis and prognosis.* Washington, D.C.: Central Intelligence Agency, 1976 (RP 76-10030).
Milgram, S., & Shotland, R.L. *Television and antisocial behavior: Field experiments.* New York: Academic Press, 1973.
Milgram, S., & Toch, H. Collective behavior: Crowds and social movements. In G. Lindzey & E. Aronson (Eds.), *The handbook of social psychology* (Vol.5). Reading, Mass.: Addison-Wesley, 1968.
Miller, A.H. On terrorism. *Public Administration Review*, 1977 (July-August), 429–435.
Miller, A.H. Negotiations for hostages: Implications from the police experience. *Terrorism*, 1978, *1*, 125–146.
Miller, A.H. Hostage negotiations and the concept of transference. In Y. Alexander, D. Carlton, & P. Wilkinson (Eds.), *Terrorism: Theory and practice.* Boulder, Colo.: Westview Press, 1979.
Miller, A.H. Terrorism and the media: A dilemma. *Terrorism: An International Journal*, 1979, *3*, 79–89.
Miller, A.H. *Terrorism and hostage negotiations.* Boulder, Colo.: Westview Press, 1980.
Miller, A.H. Responding to the victims of terrorism: Psychological and policy implications. In R. Shultz & S. Sloan (Eds.), *Responding to the terrorist threat: Security and crisis management.* New York: Pergamon Press, 1980.
Miller, J. Terrorists. *New York Times*, July 18, 1976, p.7.
Miller v. California, 413 U.S.15 (1973).
Milte, K., Bartholomew, A.A., O'Hearn, D.J., & Campbell, A. Terrorism: Political and psychological considerations. *Australian and New Zealand Journal of Criminology*, 1976, *9*, 89–94.
Moore, B. *Terror and progress (U.S.S.R.).* Cambridge, Mass: Harvard University Press, 1954.
Moore, J. Terrorism and political crimes in international law. *American Journal of International Law.* 1973, *67*, 87–92.
Moore, J. Toward legal restraints on international terrorism. *American Society of International Law Proceedings*, 1973, *67*, 88–94.
Moos, R.H. The effects of pornography: A review of the findings of the Obscenity and Pornography Commission. *Comments on Contemporary Psychiatry*, 1972, *1*, 123–131.

Moss, R. *Urban guerrillas: The new face of political violence.* London: Temple Smith, Ltd., 1972.
Moss, R. *The war of the cities.* New York: Coward, McCann, and Geoghan, 1972.
Moss, R. International terrorism and western societies. *International Journal,* 1973, *28,* 418–430.
Mosse, H.L. Terrorism and mass media. *New York State Journal of Medicine,* 1977, *77,* 2294–2296.
Motta, L.G. (Ed.). International terrorism. *Stanford Journal of International Studies,* 1977, *12,* 1–192.
Motto, J.A. Suicide and suggestibility: The role of the press. *American Journal of Psychiatry,* 1967, *124,* 252–256.
Motto, J.A. Newspaper influence on suicide: A controlled study. *Archives of General Psychiatry,* 1970, *23,* 143–148.
Murray, J.P. Television and violence: Implications of the Surgeon General's research program. *American Psychologist,* 1973, *28,* 278–472.
Murray, J.P., & Kippax, S. Television diffusion and social behavior in three communities: A field experiment. *Australian Journal of Psychology,* 1977, *29,* 31–43.
Murray, J.P., & Kippax, S. From the early window to the late night show: International trends in the study of television's impact on children and adults. In L. Berkowitz (Ed.), *Advances in experimental social psychology* (Vol. 12). New York: Academic Press, 1979.
Murray, J.P., Nayman, O.B., & Atkin, C.E. Television and the child: A research bibliography. *Journal of Broadcasting,* 1972, *26,* 21–35.
Murray, J.P., Rubinstein, E.A., & Comstock, G.A. (Eds.), *Television and social behavior (Vol. 2): Television and social learning.* Washington, D.C.: U.S. Government Printing Office, 1971.
Nafziger, R.O., Engstrom, W.C. & Maclean, M.S. The mass media and an informed public. *Public Opinion Quarterly,* 1951, *15,* 105–114.
National Broadcasting Company (NBC). *Recent developments involving violence on television: A status report.* New York: NBC Department of Social Research, 1977.
National Commission on the Causes and Prevention of Violence. *To establish justice, to insure domestic tranquility.* Department of Health, Education, and Welfare, 1972.
National Governors' Association Center for Policy Research. *Domestic Terrorism.* Washington, D.C.: U.S. Government Printing Office, 1979.
National News Council. Statement on terrorism and the media. *Columbia Journalism Review,* 1977, May-June, 1981.
Near v. Minnesota, 283 U.S. 697, 716 (1931).
New York Times v. Sullivan, 376 U.S. 254 (1964).
New York Times v. United States, 403 U.S. 713, 727 (1971).
New Zealand Psychological Society. Submission to the select committee on the Cinematographic Films Bill and the Cinematographic Films Amendment Bill. *New Zealand Psychologist,* 1976, *5,* 98–105.

Noelle-Neuman, E. Return to the concept of powerful mass media. *Studies in Broadcasting*, 1973, *9*, 66-112.

Norton, A.R., & Greenberg, M.H. *International terrorism: An annotated bibliography and research guide.* Boulder, Colo.: Westview Press, 1980.

O'Ballance, E. *Language of violence: The blood politics of terrorism.* San Rafael, Calif.: Presidio Press, 1979.

Ontario Psychological Association submission on violence in the media. In *Report of the Royal Commission on Violence in the Communications Industry (Vol. 1): Approaches, conclusions, recommendations.* Toronto: Queens Printer for Ontario, 1976.

Paisley, M.B. *Social policy research and the realities of the system: Violence done to TV research.* Stanford, Calif.: Stanford University Institute of Communication Research, 1972.

Paust, J.J. Terrorism and the international law of war. *Military Law Review*, 1974, *64*, 1-36.

Paust, J.J. A survey of possible legal responses to international terrorism: Prevention, punishment, and cooperative action. *Georgia Journal of International and Comparative Law*, 1975, *5*, 431-469.

Paust, J.J. Response to terrorism: A prologue to decisions concerning private measures of sanction. *Stanford Journal of International Studies*, 1977, *12*, 67-78.

Paust, J.J. International law and control of the media: Terror, repression, and the alternatives. *Indiana Law Journal*, 1978, *53*, 621-677.

Payne, D. Newspapers and crime: What happens during strike periods? *Journalism Quarterly*, 1974, *51*, 607-612.

Payne, D., & Payne, K. Newspapers and crime in Detroit. *Journalism Quarterly*, 1970, *47*, 233-238.

Pember, D.R. *Mass media in America.* Chicago: Science Research Associates, 1977.

Pepitone, A. The social psychology of violence. *International Journal of Group Tensions*, 1972, *2*, 19-32.

Peterson, T., Jensen, J.W., & Rivers, W.L. *The mass media and modern society.* New York: Holt, Rinehart & Winston, 1965.

Peterson. W.A., & Gist, N.P. Rumor and public opinion. *American Journal of Sociology*, 1951, *57*, 159-167.

Phelps, E. Neurotic books and newspapers as factors in the mortality of suicide and crime. *Bulletin of the American Academy of Medicine*, 1911, *12*, 264-306.

Phillips, D.P. The influence of suggestion on suicide: Substantive and theoretical implications of the Werther effect. *American Sociological Review*, 1974, *39*, 340-354.

Phillips, D.P. Motor vehicle fatalities increase just after publicized suicide stories. *Science*, 1977, *196*, 1464-1465.

Phillips, D.P. Airplane accident fatalities increase just after newspaper stories about murder and suicide. *Science*, 1978, *201*, 748-749.

Phillips, D.P. Suicide, motor vehicle fatalities, and the mass media: Evidence

towards a theory of suggestion. *American Journal of Sociology*, 1979, *84*(5), 1150–1174.
Phillips, D.P. The deterrent effect of capital punishment: New evidence on an old controversy. *American Journal of Sociology*, 1980, *86*, 139–148.
Piepe, A., Crouch, J., & Emerson, M. Violence and television. *New Society* (London), 1977, *41*, 536–538.
Pierre, A.J. The politics of international terrorism. *Orbis*, 1976, *19*, 1251–1269.
Pinderhughs, C.A. Televised violence and social behavior. *Psychiatric Opinion*, 1972, *9*, 28–36.
Pool, I. de S. Government and the media. *American Political Science Review*, 1976, *70*, 1234–1241.
Price, H.E., Jr. The strategy and tactics of revolutionary terrorism. *Comparative Studies in Society and History*, 1977, *19*, 52–66.
Publicity crimes. *New Yorker*, 1974, *50*, 27ff.
Quandt, R.E. Some statistical characterizations on aircraft hijacking. *Accident Analysis and Prevention*, 1974, *6*, 115–123.
Quinney, R. *The social reality of crime*. Boston: Little, Brown, 1970.
Rand Corporation. *New Modes of conflict: Urban guerrilla warfare and international terrorism*. Santa Monica, Calif.: Rand Corporation, 1978.
Rapoport, D. *Terrorism and assassination*. Toronto: Canadian Broadcasting System, 1971.
Redlick, A.S. The transnational flow of information as a cause of terrorism. In Y. Alexander, D. Carlton, & P. Wilkinson (Eds.), *Terrorism: Theory and practice*. Boulder, Colo.: Westview Press, 1979.
Report of the Commission on Obscenity and Pornography. Washington, D.C.: U.S. Government Printing Office, 1970.
Review of the Operation of the Prevention of Terrorism (Temporary Provisions) Acts of 1974 and 1976. (Shackleton Report). London: Home Office, August 1978.
Revzin, P. A reporter looks at media role in terror threats. *Wall Street Journal*, March 14, 1977, p.16.
Robinson, J.P. The audience for national TV news programs. *Public Opinion Quarterly*, 1971, *35*, 403–405.
Robinson, J.P., & Bachman, J.G. Television viewing habits and aggression. In G.A. Comstock & E.A. Rubinstein (Eds.), *Television and social behavior* (Vol. 3). Washington, D.C.: U.S. Government Printing Office, 1971.
Rogers, E.M., & Shoemaker, F. *Communication of innovations: A cross-cultural approach*. New York: The Free Press, 1971.
Rosenthal, M.M. Riot news: The press, the spread of opinion, and demogeographic self-interest. *Communication Research*, 1978, *5*(2), 176–201.
Roshier, B. The selection of crime news by the press. In S. Cohen & J. Young (Eds.), *The manufacture of news*. Beverly Hills, Calif.: Sage Publications, 1973.
Roucek, J.S. Sociological elements of a theory of terror and violence. *American Journal of Economics and Sociology*, 1962, *21*, 165–172.

Roucek, J.S. Guerrilla warfare: Its theories and strategies. *International Behavioral Scientist*, 1974, *6*, 57–80.

Royal Commission on Violence in the Communications Industry. *Report of the Royal Commission on Violence in the Communications Industry.* Toronto: Queen's Printer for Ontario, 1976.

Rubin, B. *Media, politics and democracy.* New York: Oxford University Press, 1977.

Rubinstein, E.A. Television and social behavior: Social science research for social policy. *Educational Broadcasting Review*, 1972, *6*, 409–415.

Rubinstein, E.A. The TV violence report: What's next? *Journal of Communication*, 1974, *24*, 80–88.

Rubinstein, E.A. Social science and media policy. *Journal of Communication*, 1975, *25*, 194-200.

Rubinstein, E.A. Warning: The Surgeon General's research program may be dangerous to preconceived notions. *Journal of Social Issues*, 1976, *32*, 18–34.

Rubinstein, E.A., Comstock, G.A., & Murray, J.P. *Television and social behavior, Volume 4: Television in day-to-day life: Patterns of use.* Washington, D.C.: U.S. Government Printing Office, 1971.

Ryan, M., & Owen, D. A content analysis of metropolitan newspaper coverage of social issues. *Journalism Quarterly*, 1976, *53*, 634–640.

Salomone, F. Terrorism and the mass media. In M.C. Bassiouni (Ed.), *International terrorism and political crimes.* Springfield, Ill.: Charles C. Thomas, 1975.

Sandman, P.M., Rubin, D.M., & Sachsman, D.B. *The media: An introductory analysis of American mass communication.* Englewood Cliffs, N.J.: Prentice-Hall, 1972.

Schaffer, E.B. A view of violence in America. *Police Journal*, 1976, *49*, 270–276.

Schlickel, R. Violence in movies. *Review of Existential Psychology and Psychiatry*, 1968, *8*, 169–178.

Schneider, J.A. Networks hold the line against violence. *Society*, 1977, *14*, 14–17.

Schornhorst, F.T. The lawyer and the terrorist: Another ethical dilemma. *Indiana Law Journal*, 1978, *53*, 679–702.

Schramm, W. *The process and effects of mass communications.* Urbana, Ill.: University of Illinois Press, 1954.

Schramm, W. *Responsibility in mass communications.* New York: Harper, 1957.

Schramm, W. (Ed.). *Mass communications: A book of readings.* Urbana, Ill.: University of Illinois Press, 1960.

Schramm, W. Mass communication. *Annual Review of Psychology*, 1962, *13*, 251–284.

Seib, C.B. The Hanafi episode: A media event. *Washington Post*, March 18, 1977, p. A27.

Selzer, M. *Terrorist chic: An exploration of violence in the seventies.* New

York: Hawthorn Books, 1979.
Sewell, A.F. Political crime: A psychologist's perspective. In M.C. Bassiouni (Ed.), *International terrorism and political crimes*. Springfield, Ill.: Charles C. Thomas, 1975.
Shackleton Report. See: *Review of the Operation of the Prevention of Terrorism (Temporary Provisions) Acts of 1974 and 1976*.
Shaw, D. Editors face terrorist demand dilemma. *Los Angeles Times*, September 15, 1976, p.14.
Shultz, R.H. & Sloan, S. (Eds.). *Responding to the terrorist threat: Security and crisis management*. New York: Pergamon Press, 1980.
Shuttleworth, F.K., & May, M.A. The social conduct and attitudes of movie fans. In R.C. Peterson & L.L Thurstone (Eds.), *Motion pictures and the social attitudes of children*. New York: Macmillan, 1933.
Silbermann, A. The sociology of mass communications. *Current Sociology*, 1970, *18*, 1–124.
Sinclair, J. Mass media and the dialectics of social change: The Melbourne Herald and the counter culture in the late sixties. *Australian and New Zealand Journal of Sociology*, 1975, *11*, 46–49.
Singer, R.D. Violence, protest and war in television news: The U.S. and Canada compared. *Public Opinion Quarterly*, 1970, *34*, 611–616.
Singer, R.D. & Kaplan, R.M. (Eds.). Television and social behavior. *Journal of Social Issues*, 1976, *32*, 1–247.
Small, W. *To kill a messenger: Television news and the real world*. New York: Hastings House, 1970.
Smart, I.M.H. The power of terror. *International Journal*, 1975, *30*, 225–237.
Smith, W.H. International terrorism: A political analysis. *Yearbook of World Affairs*, 1977, *31*, 138–157.
Snyder, D. Collective violence. *Journal of Conflict Resolution*, 1978, *22*, 499–529.
Sobel, L.A. (Ed.) *Political terrorism*. New York: Facts on File, Inc., 1978.
Souchon, H. Hostage-taking: Its evolution and significance. *International Criminal Police Review* (St. Cloud), 1976, *31*, 168–173.
Steiner, G.A. *The people look at television*. New York: Knopf, 1963.
Stephans, D. The electronic whipping boy. *Mental Health*, 1967, *26*, 12–14.
Sterling, C. The terrorist network. *Atlantic Monthly*, 1978, *242*, 37-43ff.
Stern, J.C. News media relations during a major incident. *Police Journal* (Chichester), 1976, *49*, 256–260.
Stevenson, R.L. *The uses and non-uses of television news*. Paper presented at the meeting of the International Society of Political Psychology, New York, 1978.
Streng, F., & Stozer, H.V. Kriminalitaet und publicity: Zur kriminalogischen Wirkung einer bestimmten Kriminalberichterstattung [Criminality and publicity: Crime producing effect of criminal reporting]. *Kriminalistik* (Hamburg), 1977, *31*, 499–500.
Stouse, J.C. *The mass media, public opinion, and public policy analysis: Linkage explorations*. Columbus, Ohio: Charles Merrill, 1975.

Suicide after watching television. (Letter to the Editor). *Journal of the American Medical Association*, 1958, *167* 497.

Surgeon General's Scientific Advisory Committee on Television and Social Behavior. *Television and growing up: The impact of televised violence.* Washington, D.C.: U.S. Government Printing Office, 1972.

Sussman, B. Media leaders want less influence. *Washington Post*, September 29, 1976, p.A1.

Tannenbaum, J.A. The terrorists: For world's alienated, violence often reaps political recognition. *Wall Street Journal*, January 4, 1977, p.1ff.

Tannenbaum, P.H., & Greenberg, B.S. Mass communication. *Annual Review of Psychology*, 1968, *19*, 351–386.

Tayler, E. The terrorists. *Horizon*, 1973, Summer, 58–64.

Tedeschi, J.T., & Lindskold, S. Collective behavior. In J. Tedeschi (Ed.), *Social psychology: Interdependence, interaction.* New York: Wiley, 1976.

Television Research Committee. *Second Progress Report and Recommendation.* Leicester, England: Leicester University Press, 1969.

Terrorism and censorship. *Time*, March 28, 1977, p.57.

Terrorism and social control. *Ohio Northern University Law Journal*, 1979, *6*, 1–143.

Terrorism and the media. *Indiana Law Journal*, 1978, *53*, 619–777.

Terrorism and the media. Proceedings of a conference sponsored by the Ralph Bunch Institute for Studies on the United Nations, the Institute for Studies in International Terrorism, and the Institute on Human Relations in November of 1977 in New York City.

Terrorism: Police and press problems. Proceedings of a conference sponsored by the Oklahoma Publishing Company and the University of Oklahoma in April of 1977 in Oklahoma City, Oklahoma.

Terrorists and hostage coverage. Proceedings of a conference sponsored by the Radio and Television News Directors' Association in November of 1977 in Washington, D.C.

Terry, H.A. Television and terrorism: Professionalism not quite the answer. *Indiana Law Journal*, 1978, *53*, 745–777.

There should be no free publicity for terrorists. *Financial Weekly*, July 13, 1979, p.9.

Thornton, T.P. Terror as a weapon of political agitation. In H. Eckstein (Ed.), *Internal war: Problems and approaches.* London: Collier-Macmillan, Ltd., 1964.

Tobin, R.L. More violent than ever: Preoccupation with bad news in the mass media. *Saturday Review*, 1968, *51*, 79–80.

Toch, H. *The social psychology of social movements.* Indianapolis, Ind.: Bobbs-Merrill, 1965.

Tucker, C. The night TV cried wolf. *Saturday Review*, October 1, 1977, p. 56.

Turner, R. The public perception of protest. *American Sociological Review*, 1969, *34*, 815–831.

Turner, R.H., & Killian, L.M. *Collective behavior.* Englewood Cliffs, N.J.: Pren-

tice-Hall, 1957.
Two sides of the coin on media and terrorists. *Broadcasting*, April 4, 1977, p.78.
United Nations Secretariat. *International terrorism: A select bibliography.* New York: United Nations, 1973.
United States Department of Justice, Federal Bureau of Investigation. *Terrorist Activities: A bibliography.* Quantico, Va.: FBI Academy, 1973.
United States Department of Justice, Law Enforcement Assistance Administration, National Advisory Committee on Criminal Justice Standards and Goals. *Disorders and terrorism: A report of the task force on disorders and terrorism.* Washington, D.C.: U.S. Government Printing Office, 1976.
United States Department of Justice, Law Enforcement Assistance Administration, National Institute of Law Enforcement and Criminal Justice. *Terrorism: A selected bibliography.* Washington, D.C.: U.S. Government Printing Office, 1976.
United States Department of Justice, Law Enforcement Assistance Administration, National Institute of Law Enforcement and Criminal Justice. *Terrorism.* Washington, D.C.: U.S. Government Printing Office, 1977.
United States Department of Justice, Law Enforcement Assistance Administration, National Insitute of Law Enforcement and Criminal Justice. *Terrorism.* Rockville, Md.: NILECJ, 1978.
United States Senate. *Terroristic activity: International terrorism.* Hearings Before the Subcommittee to Investigate the Administration of the Internal Security Act and Other Internal Security Laws of the Judiciary, United States Senate. Ninety-fourth Congress, First Session; Part 4, May 14, 1975. Washington, D.C.: U.S. Government Printing Office, 1975.
United States Senate. *Combating international and domestic terrorism.* Hearings before the Committee on Foreign Relations on S.2236, June 8, 1978.
United States Senate. *Federal capabilities in crisis management and terrorism.* Staff report of the Subcommittee on Civil and Constitutional Rights of the House Committee on the Judiciary. Washington, D.C.: U.S. Government Printing Office, 1979.
Urry, J. *Reference groups and the theory of revolution.* London: Routledge and Keagan Paul, 1973.
Victoroff, D. Communication de masse et violence [Mass communication and violence.] *Bulletin de Psychologie* (Paris), 1977, *30*(Serial No. 328, 424–428.
Violence and television. *British Medical Journal*, 1976 (6014), 856.
Violence on TV. *British Medical Journal*, 1969, *3*(5663), 125–126.
Wadsworth, W. The newspapers and crime. *Bulletin of the American Academy of Medicine*, 1911, *12*, 316–325.
Walker, J.L. The diffusion of innovations among the American states. *American Political Science Review*, 1969, *63*, 880–899.
Wallace, R. Contagion and incubation in New York City structural fires 1964-

1976. *Human Ecology,* 1978, *6,* 423–433.
Walter, E.V. Violence and the process of terror. *American Sociological Review,* 1964, *29,* 248–257.
Walter, E.V. *Terror and resistance.* New York: Oxford University Press, 1969.
Walters, R.H. Implications of laboratory studies of aggression for the control and regulation of violence. *The Annals of the American Academy of Political and Social Sciences,* 1966, *364,* 60–72.
Warner, M. Decision-making in network television news. In J. Tunstall(Ed.), *Media sociology.* Urbana, Ill.: University of Illinois Press, 1970.
Warren, D.I. Mass media and racial crisis: A study of the New Bethel Church incident in Detroit. *Journal of Social Issues,* 1972, *28,* 111–131.
Watson, F. *Political terrorism: The threat and the response.* Washington, D.C.: R.B. Luce Company, 1976.
Weisman, P. When hostages' lives are at stake. *TV Guide,* August 26, 1978, 4–9.
Weiss, W. Effects of the mass media of communication. In G. Lindzey & E. Aronson (Eds.), *The handbook of social psychology* (Vol. 4). Reading, Mass.: Addison-Wesley, 1968.
Wertham, F. *Seduction of the innocent.* New York: Holt, Rinehart, & Winston, 1954.
Wertham, F. The scientific study of mass media effects. *American Journal of Psychiatry,* 1962, *119,* 306–311.
Westley, B.H. & Severin, W.J. Some correlates of media credibility. *Journalism Quarterly,* 1964, *41,* 325–335.
Whitehead, P.C. Sex, violence, and crime in the mass media. *Canada's Mental Health,* 1970, *18,* 20–23.
Whitehouse, M. *Cleaning up TV.* London: Blandford, 1967.
Whitman, H.J. *Terror in the streets.* New York: Dial Press, 1951.
Who's Who looks into ethical questions of covering terrorists' acts. *Broadcasting,* March 21, 1977, p.28.
Wilber, C.G. (Ed.). *Contemporary violence: A multi-disciplinary examination.* Springfield, Ill.: Charles Thomas, 1975.
Wilhoit, G.C. (Ed.). *Mass communication review yearbook* (Vol. 1). Beverly Hills, Calif.: Sage, 1980.
Wilkinson, D.Y. (Ed.). *Social structure and assassination: The sociology of political murder.* Cambridge, Mass.: Schenkman, 1976.
Wilkinson, P. *Political terrorism.* New York: Halstead Press, 1975.
Wilkinson, P. *Terrorism and the liberal state.* New York: Wiley, 1977.
Wilkinson, P. Social scientific theory and civil violence. In Y. Alexander, D. Carlton & P. Wilkinson (Eds.), *Terrorism: Theory and practice.* Boulder, Colo.: Westview Press, 1979.
Wilson, V. Terrorism works: terrorists know it. *New Orleans Times-Picayune,* April 28, 1978, p.15.
Winick, C. (Ed.). *Deviance and the mass media.* Beverly Hills, Calif.: Sage Publications, 1978.
Withey, S.B., & Abeles, R.P. (Eds.). *Television and social behavior: Beyond*

violence and children. Hillsdale, N.J.: Lawrence Erlbaum, 1980.
Wohlstetter, R. Kidnapping to win friends and influence people. *Survey*, 1974, *20*(4 Serial No.93), 1–40.
Wolf, J.B. Controlling political terrorism in a free society. *Orbis*, 1976, *19*, 1289–1308.
Wolf, J.B. Urban terrorist operations. *Police Journal* (Chichester), 1976, *49*, 277–284.
Wolfenstein, M., & Leites, N. *Movies: A psychological study*. Glencoe, Ill.: Free Press, 1950.
Yette, S.F. The mass media vs. the Black mind: Creating the behavioral statistic. In *National Minority Conference on Human Experimentation Conference*, Washington National Urban Coalition, 35–36, n.d.

Index

Abernathy, Ralph, 15
Access to information, 3,6,8,9,16,17,22,29,37,42-44,72,73
Afghanistan, 18,33,46
Aircraft hijackings, 29,30,83,100,135,149
American Airlines hijacking, 100
American Broadcasting Company (ABC), 31-32,34,59,60,92; policy guidelines, 103
American Communications Association v. Douds, 72
Anderson, Jack, 16
Arab oil boycott, 32-33,36
Arab terrorism, 14-15,27,36
Arafat, Yasser, 34,56n
Ashwood, Thomas M., 29
Associated Press, 46; policy guidelines, 103,137
Association for purpose of terrorism, 44
Atlanta Constitution, 52

Baader-Meinhof gang (West Germany), 5,25,69,93
Bagdikian, Ben, 94
Bakhtiar, Shapour, 34
Ball, George, 58
Bassiouni, Cherif, 135
Becker, Jillian, 35
Berbaum, Michael L., 10
Bernstein, Carl, 17
Black Muslims, 99
Black Panthers, 14-16
Black September, 96
Boccardi, Louise D., 137
Böll, Heinrich, 93
Bradlee, Benjamin C., 85
Branzburg v. Hayes, 40-42
Brinton, Crane, 1,5
British Airways hijacking, 30
British Broadcasting Corporation, 6,29,110-20; Agreement with Metropolitan Police (London), 114-15,123-24; INLA terrorist interview, 117-21
British ITV (Independent Television), 28,29,112,116
Burger, Warren, 8,43
Bukanin, Michael, 23

Carter, Jimmy, 18,133; administration, 5,18,19,32,36,52; & Iran hostage seizure, 52-57
Censorship, 93,94,97,104,108,115,136
Central Intelligence Agency (CIA), 106
Chalfont, Lord, 119
Chandler, Robert, 59
Chicago Sun-Times, 7,9,26,82,85,96,100; guidelines (standards), 9,102,134,143,145,159
Chicago terrorist incidents, 99-102
Chicago Tribune, 52,103,136
China, 35
Civil Rights Act, 42
Civiletti, Benjamin R., 54,149
Clutterbuck, Richard, 95
Code of Federal Regulations, 42
Columbia Broadcasting System (CBS), 9,21,32,59,60,92; guidelines (standards), 103,143-44,157-58
Columbia Journalism Review, 95-96
"Commandos", 3,32
Congress (US), 18,40-41,44-45
Constitutional rights, 1st Amendment, 3,8,9,21,37-43,45,47,71-75,78,82,97,133,146,149; 4th Amendment, 38; 14th Amendment, 38,72
Cooms, James E., 14
Cooper, H.H.A., 94
Crabbe, Tony, 113
Croatian consulate takeover (Chicago), 99
Cronkite, Walter, 60

Daily Express (London), 112
Daily Mirror (London), 112,113
Daily News (Chicago), 134,143,146,159
Daily Telegraph (Great Britain), 118,119
Defense Department (US), 149
Detente, 33,35,36
Detroit race riots, 96
deVernisy, Jacques, 35
Douglas, William O, 37,42
Downie, Leonard, 7,26,27,82,96,98

Eagleton, Thomas 16-17
Economist (London), 33

217

Edelman, Murray, 13
Editor and Publisher, 85
Egypt, 17
Emerson, Thomas I., 37
Engels, Friedrich, 23
Entebbe (Uganda) Airport incident, 92
Entertainment, 70,91,140
Environmental Protection Agency (EPA) v. Mink, 37,44
Epstein, Edward Jay, 15-16

Federal Aviation Administration, 150
Federal Bureau of Investigation (FBI), 15,85,100,101,107,149, 150
"Fellow travelers", 5
Fenyvesi, Charles, 31,138
Financial Weekly, 119
Francis, Richard, 115, 124
"Freedom fighters", 3,32
Freedom of Information Act, 37,44
Friedlander, Robert, 6,7,9,21,25; paper by, 51-66

Gallegos, William, interview with, 6,21,25,60
Gannett newspapers, 136-37
Garrett v. Estelle, 72
Georgia Bureau of Investigation (GBI), 40
Gerbner, George, 138
Germany, West (Federal Republic), anti-terrorist legislation, 44; Lufthansa raid, 29; Munich Olympic incident, 96-97; terrorism in, 5,6,22,23,25,44,93,96
Great Britain, anti-terrorist measures, 106-29; BBC interview with terrorist, 117-21; BBC/Metropolitan Police (London) agreement, 123-24; Iranian Embassy seizure, 27-29; media coverage of terrorism, 15,18,22; media standards, 7; Metropolitan Police (London) policy on relations with news media, 125-29; Northern Ireland situation, 18-19,22,23,95,107-11,116-21; police/media relations, 6-7,9; Prevention of Terrorism Act, 22,45,109,111,118,120,121; voluntary news blackout on kidnappings, 111-14
Green, Bill, 60
"Guerrilla", 32,36,93
Guidelines and standards, 7-8,21,45-46,59,61,102,107-16,123-29,133-60; BBC/Metropolitan Police (London) agreement, 114-16,123-24; CBS News Production Standards,157- 58 Courier-Journal and Louisville Times, 158-59; Chicago Sun-Times and Daily News, 159; Metropolitan Police (London) policy on media relations, 125-29; Task Force on Disorders and Terrorism, 154-58; UPI, 160; US Government spokesperson, 148-52

Hacker, Frederick, 58,107
Haig, Alexander, 19,61
Hanafi Muslim siege (Washington, D.C.), 2,7,20,26,30,31,70,74,80,82,85,96,98-99,133,137,138
Harland, Peter, 112
Harper's (magazine), 95
Havers, Sir Michael, 110n
Hearst, Patricia Campbell, 5,91
Herald (Albany, Ga.), 40
Hoge, James W., 7-9,19,20,26; paper by, 89-105
Hoggart, Simon, 18
Horner, Charles, 33,34
Horobin, Don, 112
Horstman, Preston, 138
Hostages, Americans in Iran, 6,51-61; Hanafi Muslim incident, 20,26,31; held by terrorists, 2,28-31,46,89,101,102,107,111,114,135,138,141,144-46,150,157; in common felonies, 2; media attitudes, 31; media interference, 29-30,71-75,97-99; Munich Olympics, 96-97; negotiations for release of, 30-31,73,74,79,97
Houchins v. KQED, Inc., 8,43,72
Hutchins Commission, 107

Idaho State Penitentiary, 40
Inter-Agency Working Group to Combat Terrorism, 150
International Court of Justice (ICJ), 51,56-57
International law, 51
International Pilot's Association, 29
Iran, American hostages in, 6,7,9,21,25,27,34,51-66; deportation of Iranian students from US, 54; London Embassy seizure, 27-29; relations with PLO, 33,34; Revolution (1978), 59
Iraq, 19
Ireland (Republic of), 25
Irish National Liberation Army (INLA), 6,7,22,29,118,120
Irish Republican Army (IRA), 25,109,110n,113,117,120
Isaac, Rael Jean, 36
Israel, 17,18,23,36,95,96
Italy, 34; terrorism in, 6,23,44-45,91

Jaber, Adan, 35
Jaehnig, Walter, 6,7,9,22,46; paper by, 106-22

INDEX

Jameson, Derek, 112
Javits, Jacob, 5
Jenkins, Brian, 135
Jonathan Institute (Jerusalem) Conference on Terrorism, 33,36
Justice Dept. (US), 40-42,149,150

Kaloghirou, Aloi, 111-13
KCBI-TV (Boise, Idaho), 40
KGB (Soviet Secret Police), 18,19,35
Khaalis, Hamass Abdul, 26,98-99
Khomeini, Ayatollah, 34,53,55-57,59
Kidnapping, 84-85,91,93,101,107,108,110-11,144,146,147,157; voluntary news blackout, 111-14
King, Glen, 80
Kiritsis, Anthony, 46,74,135
Knight Newspaper Company, 16
KQED, Inc. (Pacific Foundation station), 42; See also Houchins v. KQED, Inc.

Lafflin, John, 15
Laqueur, Walter, 106
Laski, Harold J., 59
Law enforcement (police), fragmentation, 76-81; guidelines, 20,83-86,125-29; insularity, 77,81; interaction with media, 1-10,19-21,43,72-75,78-86,95-104,107-14,125-29,137,139-47,153-60, media interference, 3,21,27,29-30,71-75; problems in US, 76-86; public support, 5,39-41,44-45; resistance to change, 77, 81-83; views on media, 1-2,6-21,26-29,78; views on terrorists, 1-2,6
Le Matin, 35
Lebanon, 34
"Liberators", 3
Libya, 19,33-35
Lippmann, Walter, 16,59
London Observer, 116
London Sunday Times, 116
Lorenz, Peter, 69
Los Angeles Times, 102,103
Louisville Times and Courier-Journal, 143,145,158-59
Loy, Bob, 40
Lufthansa hijacking (West Germany, 1977), 29
Lynch, John, 25

Madison, James, 37
Mahler, Horst, 25
Marighella, Carlos, 93
Mark, Sir Robert, 29,110,111
Marshall, Thurgood, 39
Marx, Karl, 23

Maynes, C. William, 58
McNee, Sir David, 29,110,114
Media, access to information, 3,6,8,9,16,17,22,29,37,42-44,72,73; dependence on sources, 18,32,39-41; diversity, 90; exploitation, 1,4,60,95,107,138; guidelines and standards, 7-8,21,45-46,59,61,102,107-16,123-29,133-60; interference with law enforcement, 3,6-9,21,27,29-30,71-75,83-86,97,98; journalistic ethics, 6; kidnapping blackout, 111-14; legal controls, 22-24,37-43; overexposure of terrorism, 31-32,58-60,136; pool coverage, 138,141,157; portrayal of terrorists, 2-4,6,7,9,24,31-37; responsibilities, 29,30,100; restrictions, 2,4,7,24,37-43,59,95,107,109; rights, See Constitutional rights; role in democracy, 6,7,19,37,46,106,148; scoop and deadline pressures, 16,17,28,30,45-46,74,138; terrorism as news, 89-105; transmitter of government opinions, 17-19,58; US Government guidelines, 148-52; See also Law enforcement, interaction with media
Merleman, Richard, 13
Metropolitan Police (London), 110; agreement with BBC, 114-16,123-24; policy relations with news media, 125-29; See also Scotland Yard
Middle East, 17-18,23; terrorism, 18,35; US policy regarding, 32-33; See also Israel; Palestine Liberation Organization (PLO)
Miller, Abraham H., introduction by, 1-10; papers by, 13-50
Mitchell, John, 42
Moore, George Curtis, 30
Moreland, Richard L., 10
Moro, Aldo, 91
Morris, Norval, 137
Moses, Earl, 85
Moss, Robert, 33-36
Mulloy, Mike, 112,113
Munich (Germany) Olympics incident (1972), 96
Murphy, Patrick V., 7-9,20,26,97,100; paper by, 76-86

National Advisory Committee on Criminal Justice Standards and Goals, guidelines, 139-43,154-58; Task Force on Disorders and Terrorism, 4,84,94-95,107-08
National Broadcasting Company (NBC), 31,59,92,136,137; policy guidelines, 103; television interview with Iranian hostage, 6,25,60
National Jewish Monthly, 138

National News Council, 20,58,102; paper on terrorism, 133-48
National Press Club, 25
National Security Council (NSC)/Special Coordinating Committee (SCC), 148-51
Nationalism, 23,24
Neave, Airey, 6,29,118
Nechaev, Sergi, 23
Neivens, Peter, 27-29,124
Neubauer, Mark, 42
New Republic, 36,51
New Scotland Yard; *See* Scotland Yard
New York Herald, 41
New York Daily News, 52
New York Times, 35,36,54,57,59,60,102,108,136; policy guidelines, 102-03
Newsweek, 57,60
Nixon, Richard, 30,32
Noel, Cleo A., 30
North Korea, 35
Northern Ireland situation, 18-19,22,23,45,95,107,116-21
Nugent, John, 41

O'Brien, Conor Cruise, 116
Observer (London), 116
Office of Foreign Assets Control (OFAC) (Treasure Dept.), 55
Oil, Arab boycott, 32-33,36; & foreign policy, 36; US suspension of imports from Iran, 52,54

Palestine Liberation Organization (PLO), 17-19,32-33,35,56n; Soviet training, 18,33-35
Pell v. Procunier, 42,43,72
Police; *See* Law enforcement (police)
Postell, Charles, 40
Powell, Jody, 133
Press; *See* Media
Press Association (Great Britain), 114
Prevention of Terrorism Act (Great Britain), 22,45,109,111,118,120,121
Privacy Protection Act, 40-41
Propaganda, 4,6,21,25,45,58-60,69,71,73,97,117,144-46
Public opinion and perception, 3-5,23,52,54,56,70-71
Publicity, 1-4,13,58-60,69-70,74,97,107,113,135-36,144
Pulitzer Prize, 16

Qaddafi, Muammar, 35
Quinn, John C., 136

Rabe, Robert, 6,9,19-20,26; paper by, 69-75

Radio-Television News Directors Association (RTNDA), 134,138
Rapid Deployment Force (US), 54
Reagan, Ronald, administration, 19
Red Army faction (West Germany), 5
Red Brigade, 45
Rees, Merlyn, 118
Retaini, Mohammed Salem, 34-35
Revolution, 1,5,22,23
Rosenfeld, Stephen, 47
Rosenthal, A.M., 102,136
Rowan, Ford, 6,21,25,60
Rukeyser, Louis, 14-15
Rusk, Dean, 53

Salinger, Pierre, 34,56n
San Francisco State College riots, 16
Saudi Arabia, 33,36
Saxbe v. Washington Post, 42,43,72
Schenck v. United States, 71
Schleyer, Hans Martin, 93
Scotland Yard, 28,29,110-15,120,126; agreement with BBC, 114-16,123-24; policy relations with news media, 125-29
Seib, Charles, 133
Sejna, General, 35
Serbian air hijacking, 100
Shakleton, Lord, 45
Shipler, David K., 35
Small, William, 92
Somalia, 29
Sommer, Michael and Heidi, 8,10,20,47,102
Sources of information, 18,32,39-41
South Africa, 23
Soviet Union, invasion of Afghanistan, 18,33; & PLO, 33-35; US foreign policy, 19
Special Air Services (SAS) (Royal Air Force), 28
Special Branch (Scotland Yard); *See* Scotland Yard
Stanford Daily, 38-39; *See also Zurcher v. Stanford Daily*
Stanford University, 38-39
State Department, 19,30,34-36,54,149,151; guidelines, 149-53; Iranian Task Force, 57
Sterling, Claire, 35
Stewart, Potter, 39,40,42
Strategic Arms Limitation Talks (SALT II), 18,19,32-33,35,36
Supreme Court, 8,9,21,37-43,71-72,133
Swan, Sir Michael, 119
SWAT teams, 28
Symbionese Liberation Army (SLA), 5,91
Syria, 19

Task Force on Disorders and Terrorism,

INDEX

4,84,94-95,107-08; guidelines, 139-43,153-60
Television, coverage of US hostages in Iran, 58-60; other terrorist coverage, 20-21,28,47,69-70,73,92,101,102,113,117-21,136,139-41; standards, 103-04
Terrorism, as news event, 89-105; British response, 109-29; foreign policy and, 32-36,61; general view of, 1-2,14,69,78,106-07,135-36; public perception, 3-5,14,23,52,54,56,70-71; publicity, 4,13,58-60,69-70,74,97,107,113,135-36,144
Terrorists, interviews with, 4,6,14,30,43,59,60,70,72,99,117-21,134,138,141,145; motivation, 2-5,14,22-23,69; negotiations with, 30-31,73,74,79,83,97,99; non-negotiation policy, 30; portrayal by media, 3-4,6,9,14-15,19-21,24,32-37,138-39,143-47; right to fair trial, 74; types, 135; view of reality, 14
Thatcher, Margaret, 6,29,117,118,120
Time (magazine), 18,36
Topping, Seymour, 103
Trethowan, Ian, 119
Turkey, 23
TV Guide, 138

Unita (Italy), 45
United Nations, 51,56
United Press International (UPI), 143,146-47; guidelines, 160
United States, foreign policy, 18,19,32-36; guidelines for government spokespersons, 148-52; and Iran hostage seizure, 51-68; Middle East policy, 18,32-35; *See also* Constitutional rights; Supreme Court
Uruguay, 23,93

Vanocur, Sander, 59
Vicker, Ray, 36
Vietnam, 35
Vietnam War, 17,92
Voice (Flint, Mich.), 39

Wald, Richard, 136,137
Waldheim, Kurt, 56
Wall Street Journal, 18,33,36
Washington Post, 6,7,20,25,27,31,47,59,60,85,96,98,99,133,137; policy guidelines, 103; *See also Saxbe v. Washington Post*
Watergate, 17
Weaver, Suzanne, 33,35
Whale, John, 116
Whittle, Lesley, 111
Wilkinson, Paul, 24,117
WMAL-TV (Washington, D.C.), 137
Woodward, Bob, 17
WTOP-TV (Washington, D.C.), 31

Young, Andrew, 18,133

Zurcher v. California, 44
Zurcher v. Stanford Daily, 38-41